IN THE NAME OF ALLAH
THE ALL-BENEFICIENT, THE ALL-MERCIFUL

BLACK THURSDAY

(English Translation of *Raziyyat Yawm al-Khamees*)

By

Dr. Muhammad Tejani Samawi

Author of: *Then I was Guided*

Translated by: Sayyid Maqsood Athar

Edited by: Sayyid Athar Maqsood S.H.Rizvi

TABLE OF CONTENTS

Translator's Foreword 9
Preface 11
   Tradition of Pen and Paper (Qirtaas) 13
   Why didn't the Prophet force the writing of the will? 19
   Interpretations of Ahl al-Sunnah scholars 20
Part One: The Matter of Will **33**
   Proofs of 'Ali's Caliphate 35
   Majority's Point of View Regarding Caliphate 37
   Mutazalite Viewpoint Regarding Caliphate 38
   Tradition of Pen and Paper (Qirtaas) 40
   What did the Prophet Want to Write? 44
   Fabrication of Traditions During Muawiyah's Reign 45
   Abu Talib's Services to Islam 47
   Canyon of Abu Talib 48
   Ali's Services to Islam 50
   1. Eve of Migration (Hijrah) 50
   2. Brotherhood 51
   3. 'Ali and the Battle of Uhad 52
   4. Ali and the Preaching of Surah Baraat 52
   5. 'Ali Goes to Yemen to Propagate Islam 53
   6. Haroon of Muhammad 53
   7. Conqueror of Khaiber 53
Part Two: A Probe into Saqifah **59**
   1. Abu Bakr 59

Analysis of the Incidents at Saqifah 67
Another reason for denial of Caliphate to Ali (a) 70
Incident of Fadak 72
Fadak in Various Hands 74
Mamoon Returns Fadak 75
Judgment Regarding Fadak 76
The Tradition of Non-Inheritance and Holy Qur'an 77
Tradition of Non-Inheritance is against Holy Qur'an 77
Demands of Express text and Reason 81
Fadak as a Gift 83
The branch testifies to the root 84
Testimony of Mubahila 85
Inconsistency in actions of the Muslim Caliph 87
Another Face of the Saqifah Regime 91
Will of the first Caliph regarding Umar 93
Shura (Consultation) 94
Shura Procedure 97
A few questions 98
2. Umar's Opinion about Shura Members 99
'Ali's protest in Shura Meeting 101
Analysis of Shura Gathering 107
Some Personal Exertions of Umar 111
Inconsistency between the practice of the Prophet and Umar 114
Mutual differences between Abu Bakr and Umar 114
Incident of Malik ibn Nuwairah 118
Yet Another (third) Face of Saqifah 120
3. Uthman ibn Affan 120

Bani Umayyah's enmity with Islam 122
Battle of Badr 122
Faith of the Umayyads 125
Favors granted to Bani Umayyah 128
Monetary Policy of Imam 'Ali 132
Wealth of Some Famous Persons 134
Governmental Policies of Uthman 135
Practice of Uthman's Governors 138
Walid ibn Uqbah 138
Walid Drinks Wine in Kufa 139
Why Walid was Appointed as a Governor of Kufa? 141
Uthman's Behavior with Companions 142
Story of Abdullah ibn Masood's Victimization 146
Allegations of Uthman's Rivals 148
Disloyalty of Relatives 150
Repentance of a Person who Repented soon 151
Amr ibn al-Aas and Uthman 152
Uthman and Mother of Believers, Ayesha 153
Bani Umayyah Conference 154
An Important Question that must be Answered 156
Uthman's Murder 158
Conspiracies of Bani Umayyah after Uthman's Murder 160
Part Three: Caliphate of Amirul Momineen (a) 165
Part Four: The Allegiance Breakers (Nakitheen) 169
Ayesha's Age-Old Hatred to 'Ali (a) 171
Reason of Talha and Zubair's opposition 177
Instigators of the Battle of Jamal in Basra 180

Crimes of Jamal Instigators ... 187
Part Five: The Unjust Group (Qasiteen) ... 191
Battle of Siffeen ... 195
Part Six: Arbitration - Apostates - Imam's Martyrdom ... 205
Character of Amr Ibn al-Aas ... 209
Amr ibn al-Aas with Muawiyah ... 211
Arbitration and the stand of 'Ali (a) ... 212
Difficulties of 'Ali (a) ... 215
Part Seven: Glimpses of the Imam's life ... 219
Constitution of his government ... 219
Ali and the Public Treasury ... 234
Humility and Justice of Ali (a) ... 236
Analysis of 'Ali's General Policies ... 238
Some of his Golden Sayings ... 239
His will to Imam Hasan (a) ... 242
Ali (a) in the verses of Holy Qur'an ... 262
Part Eight: Glimpses of Muawiyah's Character ... 265
Plight of Hujr ibn Adi ... 266
Other Examples of Muawiyah's Deceit ... 271
Taking Ziyad ibn Abih as his Brother ... 272
Sayings of Muawiyah ... 275
Ali's discourse regarding Bani Hashim and Bani Umayyah ... 276
Bibliography ... 283
Tradition Books ... 283
Biography Books ... 283
History Books ... 283
Miscellaneous ... 284

TRANSLATOR'S FOREWORD

In the Name of Allah, the Beneficent, the Merciful.

Praise be to Allah, the Lord of the worlds and benedictions be upon Prophet Muhammad and his Purified Progeny.

The Important role that translation plays in propagation of religion is known to all. Since most Islamic texts are in Arabic or Persian, it is only through translating them into English can we make them popular among the literate Muslim youth of today. It was with this aim in mind that we established this bureau and praise be to Allah, we have completed twenty years serving the Shia Muslim world.

The present book was written by Dr. Muhammad Tijani as-Samawi, the famed author of *Then I was Guided*. Those who have read other books of this author will know that he has a special style of writing, which is well arranged and lucid at the same time.

The subject of this book, as usual is a point of controversy between the two largest sects of Islam. It concerns an incident at the end of the life of the Prophet, when he asked for writing materials to dictate a will, but the people present around him said that he was talking nonsense. According to Shia people, it was a very serious matter, whereas the majority of Muslims try to justify such things, as per their habit.

In this book, you will know who that person was, who had the audacity to cast such aspersion on the Messenger of Allah (s). It is really a matter of great astonishment that millions among the Muslim nation consider him to be a leader of Islam, eligible to be followed by others!

I leave it for the readers to find out for themselves who this person is and decide if they consider him worthy of any leadership.

I thank Agha Ansariyan of Ansariyan Publications, Qom, for undertaking to publish and print this important book. As we all know, today, Ansariyan Publication is the largest publisher of Shia Islamic books in English and other foreign languages and all credit goes to the director Agha Muhammad Taqi Ansariyan for undertaking this noble task.

May the Almighty Allah give him more divine opportunity and good sense (Taufeeq) and very long life to serve the faith as much as possible.

I thank the Almighty and His Proofs, especially the Last Proof and the Twelfth Imam on the eve of whose birthday the translation of this book was completed.

Wassalaam

Sayyid Maqsood Athar
Al-Qalam Translators & Writers Bureau
Email: sayedathar@hotmail.com
Dated: 14th Shaban 1430 A.H./7th August 2009

PREFACE

Respected Readers,

Scholars have compiled books on the subject of Imamate and Caliphate in every age and articles have been written like seasons of a year, one after another.

Shahristani has rightly mentioned in *Al-Milal wan Nahl* that the conflict in Muslim nation (Ummah) regarding the matter of Caliphate exceeds those on any other issue.

I have discussed a lot about issues, which are causes of misfortune of Muslims in my previous books and by the grace of Allah, a group of Muslims has benefited much by these books. One of the reasons of their satisfaction is that I myself followed blind faith for a long period of my life and I was not able to speak out the questions in my mind. Then Almighty Allah showered His mercy on me and took me out of the trap of blind faith and granted me recognition of truth. He eliminated barriers from my path and removed curtains from my eyes, so that I could see the truth.

Therefore it becomes my duty to safeguard this truth as a part of thanksgiving and that I should make maximum use of my pen, tongue and hands in this matter.

Hence this book is written by way of thanksgiving for this bounty. As you have waited for this book for a long time, I thank you for the same. Many people were upset with me for writing this book but those who love justice have always encouraged me in this pursuit.

The people who are angry with me did not even refrain from accusing me of being a foreign agent. But inspite of discouraging conditions, I busied myself in writing and made up my mind that every accusation can be borne, but truth cannot be denied.

The book, *Black Thursday* is a story of a grievous incident that occurred hundreds of years ago. However, the Islamic Ummah (nation) feels the pain of this incident even today and it will continue to do so forever.

You are requested to recollect that horrible incident when the last prophet Muhammad (s) was in the final days of his worldly life. The Prophet appointed Usamah ibn Zaid as the commander of his army and ordered Abu Bakr, Umar, Uthman and other Companions to join the army, but the three delayed the departure of army saying that the Prophet was not keeping well. The mother of faithful, Ayesha, was giving them reports from time to time.

She kept her father informed of every event, because she wanted him to lead the congregational prayer in Medina so that the foundation of his Caliphate may be laid.

The Prophet was in severe pain and when he saw people making a commotion, he inquired about the matter. He was told that Abu Bakr is leading the congregation.

When he heard this, he forgot all his pains and taking support of Imam 'Ali (a) and Abbas, went to the mosque and moved Abu Bakr behind and led the prayer himself.

By leading the prayer himself, the Prophet completely destroyed the foundation of Abu Bakr's Caliphate. The chief of the prophets expressed his anger over delay in the departure of Usamah's army.

A grievous incident occurred during those days in Medina. It was Thursday. The Prophet was in severe pain and the people who had stopped the departure of Usamah's army were present in his house and they visited him during his sickness. Umar was in the forefront of this group.

The Prophet asked for pen and paper, so that he could write something whereby the community may be saved from misguidance after him. He said: '*I leave behind among you two heavy things – the book of Allah and my Ahl al-Bayt. If you hold onto them, you would not get deviated after me. The two will not separate from each another till they meet me at the cistern of Kauthar.'*

Umar disobeyed the Prophet's order, saying that the Book of Allah (Qur'an) was enough for them. He also said that Muhammad was talking 'rubbish'. The Prophet got angry at this and ordered them to leave the place. The Prophet's order was disobeyed in his life itself. What have been done to his sayings after he passed away?

Umar's statements cannot be proved as good intention or personal exertion (Ijtihaad) in any manner.

The description of this incident and justifications by Ahl al-Sunnah scholars are very weak. To prove their weakness, I would like to put forward excerpts from Allamah Sayyid Abdul Husain Sharafuddin's books, An-Nass wal Ijtihaad and Al-Murajaat.

TRADITION OF PEN AND PAPER (QIRTAAS)

Compilers of traditions and historians have recorded the incident as follows:

Let us start the discussion with Bukhari's version:

Bukhari has narrated through his chain of narrators that Abdullah ibn Masood narrated from Ibn Abbas that the Prophet was in his last moments and many people had gathered in his house at that time.

The Prophet said, "I want to write a will for you so that you will never go astray after me."

Umar said, "The Prophet is affected by pain. We have the Qur'an with us and the Book of Allah is sufficient for us."

The people objected to Umar. Some of them demanded that pen and paper be given to the Prophet so that he may write the will, which would save people from going astray, while others supported Umar.

When the noise increased, the Prophet ordered the people to leave him alone.

Abdullah ibn Masood narrates that Ibn Abbas used to say: The greatest catastrophe was that the people didn't allow the Prophet to write the will by opposing one another and shouting loudly. This tradition is also recorded by Imam Muslim Nishapuri in his *Sahih Muslim* at the end of 'the book of Testaments'.

It is also narrated by Ahmad ibn Hanbal from Ibn Abbas. Apart from this, countless narrators and historians have recorded this incident.

Most narrators considered the words, '*Innan nabiyya layahjuru*' (the Prophet is talking nonsense) offensive and replaced them with *'innan nabiyya qad ghalaba alaihil waj-u'* (the Prophet is overcome by pain) meaning the Prophet is affected by pain. However the fact is that Umar had called the Prophet's words, 'rubbish'.

The narrators who came later on, considered this word offensive and replaced it. Refer to *Kitabus Saqifah*, a book by Abu Bakr Ahmad ibn Abdul Aziz Jauhari which tries to prove this point.

Many people had gathered at the Prophet's house when he was at his death bed. Umar ibn Khattab was one of them. The Prophet ordered that ink and paper be brought to him to enable him to write something for the people that they do not go astray after him.

Upon this, Umar said a few words, which meant the Prophet is affected by pain and 'we have the Qur'an with us'. 'The Book of Allah is sufficient for us'. The people gathered in the house started opposing each other. Some of them wanted that paper and ink be given to the Prophet while others supported Umar. When the commotion increased, the Prophet ordered everyone to leave the place.

From the words of Jauhari, it is clear that the phrase, 'the Prophet is affected by pain' is an explanation of the original statement of Umar.

The fact is that Umar had rejected the Prophet's words saying that they were 'rubbish'.

Hence we see that when narrators relate this incident along with the word 'rubbish', their sectarian link does not permit them to openly write about the person who called the Prophet's words 'rubbish' and who attacked his mental state.

When they reach this incident, they leave its explanation incomplete, instead of covering every detail.

Bukhari writes in chapter 'Jawaizul Wafd' of section 'Kitabul Jihad was Sair': Ibn Abbas narrated: It was Thursday. Oh! What a bad day it was! Saying this, he broke into tears and cried so much that tears flowed continuously from his eyes. Then he said: This was the day when the Prophet's affliction increased. The Prophet said: Bring paper and pen to me, to enable me to make a will for you that people do not go astray after me.People started quarreling over this point, which is not acceptable in the Prophet's presence. They said that the Prophet was talking rubbish. The Prophet ordered the people to leave him alone. Before passing away, the Prophet made three wills – first was to banish Polytheists from Arabian Peninsula, secondly, they should continue to send delegations like he did and he (the narrator) had forgotten the third one.

Of course the third forgotten thing was the same, which the Prophet wanted to write in his will, so that people do not go astray after him. It was nothing but the Caliphate of Amirul Momineen, 'Ali (a).

Political conditions forced the narrators to 'forget' this point. Similarly, a Mufti of Hanafi sect, Shaykh Abu Sulaiman Dawood narrates a tradition. This tradition is also recorded by Muslim in Sahih Muslim at the end of the 'Book of Testaments' from Saeed ibn Jubair and Ibn Abbas in a different way:

Ibn Abbas said: "It was Thursday. Oh! What a bad day it was!" Then he started to weep and tears flowed on his cheek like a garland of pearls.

After that Ibn Abbas narrates that the Prophet said: "Bring me 'paper and ink' or 'slate and ink' to enable me to make a will so that people do not go astray after me." The people said that the Prophet was talking 'rubbish'. (Refuge of Allah!)1[1]

If we go through tradition books and analyze this catastrophic incident, we come to know that the first to call the Prophet's words 'rubbish', was Umar. He uttered this sentence first and then his followers supported him.

You have already gone through the words of Ibn Abbas in the first tradition. The people gathered at the house started opposing one another. Some of them demanded that pen and paper be given to the Prophet so that he writes the will, while others supported Umar. It means they also said that the Prophet is talking rubbish.

Tibrani narrates from Umar in another tradition that when the Prophet fell sick he said, "Bring me pen and paper to enable me to write a will so that people will never go astray after me." The women behind the curtain said, "Don't you hear what the Prophet is saying?" Umar said, "You are like the women of Prophet Yusuf's time. When the Prophet falls sick, you rinse your eyes with tears and when he is healthy, you mount upon his head."

The Prophet said, "Mind it, women are much better than you."[2]

We can conclude from this incident that the Companions did not obey the Prophet. If they had done so, they would have been secure from deviation. The Companions should have obeyed the Prophet's order, not only they disobeyed him, they also gave a harsh reply that 'the Book of Allah is sufficient for us.' This reply implies that the Prophet was not at all aware of what status the Book of Allah had for

---

[1] *Sahih Muslim*, Vol. 2, Pg. 222. This tradition is also narrated by Imam Ahmad in Musnad, Vol. 1 Pg. 355. It is also narrated by other narrators.
[2] This tradition is narrated by Imam Bukhari from Ubaidullah bin Utbah bin Masood who has narrated from Ibn Abbas and Imam Muslim has also narrated it.

the people. It implies, as if these Companions had better knowledge of its benefits as compared to the Prophet.

They should have stopped here at least and should not have attacked the mental state of the Prophet. They should have avoided saying that the Prophet was talking rubbish. They should not have hurt the Prophet by uttering these words.

The Prophet was in the last moments of his life. Was it good to hurt him in this condition? They bade farewell to him by telling him such hurting words. It was as if they had not gone through the open declaration of the Book of Allah:

(وَمَا آتَاكُمُ الرَّسُولُ فَخُذُوهُ وَمَا نَهَاكُمْ عَنْهُ فَانْتَهُوا.)

And whatever the Apostle gives you, accept it, and from whatever he forbids you, keep back. (59:8)

While accusing the Prophet of talking rubbish they had forgotten this verse of holy Qur'an:

(إِنَّهُ لَقَوْلُ رَسُولٍ كَرِيمٍ. ذِي قُوَّةٍ عِنْدَ ذِي الْعَرْشِ مَكِينٍ. مُطَاعٍ ثَمَّ أَمِينٍ. وَمَا صَاحِبُكُم بِمَجْنُونٍ.)

Most surely it (the Qur'an) is the Word of an honored messenger, the processor of strength, having an honorable place with the Lord of the Dominion, one (to be) obeyed, and faithful in trust. And your companion is not gone mad. (81:19-22)

Didn't the people, who called words of the Prophet, 'rubbish', read this verse?

(إِنَّهُ لَقَوْلُ رَسُولٍ كَرِيمٍ. وَمَا هُوَ بِقَوْلِ شَاعِرٍ قَلِيلًا مَا تُؤْمِنُونَ. وَلَا بِقَوْلِ كَاهِنٍ قَلِيلًا مَا تَذَكَّرُونَ تَنزِيلٌ مِن رَّبِّ الْعَالَمِينَ.)

Most surely, it is the Word brought by an honored Apostle, and it is not the word of a poet; little is it that you believe; nor the word of a soothsayer; little is it that you mind. It is a revelation from the Lord of the worlds. (69:40-43)

Didn't the people who rejected the words of the Messenger read this verse?

(وَالنَّجْمِ إِذَا هَوَى. مَا ضَلَّ صَاحِبُكُمْ وَمَا غَوَى. وَمَا يَنْطِقُ عَنِ الْهَوَى. إِنْ هُوَ إِلَّا وَحْيٌ يُوحَى. عَلَّمَهُ شَدِيدُ الْقُوَى.)

I swear by the star when it goes down. Your companion does not err, nor does he go astray; nor does he speak out of desire. It is naught but revelation that is revealed, the Lord of Mighty Power has taught him. (53:1-5)

There are countless such verses in Qur'an, which clearly imply that the Prophet does not talk nonsense. Apart from this, common sense dictates that it is not possible for the Messenger to talk rubbish.

It is a fact that Companions knew that the Prophet was going to clarify the matter of 'Ali's Caliphate. He was going to pen down all announcements he had made regarding the Caliphate of Imam 'Ali (a). Hence Umar and his followers interrupted the conversation of Allah's Messenger. This is not a product of our imagination. Umar himself confessed thus to Abdullah ibn Abbas.[1]

If we ponder over the Prophet's words: "Bring me paper and pen to enable me to write such a will for you that you don't go astray after me," and the tradition of two weighty things (*Thaqlayn*): "I leave behind among you two heavy things. If you hold unto them tightly, you will never go astray – one is the Book of Allah and second is my progeny", the aim of Allah's Messenger becomes clear.

---

[1] Ibn Abil Hadid, *Sharh Nahjul Balagha*, Vol. 3, Pg. 140, Egypt.

WHY DIDN'T THE PROPHET FORCE THE WRITING OF THE WILL?

The Prophet asked for paper and pen at his death bed so that he could give the tradition of two weighty things (Hadith Thaqlayn) a written form.

A question arises here as to why the Prophet didn't force the writing of the will without caring for what the people were saying? Why didn't he write the will on any other day from Thursday to the day of his passing away i.e. Monday? Why did he drop the idea?

The correct answer to this is that it was the statement of Umar and his greedy followers, which hurt the Prophet badly. He dropped the idea of writing the will because there was no use of it after hearing such words. If he had written it, it could have led to violence and differences.

If the Prophet had written the will, these people would have said, "This will does not hold any importance, for it was written when the Prophet was talking rubbish."

Would the people who dared to call the Prophet's words 'rubbish' in front of him have accepted the will later on? If the Prophet had remained firm on his decision and written the will, these people would have tried to prove the will as rubbish through any means. Many books would have been written to prove that it was nonsense. Debates would have been held and all possible means would have been tried to prove the will useless. That is why the wise Messenger of Allah decided not to write the will, so that people do not get the chance to ridicule his Prophethood.

Also the Messenger of Allah knew that Imam 'Ali (a) and his followers will do as intended in his will, whether it was in written form or not. If he had written the will for those who had opposed, they would not have obeyed it at all.

THE INCIDENT OF PEN AND PAPER (QIRTAAS) AND INTERPRETATIONS OF AHL AL-SUNNAH SCHOLARS

When Allamah Sayyid Abdul Husain Sharafuddin Amili wrote the exegesis of the tradition of 'Pen and Paper' and sent it to Allamah Shaykh Salim al-Bashari, the Rector of Al-Azhar University, Egypt, the latter replied to him with interpretations and justifications of Ahl al-Sunnah scholars and also his personal observations.I present his words for the readers here: When the Prophet (s) ordered them to bring an inkpot and a piece of paper, he probably did not mean to write anything. He simply wanted to test their fidelity and obedience.

Of all the Companions who had gathered in the house, Umar al-Farooq alone was blessed with divine guidance and could understand the real purpose behind the Prophet's request. He therefore prohibited them from supplying the Prophet (s) with writing materials and they complied with the prohibition.This prohibition by Umar al-Farooq should, therefore, be regarded as a favor and one of the special privileges conferred on him by Allah. This is the answer given by some eminent scholars.

But, to be fair, this answer is incompatible with the words of the Prophet, "You will never astray thereafter," which was the condition of the command ("Bring to me writing materials"). In other words, the Prophet was saying, "If you bring to me an Inkpot and a piece of paper and I write for you a document, you will never go astray thereafter."

In view of this, it is obviously incorrect to say that the purpose of his request for writing materials was simply to test his Companions. Words of a prophet, as a rule, must be free from faults, and certainly it was better for them to supply him pen and paper than to refuse it. Moreover, the said answer is open to objection from other points of view, and they should have offered some other excuse.

What they could say at the most was that his command for bringing writing materials was not a peremptory one which would have been instantly obeyed and which was not open to examination or revision, that he who examined it was guilty of disobedience and insubordination.

On the other hand, it was a suggestion which was open to consultation, for the Companions would often seek from the Prophet (s) explanation or revision of some of his commands, particularly, Umar, who believed himself to be more competent to weigh the pros and cons and to judge the merits and demerits of a command or instruction than others and was blessed with inspiration from Allah, the High.

He wanted to save the Prophet, who was already suffering from pain, from further discomfort that would have resulted from writing the proposed document. Umar, therefore, considered it advisable not to supply the Prophet (s) with an Inkpot and a piece of paper.

Perhaps he was also afraid that the Prophet (s) might write such commands that would be beyond them to obey or comply with and they would, therefore, deserve punishment, because whatever he would write down would be imperative and final and would not leave any scope for examination and interpretation by others.Perhaps he was also afraid of the hypocrites objecting to the propriety of the document and censuring it, because the Prophet (s) had written it in a state of illness, and this would have created a big scandal. He therefore remarked, "The Book of Allah is sufficient for us," in view of the words of Allah, the Most High:

(مَا فَرَّطْنَا فِي الْكِتَابِ مِنْ شَيْءٍ.)

We have not neglected anything in the Book. (6:38)

And also:

(الْيَوْمَ أَكْمَلْتُ لَكُمْ دِينَكُمْ)

This day have I perfected for you your religion. (5:3)

As if Umar was sure that the nation would not go astray because Allah had perfected for her the faith and had completed His favor on her, so the proposed document was unnecessary!

These are the replies and you can see how unsound they are! The words of Prophet (s): "You will never go astray," indicate that his command for supply of writing materials was a firm, final and compulsory command, not open to examination, revision or consultation.It is without doubt, an incumbent duty to make all possible efforts for compliance with that which guarantees safety from error and deviation. The Prophet's feeling displeased on their disobeying his command and asking them to get out is a proof that the purpose of his command was its compulsory compliance and not reflection or consultation upon it.

They may ask why the Prophet (s) did not write down the proposed document in spite of the opposition by Companions, if writing thereof was incumbent on him, just as he did not give up the communication of the Divine Message in spite of strong opposition of infidels. In reply to this, I would say that the writing of the document was not incumbent on the Prophet (s).But it does not mean that it was not incumbent on the Companions to supply him with ink and paper when the Prophet (s) commanded them to do so, especially when he had also explicitly told them that it would save them from deviation forever and lead them to perpetual guidance.The execution of an order, as a principle, is incumbent on the person or persons ordered to do something, and not on one who issued the order, especially so when the benefit of executing the order is going to accrue solely to the person or persons ordered to do a thing. The point of discussion, therefore, is whether or not it was incumbent on the Companions to supply him with writing material; it was not incumbent on the Prophet to write down the document.

Even if it was incumbent on the Prophet (s), it was no longer binding on him after their refusal to obey and their disparaging remark, "he has talked nonsense." Had he written the document in spite of all this; it would have resulted in nothing but scandal and caused insurrection.

Some others have offered the excuse that Umar failed to understand how the proposed document would save every individual in the nation from deviation and that not a single person would go astray after the writing of the proposed document.From the words, "You will never go astray," he understood that the entire nation would not go astray and that deviation from the right path would not extend to the nation as a whole after the writing of the document.He already knew that the entire nation would never go astray and, therefore, he thought that writing the document was unnecessary. He thought that the purpose of the Prophet (s) was only to take further precaution out of his extremely merciful nature and that his command for supply of writing material was not authoritative and obligatory but open to consultation and revision.It was the urge of his extraordinary mercy and clemency that made him demand writing materials for writing a document for our further safeguard from deviation. It was this impression that prompted Umar to pass that remark and to prohibit the supply of writing materials.

These are the various excuses offered for the hasty remark and action of Umar and his supporters. But on careful consideration all these excuses appear to be faulty and unreasonable, because the Prophet's words, "You will never go astray," clearly indicate that his command was obligatory and not optional or open to consultation. His displeasure at the disparaging remark and their disobedience proves that they were guilty of omission of an obligatory duty.The correct and the best answer would, therefore, be that the disparaging remark and refusal to supply the Prophet (s) with writing materials was ill-advised, indecorous and unbecoming the Companions. It was a sudden slip on their part and a rare lapse which we do not find to be reasonable. May Allah guide those who have deviated from the right path.

You have read the letter of Shaykhul Azhar (Rector of Al-Azhar University), and seen how the Allamah has negated the stance of Umar in clear words.

In reply to this letter, Allamah Abdul Husain Sharafuddin Amili has further exhausted the proof and proved the truth as follows:

"It befits men of your learning and discretion to acknowledge the truth and to speak what is right. You have contradicted the various excuses and explanations offered by your Sunni scholars for the disparaging remark passed by the Companions and their non-compliance with his request for writing materials. There are still some aspects of those excuses and explanations which have not been examined. I will offer a few comments thereon and leave the matter to your own learned judgments.

In their first explanation, they have said that perhaps the Prophet (s) did not mean to write anything when he ordered them to bring an inkpot. His only purpose behind the order was to test their fidelity and obedience. In addition to what you have said in contradiction of this explanation, I have to point out that the remark was passed and his command was disobeyed at the time when he was under the pangs of death and was shortly to breathe his last, as is clearly stated in the tradition. It was, therefore, an occasion for apology and forgiveness or admonition and warning, and certainly not for testing his Companions. It was time for him to make a will in respect of all important matters and give final advice to his nation. A person under the pangs of death does not indulge in jokes, jests or display of humor in any other form. He is fully occupied with his own soul, his own important affairs of his relations, friends and nation, especially if the person on the deathbed is a Prophet. And why would he test their fidelity from his deathbed when he did not test it in a state of health throughout his life?"

Moreover, his words, "Get up and leave me," addressed to them when noise and nonsense increased and the quarrel developed, clearly indicate that he was displeased with them. Had the prohibition been right, he would have certainly appreciated their prohibition and expressed his satisfaction therein.He who examines the various aspects of the tradition and carefully considers their remark, "The Messenger has talked nonsense," will be convinced that they knew that what he was going to write was distasteful for them, and that is why they caused him severe mental pain by the disparaging remark and bitter quarrel and confusion in his presence. On recollecting this event, Ibn Abbas wept bitterly and called it a great misfortune, which also proves the explanation to be groundless.

The second explanation, that Umar was blessed with divine guidance and could rightly judge the merits and demerits of a thing and had inspiration from Allah, the High, is not worth paying attention to, because this would imply that Umar was right in prohibiting the supply of writing materials and not the Prophet (s) in demanding writing materials, and that the inspiration he had was truer and more appropriate than the divine revelation which governed all the utterances of the True and Trusted Prophet (s).They have explained that Umar felt pity for the Prophet (s) and wanted to save him from further inconvenience that would have resulted from writing the proposed document while he was ill and in pain. But you (whom Allah has gifted with right judgment) know that the writing of the document would have afforded pleasure and satisfaction to the Prophet (s), cooled his heart and delighted his eyes, and made him immune from deviation of his followers.His order ought to have been carried out and not ignored. When it was his aim to have ink and paper, he had also ordered them to supply him with these things, nobody should have refused to obey him.

(وَمَا كَانَ لِمُؤْمِنٍ وَّ ؟ مُؤْمِنَةٍ إِذَا قَضَى اللَّهُ وَرَسُولُهُ أَمْراً أَنْ يَكُونَ لَهُمُ الْخِيَرَةُ مِنْ أَمْرِهِمْ وَمَنْ يَعْصِ اللَّهَ وَرَسُولَهُ فَقَدْ ضَلَّ ضَلَالاً مُبِيناً)

And it behoves not a believing man and a believing woman that they should have any choice in their matter when Allah and His Apostle have decided a matter; and whoever disobeys Allah and His Apostle, he surely strays off a manifest straying. (33:36)

Moreover, the opposition by Umar and his supporters in such an important matter and their making noise and quarreling in the presence of Prophet (s) was more troublesome and painful than writing the proposed document, which would have protected his nation forever from going astray. And how could he, who would not like to see the Prophet inconvenienced with writing a document, dare to oppose him and give him a sudden shock by his words, "He has talked nonsense"?They have also said that Umar thought that it was better not to supply him with ink and paper. It is a queer, wonderful and very farfetched explanation. How could the refusal to supply the Prophet (s) with writing materials in spite of his explicit command be better than compliance with his command? Did he believe that the Messenger of Allah (s) issued orders the omission or abandonment of which was better than commissioning thereof or compliance therewith?

Still more astonishing is the explanation that Umar was afraid lest the Prophet (s) might write down commands which might be impossible for the people to obey and the omission of which might make them liable to punishment. Why was he afraid when the Prophet (s) had given the assurance, "You will never go astray after that?"Had he better knowledge of consequences of the document than the Prophet (s)? Was he more anxious about the welfare of nation, and had he more sympathy and compassion for the nation than the Prophet? Surely not!

They have also said that Umar was afraid that hypocrites would reject and censure the document written in a state of illness, and it would therefore create a scandal and cause impiety and insurrection. You know that this was impossible, because the Prophet (s) had said, "You will never go astray," which means that the document would have been a source of safety to the nation from deviation.How could it then be cause of scandal and censure by hypocrites? And if he was really afraid that hypocrites would question the document's propriety and censure it, why did he sow the seed of rejection and censure by raising an objection and prohibiting the supply of writing material, and passing the remark, "he has talked nonsense"?

While interpreting his words, "the Book of Allah is sufficient for us," they have referred to the Qur'anic verses:

(مَا فَرَّطْنَا فِي الْكِتَابِ مِنْ شَيْءٍ.)

We have not neglected anything in the Book. (6:38)

And also:

(اَلْيَوْمَ أَكْمَلْتُ لَكُمْ دِينَكُمْ.)

This day have I perfected for you your religion. (5:3)

The Reference is incorrect, because the two verses neither signify that the nation is secured forever from deviation nor guarantee the guidance of the nation to the right path. How could, on the basis of these verses, the indifference to the proposed document or disregard thereof be permissible? If the mighty Qur'an had been the cause of protection of the nation against deviation, there would not have been in this nation the present deviation and dispersion, the extinction of which appears to be almost impossible.

In their last justification of Umar, they have said that he did not understand from the Prophet's command that the proposed document would protect every individual in the nation against deviation. What he understood was that the document would prevent them from general consent of the nation on error or deviation from the right path, and he already knew that there would never be general consent in the nation on error or deviation whether the document was written or not, and that is why he objected to the supply of writing materials that day and offered resistance. To what you have stated in contradiction of this, I have to add that Umar was not so deficient in intelligence as to be unable to understand the request demanding writing materials, which was quite clear to everybody, and from which every urban and rustic person could understand that had the document been written, it would have been the cause of securing every individual in the nation from error and deviation. This is the meaning which first occurs to every mind on hearing the tradition.

Umar certainly knew that the Messenger (s) was not afraid of the general consent of his nation on error or deviation from the right path, because he had often heard the Prophet (s) say: "There will not be a general consent in my nation on deviation, and there will not be a general consent in my nation on error;" and also his words, "There will always be in my nation, a group of people who will adhere to truth and support it;" and the words of Allah:

(وَعَدَ اللَّهُ الَّذِينَ آمَنُوا مِنكُمْ وَعَمِلُوا الصَّالِحَاتِ لَيَسْتَخْلِفَنَّهُم فِي الْأَرْضِ.)

Allah has promised to those of you who believe and do good that He will most certainly make them rulers in the earth as He made rulers those before them. (24:55)

He had read in Qur'an and also heard from the Prophet (s) many other verses to the effect that all Muslims, without any exception, will never concur on error and deviation. In the face of these stipulations, no one can believe that it occurred to Umar or any other person that the Prophet (s) had ordered them to supply him with writing materials because he had the fear of the entire nation going astray. It was according to the fitness of things that Umar should have understood from the demand for writing materials what occurs to the minds of others and not that which is contradicted by precise verses of the Qur'an and genuine traditions of the Prophet (s).

Moreover, the displeasure of the Prophet (s) expressed in the words, "Get up and leave me," is a proof of their committing the sin of omitting what was one of their obligatory duties and being guilty of disobeying his command for supply of writing material.

Had the disparaging remark by Umar and his prohibition of the supply of writing materials been due to some misunderstanding, as claimed by some of his advocates, the Prophet (s) would have removed his misunderstanding and fully explained to him the purpose of his writing a document. He could also compel him and his supporters to fetch writing materials and write down the document in spite of their opposition.

But the Prophet (s) neither tried to remove the misunderstanding nor exercised any compulsion on them. He simply ordered them to get out; because he knew that the disparaging remark and non-compliance with his command were based, not on any misunderstanding, but motivated by some other consideration.

The bitter weeping and restlessness of Ibn Abbas on remembering the unfortunate event is the strongest proof of the correctness of our statement.

In fact, this unfortunate event admits no excuse. Had it been a mere excess or an occasional lapse on the part of the Companions, as you have said, it would have been treated lightly; although, this event alone proved to be a universal and crashing calamity. Verily, to Allah we belong and to Him we must return. There is neither might nor power but in Allah, the High and Mighty.

The fact is that those people didn't accord importance to Express Text (*Nass*) and acted on their personal judgments.

If an act committed against Express Text (*Nass*) can be called jurisprudence, then they were real jurists.

However, in this case, Express Text (*Nass*) of Allah and His Messenger is different and the jurisprudence of the leaders is different.

Shaykhul Azhar replied to the above explanation in the following words:

"You have surrounded the advocates of Umar and his supporters from all sides, blocked all their routes and left them no alternative, having raised a wall between them and their desire. What you have stated leaves no room for misunderstanding, and there appears to be no reason to doubt the veracity of your deductions."

We follow that jurisprudence, which is within the limits of Express Texts (*Nusoos*) and we are not ready to accept any such thought as jurisprudence, which is against Express Text (*Nass*).

The Purpose of book, Radhiyato Yaumil Khamees is not to dig out all the hostilities of the past.

The Purpose of writing this book is to present the correct form of history so that human beings can go from wrong views to the fountain of truth and reach the place of guidance.

We invite all Muslims of the world to come and search for the correct teachings of religion and try to obtain the truth, which was preached by the Prophet.

If we allow the Prophetic Practice (*Sunnah*) and teachings to illuminate our way, we will never be misguided.

We need to obey the Prophet (s). We do not need the jurisprudence of any Zaid and Bakr because it is possible for jurists to commit mistakes and it is not possible for a personality like the Prophet to commit a mistake.

No one can give an excuse later on that they were born centuries after an incident and they remained far away from the soul of Islam.

Hence I once again request the readers not to stop our endeavors in spite of these conditions, because the West is bent on destroying us, and day by day we are becoming its victims.

Did you ever wonder what the basic cause of our weakness is?

I think the basic cause of our weakness is that we have never tried to understand Islam in a correct way. We have assumed and adopted those views as Islam, which are in accordance with our desires and thoughts. If we had adopted the right soul of Islam, these wolves could never have overpowered us.

Respected Readers,

I have not written this book to earn fame or to gain titles. The main purpose of this book is to present a correct version of history to all because majority of human beings are unaware of it. The cause of this ignorance is that truth was concealed in every age and its beautiful face was always covered with a veil. In every age wine was made as water and the distorted and ugly face of truth was made beautiful using various techniques.

Therefore the majority is unaware of difference between right and wrong and distinction between a good and bad leader could not be made.

In such circumstances, I trusted Allah and tried to present the facts. I hope that Allah will make this book a beacon of light for those who are in search of truth and make it an illuminated candle in darkness.

I pray to Allah to grant me the bounty of recognition and include me among those who have got recognition and keep away from the disease of ignorance. I pray that He forgives my mistakes for He is All-Hearing and He accepts from us.

Our Lord! Accept from us; surely Thou art the Hearing, the Knowing, and turn to us (mercifully), surely Thou art the Oft-returning (to mercy), the Merciful.

For the sake of the Prophet and his Purified Progeny. May Allah bless Muhammad and the Progeny of Muhammad (s).

THE MATTER OF WILL

There are two points of views among Muslims regarding the Caliphate; one group says that it is religious as well as a worldly matter.

Caliphate is related to religion in a way that a Caliph is expected to follow religious commandments in all matters. A Caliph should be immune from mistakes and have a complete knowledge of religion. Caliphate is related to the world in a way that a Caliph is also a human being and Allah does not send revelation upon him. He has to follow the commandments of religion much in the same way as other followers do.

Further, a Caliph is chosen by Allah and it is announced to public by the prophet. A Caliph is responsible for safeguarding religion after the prophet. Teaching religious commandments in all walks of life is also the responsibility of a Caliph after the prophet. According to this point of view, the rank of Caliphate is after prophethood and Caliphate should also be as pure as prophethood.

Followers of this view believe that Allah ordered His Prophet (s) to appoint his successor and the Prophet appointed Imam 'Ali (a) as a Caliph. However after the Prophet passed away, some people kept 'Ali (a) away from his right and founded their own Caliphate. Still Imam 'Ali (a) remained rightful and he was the first successor of the Prophet. He was kept away from performing his duties as expected for a long period of time but it was not his fault. It was the fault of those who tried to bring about changes in religion.

This Group presents the following points to prove that Caliphate and Imamate is a religious matter:

The Prophet preached religious as well as worldly matters and it was necessary for him to appoint a leader for Muslims after him so that the Ummah does not get involved in differences after him. Also such a person is required for leadership of Ummah who is perfect and has complete knowledge of all religious and worldly matters and he should also have the best character. Islam is not just for Quraish or Arabs, it is for the benefit of entire humanity, hence it is necessary to appoint a person who is capable in all aspects.

1. Leaving the matter of Caliphate to the choice of the Ummah is not acceptable. It is not possible to leave such an important matter at the mercy of people because it can lead to many complications. Even if Caliphate is left to the choice of people, do all Muslims have right to it or only some specified individuals?

2. If it is the right of only some specified individuals, what is the reason for it? What is so special about this group?

3. Is the right of selecting the Caliph with only with Abu Bakr, Umar and Abu Ubaidah and other Helpers (*Ansar*) who were present at Saqifah?

4. Can the Caliphate of Saqifah be proved correct in spite of opposition from great Companions like Imam 'Ali (a) and other members of Bani Hashim; Saad ibn Ubadah and his sons, Salman Farsi, Abu Zar Ghiffari, Miqdad ibn Aswad, Ammar ibn Yasir, Zubair ibn Awwam, Khalid ibn Saeed and Huzaifah ibn Yamani and Buraira?

5. Is it correct to consider the Caliphate legal in spite of opposition of so many great personalities?

6. If the right of selecting a Caliph is given to Muslims, would they select the best personality in spite of having tribal conflicts between them?

7. The Prophet knew about conflicts between different tribes. Did he leave the matter of Caliphate to the people to increase conflicts?

8. If this right is given to people, would the selection be through written or oral votes?

9. If it is necessary to have written votes, how many such people were present who were completely illiterate? Then how could this method be implemented?

10. Would it be necessary to install polling booths in every city and town? Or some other method will be adopted?

11. Will the candidates be allowed to canvass for themselves?

12. How will this election be implemented?

13. How much time is needed to conduct this election?

14. Who will have the charge of religious matters between the time when the prophet passes away and the election of a Caliph?

The answers to above questions are absolutely necessary.

PROOFS OF 'ALI'S CALIPHATE

The Group of Muslims, which believes that Caliphate and Imamate is from Allah, has a strong and clear proof regarding it. They say that the Prophet intended to perform Hajj in 10th A.H. and announced it in entire Arabia. Muslims from all the parts of the peninsula gathered for this Hajj, which was also called the Farewell Hajj.

The Prophet was returning to Medina after performing all the rituals of Hajj when he reached a place called Ghadeer Khumm near Johfa; which is at the crossroads to Egypt and Iraq.

Almighty Allah revealed the following verse on the Prophet at this place:

$$\text{يَا أَيُّهَا الرَّسُولُ بَلِّغْ مَا أُنْزِلَ إِلَيْكَ مِنْ رَبِّكَ وَإِنْ لَمْ تَفْعَلْ فَمَا بَلَّغْتَ رِسَالَتَهُ وَاللَّهُ يَعْصِمُكَ مِنَ النَّاسِ إِنَّ اللَّهَ لَا يَهْدِي الْقَوْمَ الْكَافِرِينَ}$$

O Apostle! Deliver what has been revealed to you from your Lord; and if you do it not, then you have not delivered His message, and Allah will protect you from the people; surely Allah will not guide the unbelieving people. (5:67)

After the revelation of this verse, the Prophet ordered a pulpit to be built using camels saddles and gathered all the people. When people gathered, he delivered a sermon; then he raised the hand of Imam 'Ali (a) and announced: "Allah is my master and I am the master of all believers. 'Ali is the master of those for whom I am the master."[1]

Immediately after this, Almighty Allah announced the completion of religion in the verse:

(لِيَوْمَ أَكْمَلْتُ لَكُمْ دِينَكُمْ وَأَتْمَمْتُ عَلَيْكُمْ نِعْمَتِي وَرَضِيتُ لَكُمُ الْإِسْلَامَ دِينًا.)

This day have I perfected for you your religion and completed My favor on you and chosen for you Islam as a religion. (5:3)

When this verse was revealed, the Prophet thanked God and said: "Glory be to Allah for perfection of religion, completion of bounties and Wilayat (mastership) of 'Ali."

It must be mentioned that Shias celebrate Eid Ghadeer in the remembrance of this incident. Maqrizi has explained this celebration in the following words:

"We should know that there was no such Eid as Eid Ghadeer during the early days of Islam. Also we do not have its mention from the chaste people's words. This Eid was first celebrated in the year 352 Hijra during the time of Muizzud Daula 'Ali ibn Babawahy in Iraq, which is based on the tradition narrated by Baraa ibn Aazib quoted by Imam Ahmad in his *Musnad:* We were traveling with the Prophet, when we reached the place of Ghadeer Khumm and an announcement for congregational prayers was made. The place between two trees was swept and the Prophet offered Zuhr (noon) prayers and delivered a sermon. He addressed the people and said: "Don't you know that I have more right on believers than they have on their own self?"

---

[1] Refer Tradition of Wilayat *in Abaqaat al-Anwar* for detailed discussion.

Then he raised Imam 'Ali's hand and announced: "'Ali is the master of whomsoever I am the master. O Allah! Love one who loves 'Ali and hate those who hate 'Ali." After this Umar came to Imam 'Ali (a) and said: "O son of Abu Talib! Congratulations! You have become the master of all believing men and women."

The place of Ghadeer Khumm is three miles from Johfa and there is a spring of water over there; there are many trees covering this place.

Shias celebrate Eid on 18th Zilhajj in the memory of this incident, offering prayers all night and praying a two rakat prayer of thanksgiving in the forenoon. They put on new clothes, free slaves, distribute alms as much as possible, slaughter animals and express happiness. When Shias started celebrating this Eid, Ahl al-Sunnah also started celebrating an Eid exactly eight days after that and said that the Prophet and Abu Bakr had entered the cave on this day."[1]

MAJORITY'S POINT OF VIEW REGARDING CALIPHATE

According to the point of view of the second group of Muslims, although religious knowledge is essential for Caliphate, it is a worldly matter from beginning to end. Therefore the Prophet did not issue Express Text (*Nass*) regarding Caliphate as it is not one of the necessities of faith.

Hence we see that some Muslims gathered in Saqifah Bani Saada[2] to elect a Caliph immediately after the Prophet passed away. They handed over this honored position to Abu Bakr, who in turn passed it to Umar; who constituted a committee after him, which elected Uthman as Caliph. Imam 'Ali (a) was elected by people after the death of Uthman. These four personalities are called the Rightly-guided Caliphs (*Khulafa Rashideen*).

---

[1] *Al-Mawaiz wal-Etebar*
[2] Saqifa is a place where certain people gathered to plan evil activities and talk nonsense. *Ghiyathul Lughat*

The order of their religious merit is also same. This group says that religious commandments were completed before the Prophet passed away. The complete guidance regarding all worldly matters was delivered. Hence there was no need of a Caliph to be appointed by Allah. Ustad Abdul Fattah Abdul Maqsood supports this view in his book, *Al-Imam 'Ali ibn Abi Talib (a)*:

"Islamic Caliphate is related to worldly matters. It is a political issue much like the governmental issues prevalent today. Caliphate is based on choice and it has nothing to do with Express Text (*Nass*) because the Prophet did not clearly appoint anyone as his Caliph in the last moments of his life."

However, it is true that the Prophet had pointed it out many times, but Companions were unaware of its explanation. Also there are a few traditions, in which Caliphate is discussed clearly. For example, 'tradition of Ghadeer' and 'tradition of the Shoe-mender' can be presented as those with a clear mention of Caliphate.[1]

MUTAZALITE VIEWPOINT REGARDING CALIPHATE

Apart from the above viewpoints, there exists one more, which is similar to the above two.

These people agree with Ahl al-Sunnah viewpoint that Caliphate is a worldly matter and the Prophet did not clearly appoint any Caliph after him. However, they believe that Imam 'Ali (a) is more rightful for Caliphate than Abu Bakr because the former is the best in the entire Ummah in all aspects.

I mention a tradition of *Sharh Nahjul Balagha* by Ibn Abi Al-Hadid, which supports the above viewpoint:

"All our seniors agree that the Caliphate of Abu Bakr was correct and rightful and it was not based on any Express Text (*Nass*). His

---

[1] Refer the famous book, *Al-Ghadeer* by Allamah Amini. There are 11 volumes of this book. Available at: https://www.al-islam.org/ghadir/

Caliphate was based on consensus and other such methods, which are opined differently by our leaders.

Chiefs like Abu Uthman and Amr ibn Ubaid say that Abu Bakr has more excellence than Imam 'Ali (a). The order of excellence of the Rightly-guided Caliphs is same as that of their order of Caliphate. The seniors of Baghdad, be they leaders or commons, opine: Imam 'Ali (a) was more virtuous than Abu Bakr. Scholars of Basra like Abu 'Ali Muhammad ibn Abdul Wahhab al-Jabal, Shaykh Abu Abdullah al-Husain ibn 'Ali al-Baseei and Chief Qazi Abdul Jabbar ibn Ahmad and Abu Muhammad Hasan ibn Mutawayyah also support this viewpoint.

Also Abu Huzaifah, Asl ibn Ataa and Abil Hudail Muhammad ibn Hudail al-Allaaf opine that we must keep quiet in the matter of excellence of Imam 'Ali (a) and Abu Bakr. However it is a fact that 'Ali (a) was more virtuous than Uthman.

I personally support the viewpoint of seniors of Baghdad and consider Imam 'Ali (a) better than all other Muslims."

This great personality of Motazela sect writes in another place in *Sharh Nahjul Balagha* that the Motazela sect has arrived at the following conclusion after a lot of debate regarding the matter of excellence:

"Imam 'Ali (a) was the most virtuous person in entire Muslim Ummah. People kept him away from Caliphate due to certain reasons. No texts existed regarding Caliphate of Imam 'Ali (a). Those texts, which were present, had a lot of similarity in their meanings. Imam 'Ali (a) initially opposed the Caliphate of Abu Bakr but accepted it later on.

If 'Ali (a) had continued opposition we would have considered Abu Bakr's Caliphate invalid for we believe that Imam 'Ali (a) is the rightful owner of Caliphate. It was rightful for him to become a Caliph or hand it over to someone else. Over here, we can see that he had accepted the Caliphate of others. Therefore we also follow him by accepting those persons as Caliphs. We accept whatever Imam 'Ali (a) had accepted."[1]

We can explain the view of this group by saying that they consider Imam 'Ali (a) more virtuous than Abu Bakr and consider the former as more rightful to Caliphate than anyone else. However, they believe that there was no Express Text (*Nass*) regarding this. Considering this, Imam 'Ali (a) was a Caliph as per legal ruling. However, as Abu Bakr was appointed a Caliph due to odd conditions, Imam 'Ali (a) did not oppose it much. Hence the Caliphate of Abu Bakr is also correct.

The issue of Caliphate is a cause of differences in every age and all other differences stem from this issue alone. This issue is controversial from the time the Prophet passed away till now. Every sect has tried to prove its own view regarding Caliphate and to refute the stand of others.

It is very difficult for a student of History to accept each of the three viewpoints as correct because if we accept one of them, others will be proved wrong.

If someone rejects Express Text (*Nass*) and the Prophet's will, he believes that the Prophet was not at all worried about the future of Muslim Ummah. He was least bothered about the division of Ummah into numerous sects and had no problem about the Ummah falling prey to worse conditions.

Historical facts prove this viewpoint useless and invalid. Consider the example of tradition of Pen and Paper (*Qirtaas*), which is discussed in length in the earlier pages, however I would like to present it over here also.

TRADITION OF PEN AND PAPER (QIRTAAS)

Ibn Athir writes in his *Kaamil Fit Tarikh*, Vol. 2 Pg. 217:

---

[1] *Sharh Nahjul Balagha,* Ibn Abil Hadid Mutazali 72/2 first edition, Egypt

When the illness and pain of the Prophet increased, he said, "Bring me paper and pen to enable me to write something for you such that you will never go astray." Upon this, people started to fight amongst themselves, which is not acceptable in the Prophet's presence. People repeatedly said that the Prophet was talking rubbish. The Prophet said, "My pain is not as severe as what you people are calling me to." The Prophet mentioned three things in his will:

1. Banish polytheists from Arabian Peninsula.

2. The practice of sending delegations should be continued in the same way as I used to do.

...and the third thing is concealed on purpose by saying that the narrator has forgotten it.

Bukhari has narrated this tradition in the following words: When the illness and pain of the Prophet increased he said, "Bring me paper and pen so that I write something for you such that you will never go astray." Upon this, people started to fight amongst themselves, which is not acceptable in the Prophet's presence. People repeatedly said that the Prophet was talking rubbish. The Prophet said, "My pain is not as severe as what you people are calling me to." The Prophet mentioned three things in his will:

1. Banish polytheist from Arabian Peninsula.

2. The practice of sending delegations should be continued in the same way as I used to do.

The narrator stopped here or said that he has forgotten the third point.

Bukhari has also narrated this tradition from another chain as follows:

Ibn Abbas narrates that the Prophet was in his last moments and many people had gathered in his house at that time. The Prophet said,

"I want to write a will for you so that you will never go astray after me."

Some people said, "The Prophet is affected by pain. We have the Qur'an with us; the Book of Allah is sufficient for us." People gathered in the house started opposing one another on this point. When the noise increased, the Prophet ordered the people to leave him alone.

This tradition is narrated by Ibn Saad in *Tabaqaat-e-Kubra* Vol. 4, Pg. 60 and 61 as follows:

When the Prophet was in his last moments, a lot of people including Umar had gathered at his place. The Prophet said: Bring me paper and pen to enable me to write a will for you so that you don't go astray after me. Umar said: The Prophet is affected by pain and we have the Qur'an with us. The Book of Allah is sufficient for us. Those present at the scene started opposing one another and when the noise increased, the Prophet ordered the people: Get up and leave the place.

After reading this tradition, you can decide for yourself whether the reply of Umar was appropriate as far as the Prophet's personality is concerned. Do the etiquettes of companionship permit such replies? Does the religion of Islam allow someone to disgrace the Prophet's words by calling them rubbish?

Put the words of Umar aside and refer to this verse of holy Qur'an:

(وَمَا يَنْطِقُ عَنِ الْهَوَى. إِنْ هُوَ إِلَّا وَحْيٌ يُوحَى.)

Nor does he speak out of desire. It is naught but revelation that is revealed. (53:3-4)

What is the legal value of Umar's words in view of this verse? I would like to leave the judgment to readers who like justice. It is strange that the Companions also posed a number of questions to the Prophet, which had very little importance as compared to the issue of

Caliphate. Ibn Khaldun writes in his *Tarikh:* The Companions asked the Prophet who would give him the funeral bath. The Companions also asked what his shroud should be of. The Prophet replied that he should be shrouded in his own clothes or in a cloth from Egypt or Yemen. The Companions asked who would lower him in the grave and the Prophet replied that it should be someone from his family.

In this tradition, we see that Companions go on asking the Prophet about his shroud, burial and grave. Didn't they ask him who his successor will be? Didn't the Prophet himself tell the Companions about his successor?

Ibn Khaldun writes on the same page: After this the Prophet said, "Bring me paper and pen to enable me to write something for you such that you will never go astray after me. The people started quarrelling on this. Some said that the Prophet was talking rubbish. The Prophet said: "My pain is better than what you are calling me to?"[1]

Dear readers!

You decide, why the Prophet wasn't allowed to write the will. Why was this opposition made? What was the need of this mayhem? Was it because he was going to make a will regarding the Caliphate of a person about whom he had spoken a number of times during his lifetime? So that no one has a doubt in his mind regarding his Caliphate.

Umar was well aware of this fact. He could guess the Prophet's intention and hence he opposed him. It is quite strange that narrators say that the Prophet willed regarding three things. They have even described two of them and Abu Bakr had even acted on them. However, the third point was forgotten by the narrator or he had not narrated it on purpose.

---

[1] *Tarikh Ibn Khaldun*, Vol. 2, Pg. 297

The Prophet wanted to write down this third point, and that is why the people tried to misbehave with the Prophet calling his words 'rubbish'. It is strange that three things were actually included in the will out of which, two were mentioned by the Prophet in his senses while he was blamed of talking rubbish at the third point.

WHAT DID THE PROPHET WANT TO WRITE?

Now the question arises as to what the Prophet wanted to write in his last moments? The answer is given by Umar in his own words. Ahmad ibn Abi Tahir has narrated it in his *Tarikh Baghdad* through his chain of narrators. Ibn Abil Hadid has also mentioned it in *Sharh Nahjul Balagha* Vol. 3, Pg. 97. This tradition can be summarized as follows: Abdullah Ibn Abbas was walking along with Umar. Umar said, "O Ibn Abbas! If you hide this fact, it would be obligatory for you to sacrifice a camel…Does 'Ali have desire for Caliphate even now?"

Ibn Abbas replied in affirmative. Umar said, "Does 'Ali think that the Prophet had willed regarding his Caliphate?"

Ibn Abbas again replied in affirmative. Umar said, "The Prophet had pointed it out in his life a number of times but he didn't make it clear. The Prophet desired to write it down in the last moments of his life and was fully prepared to mention 'Ali's name. I stopped him from doing so keeping the benefit of Islam and Muslims in mind. The Prophet too understood from my resistance that I have understood his intentions and hence he dropped the idea."

If this tradition is correct, it means that Umar was more concerned for the benefit of Islam than the Prophet. If this is the case, Allah should have made Umar the prophet instead of Prophet Muhammad.

If we ignore the worldly aspect of Caliphate to make the discussion simpler, disregard the historical facts presented by the first group and accept only those historical facts that are present in books of the second group, then only we will be able to derive a better solution.

It is worth asking here why couldn't Imam 'Ali (a) attain the Caliphate after the Prophet passed away?

Before replying to this question from books of Ahl al-Sunnah, I would like to state that these answers will be brief because most historical facts regarding this incident have been distorted and every possible change was made during the time of Umayyads and Abbasids.

We can clearly see how the progeny of Abu Talib was made the target of oppression. The regimes of that time had extreme hatred for Ahl al-Bayt. Scholars and tradition narrators of that time earned a large amount of wealth through fabrication of traditions disparaging the Household of the Prophet. They made enmity of Muhammad's Progeny as means of gaining proximity to the rulers. Excellences of Muhammad's progeny, which could not be hidden, were associated with others.

In spite of all this, it is a miracle of truthfulness of Muhammad's progeny that their excellences are still present in the books today along with the account of oppression they had to face.

In this book, as much as possible, I would only quote from established books of History.

FABRICATION OF TRADITIONS DURING MUAWIYAH'S REIGN

Consider the following incident as regards oppression on the Progeny of Muhammad and especially on Imam 'Ali (a):

Abul Hasan 'Ali ibn Muhammad ibn Abi Saif al-Madaini writes in his book *Al-Ahadith:* After signing the treaty with Imam Hasan (a), Muawiyah wrote to his governors: "I don't take guarantee of a person who narrates any tradition regarding the excellence of Abu Turab and his Ahl al-Bayt."

People started cursing Imam 'Ali (a) from every pulpit after this letter. They used to hate him and narrate immoral things regarding him and his family.

After this, Muawiyah wrote to his governors: "No one should accept the testimony of 'Ali and his followers."

Further he wrote to his governors: "Love all those who love Uthman and narrate his excellences. Honor such people and if someone narrates a tradition praising Uthman, send that tradition to me along with full name of the narrator."

The Governors obeyed Muawiyah's orders word by word and rewarded those who narrated excellences of Uthman. As a result the virtues of Uthman grew in large number.

Now Muawiyah sensed danger and wrote to his governors: "Traditions regarding the virtues of Uthman have increased much. When you read this letter, order the people to produce traditions regarding the other two caliphs also. Always remember that if you find a tradition about the excellence of Abu Turab, a similar tradition must be coined regarding the Companions." Muawiyah's letters were read out in public. After this, traditions regarding the Companions and first two caliphs were produced rapidly. These traditions had nothing to do with truth and reality. Jurists, judges and rulers of that time propagated these traditions everywhere.

Now let us look at the above mentioned question: Why couldn't Imam 'Ali (a) attain Caliphate?

While replying to this question, we must keep in mind the character of Imam 'Ali (a) and his sacrifices during the Prophet's lifetime including his peace treaties and battles. We will be able to solve this complexity if we understand the reasoning behind his peace treaties and battles during the Prophet's time.

Let us divide the question into two parts in order to answer it effectively:

1. Did Imam 'Ali (a) deserve Caliphate?
2. If yes, why was he kept away from it?

We will have to study the life history of Imam 'Ali (a) to answer the first question and also have to remember the sacrifices of his parents.

ABU TALIB'S SERVICES TO ISLAM

Even a common student of Islamic history is aware of how well Abu Talib carried out the job of safeguarding Allah's Messenger. We can compile an entire book if we try to explain the sacrifices of Abu Talib.

I present here a few examples of Abu Talib's sacrifice from *Sirat Ibn Hisham:*

When the Prophet started preaching religion, he invited the people of Mecca to divine unity and criticized their hand-made idols. Quraish were enraged at this but when they saw Abu Talib guarding the Prophet, they sent to him a delegation comprising of Quraishite chiefs; Rabia ibn Abdus Shams's son Utbah, Shaybah and Abu Sufyan were in the forefront of this delegation.

When this delegation came to Abu Talib it said: "Your nephew is talking ill about our gods and religion. Please stop him or you step aside and we shall deal with him."

Abu Talib calmed the people down and sent them away. A few days later, the people of Quraish came to Abu Talib again. This time also, Abu Talib sent them back. When people were convinced that Abu Talib will not hand Muhammad over to them, they took along a handsome youth called Ammara ibn Walid to him. They said to Abu Talib: "You may keep Ammara ibn Walid in exchange of your nephew."

Abu Talib refused saying: "What a bad option you have proposed! Should I raise your child and hand over mine to you so that you may kill him?"

Ibn Saad writes in *Tabaqaat-e-Kubra:* When Abdul Muttalib passed away, Abu Talib adopted the Prophet for whom he had unparalleled love, to an extent that he did not love his own children so much. He used to make the Prophet sleep beside him and take him along wherever he went. He loved the Prophet more than anything else.[1]

CANYON OF ABU TALIB

Ibn Athir has mentioned this incident of sacrifice in *Al-Kamil fit Tarikh,* Vol. 2, Pg. 59-62:

When Quraish realized that Islam is progressing day by day and their courier returned unsuccessfully from the court of King Negus, they called a meeting of tribal chiefs who came to a conclusion that they shall boycott Bani Hashim and won't have any relations with them.

They wrote down this decision on a scroll and hung it in holy Kaaba. Abu Talib took Bani Hashim and Bani Abdul Muttalib to a valley, which is also known as Sheb-e-Abi Talib (Abi Talib's canyon). They spent around three years in this place, after which the Almighty Allah revealed to the Prophet that the writing of that scroll is eaten up by termites; only the name of Allah remains. The Prophet informed Abu Talib of this fact who never doubted anything told by the Prophet. Abu Talib immediately came to the sanctuary and announced to Quraish: "Your promise is eaten up by termites; only the name of Allah remains..."Then he recited the following lines:

> "Take a lesson from this scroll. When a stranger gives some news, we are surprised. Allah has wiped out all the writings of their denial and disobedience. They were challenging a rightful person with their unjust reasoning. Whatever they said was destroyed. Whoever concocts a lie will surely be falsified."

No polytheist dared to hurt the Prophet as long as Abu Talib was alive, but when he passed away, the approach of polytheists became clear and they hurt him to their hearts' content. The Prophet

---

[1] *Tabaqaat-e-Kubra* Vol. 1, Pg. 101

mentions this fact in the following words: "Quraish could not hurt me as long as Abu Talib was alive."[1]

Let us conclude the discussion on sacrifices of Abu Talib with the words of Ibn Khaldun, the historian:

The Prophet was eight years old when his grandfather, Abdul Muttalib passed away. Abdul Muttalib entrusted to his son, Abu Talib, the custody of young Muhammad. He raised the Prophet very well, watching out all his activities carefully. He had seen the childhood and youth of the Prophet in a better way. He used to see that the Prophet kept away from all practices prevalent during the period of ignorance. Three years before migration, Abu Talib and Lady Khadija passed away. The Prophet was aggrieved deeply because of the passing away of a caring uncle and a loyal wife. The Quraish who had controlled themselves out of fear of Abu Talib, started troubling the Prophet and used to throw dirt on his place of offering prayers.[2]

This is a brief account of sacrifices of the respected father of Imam 'Ali (a). Due to space considerations in this book, it is not possible to explain the sacrifices of the respected mother of Imam 'Ali (a) for the Prophet of Islam. It would be enough to say regarding her excellence that when she passed away, the Prophet brought his own shirt for shrouding her, got down inside her grave to level the earth with his own hands and himself laid down in the grave for a while before burying her.[3]

Imam 'Ali (a) was raised under the care of Abu Talib, who was a great lover of the Prophet; and Lady Fatima bint Asad, who made so many sacrifices for the Prophet. Later on he remained under the care of the Prophet and Lady Khadija.

---

[1] *Al-Kamil fit Tarikh,* Vol. 2, Pg. 59-62
[2] *Tarikh Ibn Khaldun,* Vol. 2, Pg. 171
[3] *Tarikh Ibn Khaldun,* Vol. 2, Pg. 179-180

ALI'S SERVICES TO ISLAM

This was the account of the family of Imam 'Ali (a). Now let us have a look at the character of Imam 'Ali (a) and the services he offered for the Prophet of Islam and Islam itself.

As far as mutual relation between Imam 'Ali (a) and Islam is concerned, I would like to support the words of an Egyptian scholar, Aqqad as follows:

"'Ali was a pure Muslim because of his ideal character and the new religion did not find anyone's religion as true and deep as that of 'Ali."[1]

Dr. Taha Husayn writes in his book, *Al-Fitnatul Kubra* Uthman ibn Affan, Pg. 101:

"Imam 'Ali (a) was still a child when the Prophet announced his prophethood. The former immediately accepted Islam. After the declaration, he was raised up under the care of the Prophet and Lady Khadija. He never worshipped idols in his entire lifetime."

The clear difference between senior companions and Imam 'Ali (a) is that the latter was raised up under the shade of revelations. This honor is not shared with any one else.

This was the reason why Imam 'Ali (a) emerged as a unique personality in all aspects.

The following examples must be remembered to understand the personality of Imam 'Ali (a). Take a look at the incident of the night before migration of the Prophet, to study the sacrifices made by Imam 'Ali (a).

1. EVE OF MIGRATION (HIJRAH)

Ibn Hisham narrates that when Quraish saw that Islam was progressing by the day and spreading to other cities also, especially

---

[1] *Abqariyat al-Imam,* al-Ustad Aqqad, Pg. 13

Yathrib; and they also came to know that many followers of Prophet have migrated to Yathrib, they rightly predicted that even the Prophet would leave Mecca and move to Yathrib anytime. They summoned their chiefs to discuss this problem.

The chiefs of Meccan polytheists included Utbah, Shaybah and Abu Sufyan. During the discussion, it was suggested that the Prophet should be arrested or banished but both these options were rejected by the majority.

They came to a final conclusion that a person from each Meccan tribe should come forward and put an end to the life of the Prophet on a particular night. The involvement of numerous tribes in this act will benefit in such a way that the progeny of Abde Manaf will not be able to take revenge from so many tribes. Their hold will be tightened in this way. When the Prophet sensed the presence of people from different tribes near his house, he asked Imam 'Ali (a) to sleep on this bed and cover himself with a cloak.[1]

The death of Abu Talib's son was nearly certain. When the Prophet said that his life is in danger and asked Imam 'Ali (a) to sleep in his bed, the latter boldly asked: "Will your life be saved, if I sleep here?"

The Prophet replied in the affirmative and then told Imam 'Ali (a) to return all possessions of the people of Mecca held by the Prophet as trusts.

Imam 'Ali (a) stayed in Mecca for three days after the Prophet's migration. He returned all the belongings of the disbelievers of Mecca. After completing this job, he started for Medina on foot. His feet had swollen up due to such a long walk.[2]

2. BROTHERHOOD

After migration, the Prophet made every Emigrant (*Muhajir*) a brother of respective Helper (*Ansar*).

---

[1] *Sirah Ibn Hisham*, Vol. 2, Pg. 95
[2] *Tarikh Ibn Khaldun*, Vol. 2, Pg. 187, Ibn Athir, *Al-Kamil fit Tarikh*, Vol. 2, Pg. 75

Tears flowed from the eyes of Imam 'Ali (a) as he saw this scene. The Prophet asked the reason for this. Imam 'Ali (a) said: "You have made all of your Companions brothers of each other but did not make me anyone's brother." The Prophet said: "You are *my* brother in this world and the hereafter."[1]

3. 'ALI AND THE BATTLE OF UHAD

When Muslims suffered a setback in the Battle of Uhad and the Companions climbed the mountain, Imam 'Ali (a) continued to fight with utmost selflessness and stood like a mountain in front of the enemies. The fight of the son of Abu Talib encompassed the entire battlefield. This was the time when a voice from heaven called out: "If there is any sword, it is Zulfiqar. If there is any brave youth, it is 'Ali."

When he returned home after protecting Islam and the Prophet of Islam, he handed over the sword to his wife, Lady Fatima Zahra and recited the following lines:

"O Fatima! Take this sword. This sword is worth praising. I do not fear or tremble in the battlefield. I swear by my life that I have done Jihad for the love of the Prophet and obedience of Almighty Allah."[2]

4. ALI AND THE PREACHING OF SURAH BARA'AT

Muhammad ibn Husain narrates from Ahmad ibn Mufaddal from Asbaat that Saadi said: "When the initial verses of Surah Baraat were revealed, the Prophet made Abu Bakr the leader of Hajj and handed over those verses to him and asked him to read them aloud in public.

Abu Bakr took the verses and moved on, but when he reached near the trees of a place called Zil Halifa, Imam 'Ali (a) came from behind mounted on the Prophet's camel and took the verses away from him. Abu Bakr returned to the Prophet and said: 'O Messenger of Allah! May my parents be sacrificed on you, was any verse

---

[1] *Sirah Ibn Hisham*, Vol. 2, Pg. 95-97-111
[2] *Tarikh Tabari*, Vol. 3, Pg. 154, *Murujuz Zahab*, Masoodi Vol. 2, Pg. 284

revealed regarding me?' The Prophet said, 'No, my message can be delivered either by me or 'Ali only.'"[1]

5. 'ALI GOES TO YEMEN TO PROPAGATE ISLAM

The Prophet sent Khalid ibn Walid to Yemen to preach Islam but no one accepted it on his invitation. Then the Prophet appointed Imam 'Ali (a) to propagate Islam in Yemen and ordered him to sent Khalid and his companions back to Medina.

Imam 'Ali (a) sent back Khalid and his companions immediately on reaching the place; then he read aloud the letter of the Prophet before the people of Yemen. As a result of his preaching, the tribe of Hamadan accepted Islam in a single day.[2]

6. HAROON OF MUHAMMAD

Imam 'Ali (a) participated in all battles except the Battle of Tabuk as the Prophet had appointed him as his deputy in Medina on this occasion.

Imam Muslim ibn Hajjaj has narrated this incident in the following words: "Saad ibn Abi Waqqas narrates that the Prophet told Imam 'Ali (a), 'You are to me as Aaron was to Moses. The only difference is that there would be no prophet after me.'"

Saad ibn Abi Waqqas narrates that the Prophet asked Imam 'Ali (a) to stay in Medina at the time of the Battle of Tabuk. Imam 'Ali (a) said, "You are leaving me behind with women and children?"

The Prophet said, "Aren't you pleased that you are to me as Aaron was to Moses except that there would be no prophet after me?"

7. CONQUEROR OF KHAIBER

When the Companions failed to conquer Khaiber and fled from the enemy, the Prophet announced: "Tomorrow I shall hand over the flag

---

[1] *Tarikh Tabari*, Vol. 3, Pg. 154
[2] Ibn Athir, *Al-Kamil fit Tarikh*, Vol. 2, Pg. 35

to a person who is a real man. He loves Allah and His Messenger and they too love him. Allah will make us capture Khaiber at his hands."

Umar says that it was the only occasion when he wished for leadership. He spent the entire night praying that the banner of Islam comes to him but the Prophet called Imam 'Ali (a) in the morning and handed the banner to him.[1]

Apart from these facts, the following issues must be kept in mind to prove the Caliphate of Imam 'Ali (a) immediately after the Prophet:

A. Imam 'Ali (a) had good understanding of the essence of the religion of Islam and he encompassed all aspects of faith. Often Imam 'Ali (a) used to sit and talk with the Prophet in private and people were completely unaware of these discussions. He used to benefit as much as he could from the Holy Prophet (s) regarding the meaning and interpretation of Qur'an.

If Imam 'Ali (a) did not question first, the Prophet used to commence the discussion. People other than Imam 'Ali (a) were divided into a few types:

1. Some were such that they used to hesitate in posing questions to the Prophet and they used to pray for some ignorant one to come forward and ask the Prophet so that they can hear something.

2. Some people were extremely foolish who had nothing to do with reality.

3. Some people were away from knowledge because of their excessive involvement in worship or in worldly matters.

4. Some people had hatred of Islam hidden in their hearts and used to consider religious knowledge as waste of time.[2]

---

[1] *Sahih Muslim*, Vol. 2, Pg. 324
[2] Ibn Abil Hadid, *Sharh Nahjul Balagha*, Vol. 3, Pg. 17

B. The Prophet used to send Imam 'Ali (a) to different places in order to appoint him as his successor and to develop self-confidence and he always returned successful.

Whenever the Prophet sent out an expedition he used to make 'Ali the leader, if the latter was included in it.

Imam 'Ali (a) never went out on an expedition under anyone's leadership.

The worst scenario of history is that Abu Bakr, during his reign trained Umar in intellectual and practical aspects and the person he himself had taught was appointed as his successor and people also accepted his Caliphate. However when the Prophet appointed a person as his successor, whom he had taught all his life, nobody accepted it!

C. Usamah's Army:

The Prophet wanted to pave way for the Caliphate of Imam 'Ali (a) before he passed away. He wanted to send all those people out of Medina who could have opposed it. So let us have a look at the incident of Usamah's army as narrated by Ibn Saad:

Four nights before the end of the month of Safar, it was Monday of 11 A.H. when the Prophet ordered an attack on Rome.

He called Usamah ibn Zaid in the morning and told him: "You take the army with you to the place where your father was martyred. Crush that area with the hooves of your horses. Attack the people of Abna in the morning and take care that they remain unaware of your arrival. If Allah gives you success, do not stay there for long. Take your guides and spies and come back."

The Prophet's illness increased on Wednesday and he readied a banner with his own hands on Thursday and said: "Usamah, march forward, taking the name of Allah; do Jihad and fight with the deniers of divine unity."

The Prophet handed that banner to Buraidah ibn Haseen Salmi. Usamah's army gathered at a place called Jarf. The chiefs of Emigrants and Helpers were also present in that army. Abu Bakr, Umar and Abu Ubaidah ibn Jarrah were enlisted first in that army. They objected to Usamah's leadership and said that a young boy has been made the leader of Emigrants.

The Prophet was much annoyed when he learnt of people's objection. He came out of his house with a cloth tied around his forehead, climbed the pulpit and said:

"O people! How can you object to Usamah's leadership? Remember, this habit of objecting is not new for you. Earlier also you had objected to the leadership Usamah's father.

By Allah! He was worthy of that leadership. After him his son is also worthy of being a leader. Usamah and his father are among those people I love most. Both father and son are good. I advise you to be good to them. They are among the best ones."

Then the Prophet left the place and returned to his house. This sermon was delivered by the Prophet on Saturday, 10th Rabiul Awwal.

After this, the Prophet's illness increased and he used to repeatedly ask Usamah's army to leave for the expedition.

The Prophet's pain intensified on Sunday. When Usamah came to take leave of him, his illness had become so serious that Usamah could not talk to him much. The Prophet raised his hands for prayer and then rested them on Usamah's head.

Usamah understood that the Prophet was praying for him. Then Usamah came to his army and ordered them to march forward taking the name of Allah. The army had hardly moved when the Prophet passed away.[1]

---

[1] *Tabaqaat Ibn Saad*, Vol. 4, Pg. 3-4

The words of Ibn Saad can be summarized as follows:

1. The Prophet readied an army to fight against Syria and Rome before he passed away.

2. Usamah, who was a young boy, was made the commander of that army.

3. People who had brought faith in the beginning of Islam, especially Abu Bakr, Umar and Abu Ubaidah ibn Jarrah were enlisted in the army.

4. When the expedition was delayed, in spite of his sickness, the Prophet came out of his house with a cloth tied around his forehead and went to the mosque.

5. He expressed his annoyance over those who had objected to Usamah's leadership and also remarked that it was an old habit of theirs. Earlier, they had objected to the leadership of Usamah's father, Zaid. However, Zaid was worthy of leadership. Similarly Usamah is worthy of leadership in spite of their criticism.

6. The army did not obey the Prophet's command in spite of repeated orders to move. They halted at a place called Jarf.

7. Why was the Prophet eager to send the army on expedition in the last days of his life?

8. What was the purpose of sending Abu Bakr, Umar and the chiefs of Emigrants under the leadership of a young boy?

9. Why did people delay the expedition in spite of repeated orders?

Was it because the Prophet wanted to eliminate every possible hindrance before he passed by and pave the way for the Caliphate of Imam 'Ali (a) in Medina?

Was there some link between dispatching Usamah's army and asking for pen and paper?

Only if Usamah hadn't delayed the expedition due to opposition from Abu Bakr and Umar and moved ahead with the army, the history of Islam would have been written in a different way. The Muslim community would not have faced such disgrace today.

A PROBE INTO SAQIFAH

1. Abu Bakr

The Outcome of earlier discussion is that Imam 'Ali (a) was rightful to Caliphate immediately after the Prophet, because he had deep relations with the Prophet of Islam and Islam itself. Islam as well as the Prophet of Islam considered him worthy of Caliphate and Imamate.

Imagine if people had presented the following proofs in support of 'Ali's candidature in Saqifah of Bani Saada:

(1) 'Ali was most proximate to the Prophet.

(2) 'Ali was raised under the Prophet's care.

(3) He was responsible for returning possessions of the people kept with the Prophet as trusts after the latter migrated.

(4) The Prophet made him his brother.

(5) He was the Prophet's son-in-law.

(6) The Prophet's progeny would continue from 'Ali.

(7) He was the commander of the Prophet's army in all battles.

(8) He is to Prophet as Haroon was to Moosa.

(9) He is the gate of the city of knowledge.

(10) He is the gate of the house of wisdom.

(11) He is the reflection of the virtues of prophets.

(12) He is a part of the light of the Prophet.

(13) He is the son of parents who raised the Prophet.

(14) He was born in holy Kaaba.

(15) He never worshipped idols.

(16) His love is compensation of the messengership of the Holy Prophet (s).

(17) He was a proof of truthfulness of Islam in imprecation ceremony (*Mubahila*).

(18) He is one of the pure members of the cloak of purity.

(19) He has complete knowledge of the Book.

(20) He bought divine pleasure in exchange of his life.

If it had been the case and Muslims had elected him for leadership, they would not have faced such deviations and the history of Islam would have been written with gold. Dr. Taha Husayn had mentioned correctly in the following words:

"'Ali is worthy of Caliphate without any doubt due to his proximity to the Prophet and Islam, his sacrifices, his perfect character, attachment with religion, knowledge of Qur'an and Prophetic Practice (*Sunnah*)."[1]

Ibn Hajar Asqalani narrates the important virtues of Imam 'Ali (a) in the following words:

"'Ali ibn Abi Talib was the first to accept Islam according to most scholars. He was raised up under the Prophet's care and was not separated from him at any time. He participated in all battles except the Battle of Tabuk as on this occasion he remained in Medina on the Prophet's order. And the Prophet had said: 'O 'Ali! Aren't you pleased that you are to me as Haroon was to Moosa?'"

Imam 'Ali (a) was the commander of the army in most battles. When the Prophet was making Companions, brothers of each other, he made Imam 'Ali (a) his brother. There are countless virtues of Imam 'Ali (a). Ahmad ibn Hanbal says: "There is no Companion except

---

[1] *Al-Fitnah al-Kubra Uthman bin Affan*, Pg. 102-103

Imam 'Ali (a) for whom so many traditions praising his virtue are present."[1]

Some scholars say that the reason behind so many traditions narrating the virtues of Imam 'Ali is that the Umayyads had tried every means to conceal them. Hence the narrators thought that it was their religious responsibility to publish the virtues of Imam 'Ali (a). The sky has never witnessed a scholar like Imam 'Ali (a). The Prophet had announced in the Battle of Khaiber: Tomorrow I shall hand the banner to a person who loves Allah and His Messenger and they too love him. Allah will grant victory at his hands. On the next day, the Prophet handed over the banner to Imam 'Ali (a). Umar used to say: This was the only day when I desired leadership. The Prophet handed over the verses of Surah Baraat to 'Ali (a) to preach. He said that the verses of Qur'an can only be preached either by him or by someone who is from him.

Also, the Prophet had said: 'Ali is my successor in this world and in the hereafter.

The Prophet had gathered 'Ali, Fatima, Hasan and Husain in a cloak and said:

(إِنَّمَا يُرِيدُ اللَّهُ لِيُذْهِبَ عَنكُمُ الرِّجْسَ أَهْلَ الْبَيْتِ وَيُطَهِّرَكُمْ تَطْهِيراً.)

Allah only desires to keep away the uncleanness from you, O people of the House! and to purify you a (thorough) purifying.[2]

Imam 'Ali (a) covered himself with a cloak and slept on the Prophet's bed to save his life during the night when the latter migrated to Medina.

The Prophet used to tell Imam 'Ali (a): You are the chief of all believers after me.

---

[1] Ibn Hajar Asqalani, *Al-Isabah fi Tamiz al-Sahaba*, Vol. 2, Pg. 501-502
[2] Surah Ahzaab 33:33

The Prophet ordered the doors of all houses opening inside the mosque to be closed permanently except that of Imam 'Ali (a). Imam 'Ali (a) was allowed to pass from the mosque any time as there was no other way for him to pass by.

The Prophet ordered a pulpit to be made out of camel saddles. Then he raised the hand of Imam 'Ali (a) in front of thousands of people and announced: "'Ali is the master for whom I am the master."

The Prophet called 'Ali, Fatima, Hasan and Husain when the following verse of holy Qur'an was revealed:

فَمَنْ حَاجَّكَ فِيهِ مِنْ بَعْدِ مَا جَاءَكَ مِنَ الْعِلْمِ فَقُلْ تَعَالَوْا نَدْعُ أَبْنَاءَنَا وَأَبْنَاءَكُمْ وَنِسَاءَنَا وَنِسَاءَكُمْ وَأَنْفُسَنَا وَأَنْفُسَكُمْ ثُمَّ نَبْتَهِلْ فَنَجْعَلْ لَعْنَةَ اللَّهِ عَلَى الْكَاذِبِينَ.

"But whoever disputes with you in this matter after what has come to you of knowledge, then say: Come let us call our sons and your sons and our women and your women and our near people and your near people, then let us be earnest in prayer, and pray for the curse of Allah on the liars."[1]

He prayed: O Lord! These are my Ahl al-Bayt. Imam Tirmidhi narrates from Imran ibn Haseen a tradition of the Prophet: "Ultimately what do you want from 'Ali? 'Ali is from me and I am from 'Ali without any doubt. He is the chief of all believers after me."

Now the same question arises. Why was Imam 'Ali (a) kept away from Caliphate in spite of so many virtues?

We will have to study the events in the Prophet's last moments and after he passed away. We must also remember that Imam 'Ali (a) was busy all the time in the burial of the Prophet after he passed away. On the other hand, the politically inclined people left his body

---

[1] Surah Aale Imran 3:61

and gathered in Saqifah of Bani Saada and established their Caliphate.[1]

According to Umar, one of the reasons behind keeping Imam 'Ali (a) away from Caliphate is that Arabs could not bear to see both prophethood and Caliphate in a single family.

To summarize this incident, the Prophet passed away in 11 A.H. and Imam 'Ali (a) became involved in his burial. The political waves were flowing all around outside the Prophet's house. The topic of Caliphate was the most favorite one.

Saad ibn Abu Ubadah reached Saqifah of Bani Saada along with the chiefs of Aws and Khazraj tribes. Umar and Abu Ubaidah were discussing the issue of Caliphate in the mosque. Other groups were busy holding discussions at different places.

When Abu Bakr heard the news of the Prophet's passing away, he came to the Prophet's house from Sunh locality. He saw Umar standing at the door with his sword unsheathed. He was threatening people saying: "I shall kill whoever says that the Prophet has passed away. The Prophet hasn't passed away. He has gone to the heaven like Prophet Isa. He will return after some days and cut off the nose and ears of hypocrites."

As a result of this heartrending tragedy, Umar had apparently lost his senses. Suddenly someone informed him about the activities prevailing in Saqifah. This same person who had lost his senses suddenly became conscious and sent a person to Abu Bakr. The person told Abu Bakr that Umar wanted to seek advice from him in an extremely serious matter.

As soon as Abu Bakr got the news, he came out of the house. Then both of them went to Saqifah of Bani Saada. Over there, chiefs of

---

[1] Keeping this incident in mind, Rumi, the mystic says: "Since the Companions were having love for the world they left the Prophet unshrouded." Abu 'Ali Qalandar Panipati has praised 'Ali (a) saying: "An Imam who on the day of the passing away of the Prophet left the caliphate and sat down to mourn the Messenger of Allah (s)."

Aws and Khazraj tribes were bent upon declaring Saad ibn Ubadah as their Caliph.

However in such a case, Imam 'Ali (a) did what he should have done. He remained busy with the Prophet's burial.

Abbas, the Prophet's uncle was aggrieved because of his passing away. He wanted to pay allegiance to Imam 'Ali (a) in this state but Imam 'Ali (a) rejected it straightaway saying that the Prophet's body was not even buried and he could not accept Caliphate at such a moment.

Abu Sufyan ibn Harb came to Imam 'Ali (a) thrice and asked him to take hold of Caliphate. He had said: "If you want I can fill up the streets of Medina with troops in order to end this unpleasant rule." However, Imam 'Ali (a) rejected him straightaway saying: "How come you have become a well-wisher of Islam? You want to play the role of a Caliph-maker?"

Even though Helpers had arranged the meet at Saqifah, they failed to gain any benefit from there. A small account of this probe is as follows:

The people of Aws and Khazraj tribes gathered in Saqifah of Bani Saada. Saad ibn Ubadah was one of them.

Saad was sick and could not speak loudly. He had appointed one of his sons to speak for him. Hence his son spoke out to public loudly whatever Saad wanted to say. Saad said:

"O Helpers (Ansar)! You hold a high rank in religion. No tribe in entire Arabia has a virtue, which you people have. The Prophet preached the worship of Allah and asked people to keep away from idols in Mecca for a number of years. All the tribes except a few people opposed him. Almighty Allah has given you this honor. Allah sent His Prophet to you and chose you to help the religion.

You proved tough before the enemies of religion and you presented more sacrifices for the sake of Islam than any other tribe. Allah's

Messenger remained pleased with you till he passed away. Strengthen yourselves. You are more rightful to kingship than anyone else."

This news reached Umar, the man who had lost his senses due to grief of the Prophet. Immediately he came to the door of the Prophet's house and called Abu Bakr and they set out for Saqifah. Abu Bakr announced over there:

"We, Emigrants were the first to accept Islam and we are from the clan of the Prophet. You all are helpers of Allah and our brothers according to Book of Allah. You are our partners in religion and we love and honor you more than others. You have always made sacrifices and I expect sacrifice from you even now. You have Abu Ubaidah and Umar ibn Khattab in front of you. You may pay allegiance to whomever you wish. According to me, both of them are worthy of it."

Umar and Abu Ubaidah said that it was not possible for anyone to take the post of Caliph in the presence of Abu Bakr. And that the latter was more rightful for it. At this moment, Habbab ibn Mundhir stood up from the Helpers and said:

"O Helpers! Maintain your unity. It was your land where worship of Allah was done freely. You only had given refuge to Allah's Messenger. You had helped him and after migration, the Prophet came to you only…In spite of this, if these people do not agree with your rule then there should be a leader each for both the groups."

Umar said that it was not possible. When Bashir ibn Saad of Khazraj sensed that the Helpers are trying to surrender the leadership to Saad ibn Ubadah, he remembered the ancient enmity between Aws and Khazraj tribes. He did not like Saad as leader because Saad was from Aws and he thought that the leadership would go to Aws. He thought that this would be something to boast of, for the progeny of Aws, which could be a cause of weakness of Khazraj and he knew that kingship cannot come to his tribe. He thought that it was better to hand it over to an Emigrant instead of letting it fall into the hands of Aws tribe.

With this in mind, he stood up and announced: "O Helpers! It is true that we have served Islam. However, we must keep this fact in mind that we did Jihad only for the sake of pleasure and obedience of Allah and His Messenger.

Muhammad belonged to the tribe of Quraish and hence only the latter has the right to his inheritance. Fear Allah and keep away from fighting them."

Abu Bakr stood up and said: "Umar and Abu Ubaidah are present here. You may pay allegiance to whomever you like."

Both said: "By Allah! How can we command you? You extend your hand so that we may pay allegiance."

Abu Bakr stretched his hand and Basheer ibn Saad paid him allegiance even before Umar and Abu Ubaidah.

Habbab ibn Mundhir stood up and called out: "O disobedient one! O enemy of the community, Basheer! You have done this out of jealousy. The tribe of Aws thought that if they remained behind Khazraj in paying allegiance, Khazraj will become dearer to the rulers. Hence Usaid ibn Khuzair from Aws also paid allegiance and then the entire tribe followed suit.

Saad ibn Ubadah was carried to his house on a bed. He did not pay allegiance as long as he lived. Later he went to Syria and was murdered there during the last days of Abu Bakr's Caliphate. It was alleged that some jinn had shot him dead with arrows at night; however, reporters say that it was the wicked Khalid ibn Walid.

Sometime after this allegiance, Baraa ibn Aazib came to the Prophet's house and saw that the Prophet was not yet buried. He announced: "I have seen with my own eyes that Umar and Abu Ubaidah are forcing each passer-by to pay allegiance to Abu Bakr."[1]

ANALYSIS OF THE INCIDENTS AT SAQIFAH

We have already probed into the incident of Saqifah entirely. The character of Umar in these events is clear to all who are not blind.

1. We want to know the reason why Umar did not come to the Prophet's house for presenting condolences. Even if he had no interest in 'Ali and his progeny, he should at least come to comfort his own daughter (Hafasah) who was widowed recently. He could have also got the honor of participating in the burial of the Prophet.

2. If he didn't want to condole the aggrieved family, why didn't he go inside to call Abu Bakr when he got the news of Aws and Khazraj?

3. Why did he send someone else to call Abu Bakr instead of going in himself? Why did he wait for Abu Bakr outside?

4. There were many Companions gathered in the house of the aggrieved family. Why Umar chose to seek advice only from Abu Bakr?

5. Was the presence of Abu Bakr inside the house and waiting of Umar at the door a coincidence or it was preplanned?

6. What was the decision taken by Umar and Abu Ubaidah before Abu Bakr arrived?

7. Abu Bakr had narrated the virtues of Emigrants. Were all Emigrants included in those virtues or only Umar and Abu Ubaidah?

8. Abu Bakr had narrated two reasons to prove Emigrants' right to Caliphate.

A. They were the first to accept Islam

---

[1] Abdul Fattah Abdul Maqsood, *Al-Imam 'Ali bin Abi Talib*, Vol. 1, Pg. 149

B. They were from the Prophet's clan

If the two above mentioned reasons are criteria for Caliphate, who is more eligible for Caliphate than Imam 'Ali (a)? The reasons are:

1. He was the first to accept Islam

2. He was nearer in relation to the Prophet than Abu Bakr

Then why Imam 'Ali (a) was not appointed Caliph as per the standard put forward by Abu Bakr?

9. If Caliphate is the right only of Emigrants why Abu Bakr selected only two persons from them, viz. Umar and Abu Ubaidah?

Can anyone give the reason for this selection? Was this selection without preference?

10. If it was necessary to appoint a Caliph from Emigrants, Abu Bakr could have advised the Helpers to elect any one from Emigrants as the leader. Why didn't he do that?

11. What was the logic behind putting forward only two names out of so many Emigrants?

12. Why did Umar and Abu Ubaidah reject the offer of Abu Bakr? Why did they prefer the leadership of Abu Bakr? What is the logical reason behind it?

13. Were all links in Saqifah procedure joined coincidently or everything was preplanned? It is absolutely necessary for students of History to know the answers of these questions.

14. Was there any relation between the events at Saqifah and army of Usamah? Did the discussion held between Umar and Abu Ubaidah in the mosque had any relation to Saqifah?

Two persons accompanied Abu Bakr to Saqifah. Didn't the friendship of these three persons prove beneficial in Saqifah?

15. Where were other Emigrants when only a few people had gathered at Saqifah to appoint a Caliph?

16. The enmity of Aws and Khazraj popped out in Saqifah. Was it a coincidence or was it backed by a preplanned conspiracy?

17. If some conspiracy was involved in the creation of this dispute, would you like to probe into it?

18. Was the election of Caliph more important than the Prophet's burial?

19. Couldn't Abu Bakr ask the Muslims to wait till the Prophet was buried?

Why was he in such a hurry that he left the Last Prophet who was also his son-in-law, behind, without burying? He could have at least waited till the burial. Did he not express his lack of love for his son-in-law by hastening so much?

20. Is there any link between the complex events at Saqifah, the tradition in which the Prophet asked for pen and paper and the incident of Usamah's army? It is necessary for the students of history to know the answers of above mentioned questions also. I personally believe that Umar played a central role in all these events. He was the one who had discussed the issue with Abu Ubaidah earlier and drafted a plan. He called Abu Bakr to accomplish it. After this, these main characters of Islamic history finalized a plan on way to Saqifah.

This is the reason why Abu Bakr was putting forward the names of these two persons and vice versa.

Did the entire Muslim Ummah made them their representative and send them to Saqifah? The fact is that not even a part of the Ummah was present in Saqifah.

Who gave the permission to this small group to decide the future of the entire Ummah?

It is a fact that when Abu Bakr was called, no advice regarding the leadership of Islam was taken from any Muslim before or after that. It is impossible to neglect the whole incident of Saqifah calling it a coincidence. It was a thing planned a long time ago. One in which the role of Umar is exposed.

ANOTHER REASON FOR DENIAL OF CALIPHATE TO ALI (A)

You have already read the incident of passing away of the Prophet and the Caliphate of Abu Bakr. Why Imam 'Ali (a) was denied Caliphate?

One important reason behind it is given by Hafiz in the following words, which we quote here for our readers who prefer justice:

Imam 'Ali (a) had intricate relations with Quraish. Quraish had severe envy for Imam 'Ali (a) because he had killed their chiefs in battles. He had weakened their hold. He had demeaned their honor. The envy could not be removed from their hearts even after accepting Islam.

Just imagine that if you have been a disbeliever for a year or two (God forbid!) and your brother or son was killed in a battle against Islam and later you become a Muslim. However, will all the strained relations and hatred be eliminated immediately? Would you embrace the person who killed your brother or son? It is really difficult! It is possible only when you have accepted Islam from the depths of your heart.

However, in contrast to this, most Arabs accepted Islam either under compulsion or to gain something.

Many of them had recited the formula of Faith (*Kalimah*) to safe their lives, while others had done it to demean the tribes with whom they had enmity. You must remember that a number of disbelievers were killed in battles by Imam 'Ali (a) and other Muslims. However, the heirs of those disbelievers held only Imam 'Ali (a) responsible for their death. They used to consider Imam 'Ali (a) as their enemy and killer of their relatives.

Their hearts were not cleansed even after accepting Islam. The fire of hatred for Imam 'Ali (a) blazed in their hearts. They were always ready to take revenge from Imam 'Ali (a). By denying Caliphate, they had taken the first installment of their revenge and they expressed it whole heartedly in Kerbala. The family of Imam 'Ali (a) was martyred in Kerbala despite their thirst and hunger only to revenge this.[1]

If the Islamic Ummah had any feeling of justice, it should have postponed the issue of Caliphate and allegiance till the Prophet's burial. Any person who has a heart will be moved on knowing that people did not attend the funeral of that great personality, whose Caliphate and succession was planned by them. No one came to offer condolence to his near and dear ones. Why did the love and friendship end as soon as the Prophet passed away?

Imam 'Ali (a) loved the Prophet very much and he fulfilled his obligation. He gave preference to the Prophet's funeral over gaining political power. The politically motivated people took the advantage of this. Imam 'Ali (a) always liked peace treaties and understanding. The greatness of Imam 'Ali's peaceful character can be seen from the fact that he did not fight the Caliphate structured in Saqifah. He observed silence for the safety Islam and holy Qur'an. He sacrificed his correct decisions for the benefit of Islamic Ummah.

Imam 'Ali (a) describes this policy of peace in *Nahjul Balagha* as follows:

Almighty Allah was made Muhammad the admonisher of all the worlds. When he passed away the Muslims fought with each other for his Caliphate.

---

[1] Ibn Abil Hadid, *Sharh Nahjul Balagha*, Vol. 3, Pg. 283, Egypt

By Allah! I had never thought that Arabs will take Caliphate away from the family of the Prophet. I had never thought that people would leave me and appoint someone else as their leader. When I saw people paying allegiance to a person, I did not oppose them forcefully because I knew that if I did so, most people will leave Islam...

In such conditions, I thought that I should bear personal loss in order to safeguard Islam.[1] I did not want to take the kingdom for a short time and cause permanent loss to Islam. The loss of Islam was more hurting to me than loss of my rule."

What can be a better proof of Imam 'Ali's peace-loving nature than the fact that he objected to the three caliphs during their rule only in religious matters.

History of the universe will fail to present such a peace-loving person like Imam 'Ali (a) because he sacrificed his rights and those of his wife for the sake of benefit of Islam. Lady Fatima Zahra was denied inheritance of her father, Fadak, which was gifted to her by her father. In spite of this, Imam 'Ali (a) did not let peace let go off his hands. Apart from this, during the early days of Abu Bakr's Caliphate, it was seen that Umar came to the house of Imam 'Ali (a) along with his followers. They stood at the door and brought wood to burn down his house. Is it possible to stop the people from talking about these historical incidents?[2]

INCIDENT OF FADAK

The brief account of Fadak is that it is a hamlet of Hijaz, near Medina. Jews inhabited it for hundreds of years, and as the land was very fertile, Jews used to cultivate it.

---

[1] Ibn Abil Hadid, *Sharh Nahjul Balagha*
[2] Abdul Fattah Abdul Maqsood, Al-Imam *'Ali bin Abi Talib* vol. 1, pg. 216

In 7 A.H., the people of Fadak surrendered their land to the Prophet. Fadak was now a personal property of the Prophet. Almighty Allah says in Surah Hashr:

(وَمَااَفَاءَ اللّٰهُ عَلٰى رَسُوْلِهٖ مِنْهُمْ فَمَا اَوْجَفْتُمْ عَلَيْهِ مِنْ خَيْلٍ وَّ؟ رِكَابٍ وَلٰكِنَّ اللّٰهَ يُسَلِّطُ رُسُلَهٗ عَلٰى مَنْ يَّشَاءُ وَاللّٰهُ عَلٰى كُلِّ شَيْءٍ قَدِيْرٌ.)

And whatever Allah restored to His Apostle from them, you did not press forward against it any horse or a riding camel, but Allah gives authority to His apostles against whom He pleases, and Allah has power over all things.[1]

The Prophet had sowed seven date seeds in Fadak and gifted the entire Fadak property to his daughter, Lady Fatima Zahra. It was used by Lady Sayyada only after it was gifted to her. After the Prophet's passing away, Abu Bakr made Imam 'Ali (a) and Fatima his political victims and confiscated Fadak. Fadak was used by the family of Prophet Muhammad (s) before. The letter of Imam 'Ali (a) is a proof of this seizure of land. He had mentioned in that letter as follows:

"It was the only land owned by us under the sky. Even then people looked at it with greedy eyes. The other party did not feel ashamed while snatching it away. Allah is the best judge."[2]

Lady Fatima Zahra was sole legal owner of that property. It was necessary for the Caliph to leave the Prophet's gift untouched. If the Caliph had any legal dispute in this matter he should have filed a suit and allowed it to remain in the custody of Lady Sayyada.

The strangest point in this case is that Abu Bakr always believed that Fadak was not Lady Sayyada's property and that it was the property of Muslims. Hence he seized this land on the first day of his rule. Lady Sayyada was claimant in this case and Abu Bakr the defendant.

---

[1] Surah Hashr 59:6
[2] Ibn Abil Hadid, *Sharh Nahjul Balagha*, Vol. 4, Pg. 28, Letter no. 45

The cataclysm of this incident is that the opposition party was the judge. It is clear that the petition was against Abu Bakr or at least against Muslim Ummah led by Abu Bakr. In both cases, Abu Bakr was defendant and he had no right to adjudicate this case whatsoever.

FADAK IN VARIOUS HANDS

Before describing the details of Fadak, it is necessary to mention that Fadak was a public property during the rule of Abu Bakr and Umar.

During Uthman's rule, the entire property was handed over to Marwan ibn Hakam. O God! Can anyone tell us if what Uthman did was right?

Ahl al-Sunnah scholars present the character of Abu Bakr as an example here. We must ask them why Uthman did not follow Abu Bakr and acted differently. Which of the two Caliphs was right in this matter?

When Fadak was under the custody of the Prophet's daughter, Muslim Ummah could not bear to see it. Now when it came under the custody of Marwan, why are people quiet? Abu Bakr had said that Fadak is not the personal property of any Muslim. It belongs to the entire Muslim Ummah.

When Muawiyah ibn Abu Sufyan came to power, he divided Fadak into three parts. A third was given to Marwan ibn Hakam, a third to Amr ibn Uthman ibn Affan, the son of Uthman and a third was given to his son, Yazid ibn Muawiyah ibn Abu Sufyan.

When Marwan came to power after Yazid, he did what the third Caliph had done by disassociating his other two partners and seized the entire property.

Afterwards Fadak became the property of his son, Abdul Aziz. When Umar ibn Abdul Aziz came to power, he handed over Fadak to Fatima's progeny. When Umar ibn Abdul Aziz died, Yazid came to power from Bani Umayyah. He seized Fadak from Fatima's progeny and handed it over to Marwan's progeny. Fadak remained with Marwan's progeny till the end of Umayyad rule.

When the Umayyad rule ended, the Abbasid Caliph, Abul Abbas Saffah handed over Fadak to Fatima's progeny.

Mansoor Dawaniqi took it back from Fatima's progeny. After that, his son, Mahdi returned it to Fatima's progeny. It was seized again by Hadi and Rashid. Mamoon Rashid the Abbaside gave it back and Mutasim snatched it away later.

Historians haven't narrated what happened after that.

It proves that Fadak was like a toy for the rulers. They used to hand it over to whomever they wished and seized it whenever and whatever part of it they liked. The writings of Mamoon Rashid at the time of returning Fadak back are enlightening, for he has explained about the inheritors of Fadak in detail.

MAMOON RETURNS FADAK

The Historian, Balazari narrates what Mamoon Rashid wrote. In 210 A.H., Mamoon gave order that Fadak be returned to its legal owners. He wrote the following to his governor Qathm ibn Ja'far in Medina:

"Amirul Momineen holds a high religious position in front of Allah as the successor of his last messenger. This position and nearness demands that he should follow Allah's Messenger in actions. He should obey the Prophet's orders and make sure that he gives the possession of things gifted by the Prophet to their original owners.

That the Prophet gifted Fadak to his daughter, Lady Fatima Zahra is as daylight, without any doubt.

Hence Amirul Momineen suggests that Fadak be returned to its original owners. Amirul Momineen should seek nearness of Allah through this act. Also he wants to become a follower of the Prophetic Practice (*Sunnah*) through this justice."

Mamoon then ordered his clerks to enter it in official records.

"After the Prophet's passing away, it was announced every year during Hajj: Whoever has something granted to by the Prophet they should come forward and take it. In spite of this, why was the Prophet's daughter kept away from her right?

Mamoon Rashid had written to his slave, Mubarak Tabari that the entire property of Fadak should be returned to Fatima's progeny. The help of Muhammad ibn Yahya ibn Zaid ibn 'Ali ibn Husain ibn 'Ali ibn Abi Talib and Muhammad ibn Abdullah ibn Hasan ibn 'Ali ibn Husain ibn 'Ali ibn Abi Talib must be taken in this matter. Arrangements must be made to increase the yield."

The above letter was written in 210 A.H.[1]

JUDGMENT REGARDING FADAK

"So many calamities befell me; that if they had fallen upon days they would have turned into nights." (From the Lamentation of Fatima Zahra)

Allah's Messenger was granted Fadak by Allah, which he gifted to his daughter upon divine commands and Lady Fatima utilized its income during the Prophet's lifetime. After the Prophet's passing away, Abu Bakr dismissed all the servants from Fadak and usurped it. Lady Zahra went to Abu Bakr when she got this news and demanded her right.

Abu Bakr presented an astounding tradition in reply. He said that the Prophet has said: "We prophets neither inherit nor leave any inheritance. Whatever we leave behind is charity."

---

[1] Balazari, *Futuhul Buldan*, Pg. 46-47

THE TRADITION OF NON-INHERITANCE AND HOLY QUR'AN

Only narrator of this tradition is Abu Bakr. A similar tradition is narrated also by Abu Bakr only. After the Prophet's passing away, people had difference of opinion as to where should he should be buried. At that moment, Abu Bakr said that the Prophet has said: "All prophets were buried at the place they passed away." While the historian, Tabari says that there are numerous prophets who were buried at places different from where they had passed away.

Lady Zahra did not accept the tradition of non-inheritance because if the Prophet's progeny does not inherit, the Prophet should have told his daughter that she would not inherit him. Abu Bakr's words mean that the Prophet did not inform his heir and secretly conveyed this fact to a person who had no relation with it. This tradition of non-inheritance was not heard by Imam 'Ali (a) because if he had done so, he would have never allowed his wife to demand her right. Also why did the Prophet tell this important thing only to Abu Bakr? Why didn't he inform other Muslims also?

TRADITION OF NON-INHERITANCE IS AGAINST HOLY QUR'AN

The stand of Lady Fatima was strong regarding above mentioned tradition of non-inheritance. She had rejected this tradition saying that it was against holy Qur'an.

1. Almighty Allah says in holy Qur'an: Allah enjoins you concerning your children:

(فُيُوصِيكُمُ اللَّهُ فِي أَوْلَادِكُمْ لِلذَّكَرِ مِثْلُ حَظِّ الْأُنْثَيَيْنِ.)

The Male shall have the equal of the portion of two females.[1]

---

[1] Surah Nisa 4:11

2. Almighty Allah has said regarding the inheritance of everyone as follows:

(وَلِكُلٍّ جَعَلْنَا مَوَالِيَ مِمَّا تَرَكَ الْوَالِدَانِ وَالْأَقْرَبُونَ.)

And to every one we have appointed heirs of what parents and near relatives leave.[1]

Readers are requested to pay attention to the phrase, "and to everyone." It is explicitly said in this tradition regarding inheritance of "everyone."

Refer to all the verses regarding inheritance, but you won't find a single verse stating that people have their heirs while prophets do not. If there is a verse denying inheritance of the prophet it should be brought forward. I challenge the whole world till Judgment Day to bring forward such a verse.

Three parts of the tradition of non-inheritance are as follows:

1. Prophets do not inherit anyone

2. The progeny of prophets does not inherit them

3. Whatever prophets leave behind is charity

Holy Qur'an rejects all the three points of this tradition.

Almighty Allah says in holy Qur'an:

(وَوَرِثَ سُلَيْمَانُ دَاوُودَ.)

And Sulaiman was Dawood's heir.[2]

If a prophet cannot be the heir of anyone, how Prophet Sulaiman can be the heir of Prophet Dawood?

This proves that the first point of this tradition is incorrect.

---

[1] Surah Nisa 4:33
[2] Surah Naml 27:12

Also the Almighty Allah has mentioned in the verse that Prophet Sulaiman became the heir of Prophet Dawood.

Hence Sulaiman (a) became the heir of a prophet. If the second point of the above mentioned tradition is correct that there is no heir for a prophet, how could someone inherit prophet Dawood? Why wasn't his property given as charity? Hence this single verse has proved all three parts of the tradition of non-inheritance incorrect.

The supplication of Prophet Zakariya (a) is mentioned in Qur'an as follows:

(قَالَ رَبِّ إِنِّي وَهَنَ الْعَظْمُ مِنِّي وَاشْتَعَلَ الرَّأْسُ شَيْبًا وَلَمْ أَكُن بِدُعَائِكَ رَبِّ شَقِيًّا. وَإِنِّي خِفْتُ الْمَوَالِيَ مِن وَرَائِي وَكَانَتِ امْرَأَتِي عَاقِرًا فَهَبْ لِي مِن لَّدُنكَ وَلِيًّا. يَرِثُنِي وَيَرِثُ مِنْ آلِ يَعْقُوبَ وَاجْعَلْهُ رَبِّ رَضِيًّا. يَا زَكَرِيَّا إِنَّا نُبَشِّرُكَ بِغُلَامٍ اسْمُهُ يَحْيَى لَمْ نَجْعَل لَّهُ مِن قَبْلُ سَمِيًّا.)

He said: My Lord! Surely my bones are weakened and my head flares with hoariness, and, my Lord! I have never been unsuccessful in my prayer to Thee. And surely I fear my cousins after me, and my wife is barren, therefore grant me from thyself an heir. Who should inherit me and inherit from the children of Yaqoob, and make him, my Lord, one in whom Thou art well pleased. O Zakariya! Surely we give you good news of a boy whose name shall be Yahya: We have not made before anyone his equal.[1]

Read the above mentioned verse repeatedly. Prophet Zakariya has asked for an heir and the Almighty Allah granted him one and selected a name for him.

If there is no inheritance for prophets, why Prophet Zakariya asked for an heir from Allah?

Even if he asked for it, why didn't Allah silence him saying: "You are a prophet? What are you saying? There is no inheritance for a prophet. You should not ask for an heir."

---

[1] Surah Maryam 19:6

If there are no heirs of prophet, why the Almighty Allah granted him one and selected a name for him?

Lady Sayyada recited the above mentioned verse and rejected the tradition of non-inheritance. However, Abu Bakr refused to restore her rights in spite of it.

Finally Lady Sayyada said: "Now mount your Caliphate after putting a bridle to it. I will meet you on Judgment Day. Allah will arbitrate on that day and the liar will be at loss.

O son of Abu Qahafa! Does the Book of Allah say that you can become the heir of your father while I cannot do so? You are talking strange things.

Have you left the Book of Allah purposely? Didn't you hear the words of Allah: Relatives are inheritors of each other in the Book of Allah? Did Allah reveal a verse regarding non-inheritance of my father? Or you say that people of two communities cannot inherit each other? If yes, didn't I and my father belong to the same community? Are you aware of general and particular matters of holy Qur'an more than my father and my cousin?"

After presenting these proofs and verses of holy Qur'an, Lady Sayyada noticed that they had no effect on the Caliph. She became annoyed and returned home crying.

She knew it before that the Caliph would not return Fadak to her. She went there only to exhaust the argument. She proved it to the world that when her father had intended to write a tradition a few days ago, it was the same group, which had said that they do not need a tradition and the Book of Allah was sufficient for them. When she recited the verse of holy Qur'an, they replied to her by narrating a tradition.

Hence Lady Sayyada proved to the world that those who had rejected the tradition earlier were now rejecting the verses of holy Qur'an also. She knew it before that she won't get her right back because the people who could snatch the Caliphate of her husband a few days before could also seize Fadak from her.

TRADITION OF NON-INHERITANCE AND DEMANDS OF EXPRESS TEXT AND REASON

Let us view the tradition narrated by Abu Bakr in the light of the Prophet's life history.

Allah's Messenger never excepted himself from the commandments of the pure law of Shariah.

1. It would be wrong to say that a prophet should neither offer prayer nor observe fast (God forbid!).

It would be wrong because a prophet cannot be exempted from the commandments of Shariah. Therefore, as a prophet is not exempted from prayer, fast and other Islamic commandments, he can also not be exempted from the commandment of Islam regarding inheritance.

2. Wasn't there a political aim behind rejecting a simple Islamic commandment in the case of Fadak?

3. Was Abu Bakr trying to suppress his political rival, Imam 'Ali (a) and his family by denying inheritance to Lady Sayyada?

4. Is this matter linked to political economics?

Was it intended to deprive Imam 'Ali (a) and his family from the leftover bread also?

5. Was it intended to weaken Imam 'Ali (a) financially and stop him from contesting for the post of Caliphate?

6. Was it intended to consider those people apostate who rejected the Caliphate of Abu Bakr and bar them from benefits, from Zakat and attack them? Was this reasoning behind usurping Fadak? Did they fear that if Fadak remains in possession of 'Ali, he would help their rivals financially?

7. Was it intended to demean the honor of the progeny of Muhammad by usurping Fadak? Did they intend to show it to the people that the Prophet himself had deprived his people from inheritance?

Did they try to prove that those people who have no right of inheriting the prophet had no right to Caliphate?

8. Were many people involved in seizing Fadak?

9. Even if the tradition narrated by Abu Bakr is considered valid, is it applicable only for the Prophet or to all the prophets?

10. Why did the Prophet want to keep his loving daughter away from his inheritance?

11. Did the Prophet fear that his daughter and son-in-law will misuse it after him (God forbid)?

12. If yes, why did he hand it over to his daughter?

13. Did this apprehension arise because she had misused it during the Prophet's lifetime?

14. If yes, when and how did it happen?

Allamah Ibn Abil Hadid Mutazali has narrated a beautiful debate on this matter between the Chief Qazi and the ensign of guidance (*Alamul Huda*) Sayyid Murtuza. The former rejected inheritance of prophets while the latter tried to prove it.

The stand of Chief Qazi was that the inheritance of prophets mentioned in holy Qur'an is regarding their knowledge and virtues and not regarding their property.

Sayyid Murtuza's stand was that inheritance is regarding wealth and land first. And this relation is true. Its relation with knowledge and virtues can be metaphorical. As per the principle of holy Qur'an, metaphorical meanings are accepted only when the real meanings are in effect. What is wrong in a prophet inheriting worldly things?

There is nothing wrong logically as well as according to Shariah. It is not possible to discard the real meaning and accept the metaphorical. Even if we accept the statement of Chief Qazi that the inheritance of prophets is in relation to knowledge and virtues instead of material things, it would mean that the Prophet's progeny are inheritors of his knowledge and virtues.

If the Prophet's progeny are inheritors of his knowledge and virtues how could the Caliphate of Abu Bakr be legal in the presence of these personalities.[1]

FADAK AS A GIFT

Lady Sayyada demanded Fadak because it had been gifted to her. Imam 'Ali (a), Hasan, Husain and Umme Aiman were witnesses from Lady Sayyida's side.

However, the Caliph rejected all witnesses and said: "The course of testimony is not complete because 'Ali is Sayyada's husband, Imam Hasan and Imam Husain are her sons and Umme Aiman is her slave."

The fact is that this proof is complete in all aspects.

Refer to the following verse of Surah Aale Imran to know how strong 'Ali's proof was:

شَهِدَ اللّٰهُ أَنَّهُ لَا إِلٰهَ إِلَّا هُوَ وَالْمَلَائِكَةُ وَأُولُوا الْعِلْمِ قَائِمًا بِالْقِسْطِ لَا إِلٰهَ إِلَّا هُوَ الْعَزِيزُ الْحَكِيمُ.

Allah bears witness that there is no god but He, and (so do) the angels and those possessed of knowledge, maintaining His creation with justice; there is no god but He, the Mighty, the Wise.[2]

In this verse, Almighty Allah includes Himself, His angles and the just ones as witnesses of His unity (*Tauheed*).

---

[1] *Sharh Nahjul Balagha*, Vol. 4, Pg. 78-103
[2] Surah Aale Imran 3:18

Scholars who prefer justice are witness of Tauheed (Monotheism) and Imam 'Ali (a) should be listed foremost among the just ones because the Prophet has said regarding 'Ali's knowledge: "I am the city of knowledge and 'Ali is its gate."

As far as justice is concerned, the sky has not witnessed a just person like 'Ali. If Imam 'Ali (a) is a witness to Tauheed (Monotheism), why can't he be the witness in the matter of Fadak? It is strange that we accept Imam 'Ali's testimony in the matter of Tauheed (Monotheism) and reject it in the matter of Fadak. Imam 'Ali (a) is not only a witness to Tauheed but also a witness to the prophethood of the Prophet as mentioned in Surah Raad by Almighty Allah:

(وَيَقُولُ الَّذِينَ كَفَرُوا لَسْتَ مُرْسَلًا ۚ قُلْ كَفَىٰ بِاللَّهِ شَهِيدًا بَيْنِي وَبَيْنَكُمْ وَمَنْ عِندَهُ عِلْمُ الْكِتَابِ.)

And those who disbelieve say: You are not a messenger. Say: Allah is sufficient as a witness between me and you and whoever has knowledge of the Book.[1]

According to the correct interpretation, the phrase "whoever has knowledge of the book" implies Imam 'Ali (a).

This verse proves that Imam 'Ali (a) is the witness of the prophethood of Prophet Muhammad (s).

Now the question arises as to why the person who testified to the prophethood of the Prophet could not be allowed to testify in the matter of Fadak?

THE BRANCH TESTIFIES TO THE ROOT

The testimony of Imam Hasan and Husain was rejected saying that the branch is testifying for the root. i.e. the testimony of Imam Hasan and Husain is not acceptable as they were sons of Lady Sayyada.

---

[1] Surah Raad 13:43

The incident of Prophet Isa's birth and the problem of Lady Maryam are present in holy Qur'an. When people started taunting Lady Maryam for the birth of a child, her new-born son had testified to his prophethood and the chastity of his mother.

If the testimony of children in favor of their parents is not acceptable, why Allah made Prophet Isa (a) testify to the chastity of his mother? If this formula is accepted, what will happen to all traditions narrated by Ayesha regarding her father? There were four persons present in front of the Caliph. One of them was the claimant herself and other three were witnesses. Refer to the incident of Mubahila (imprecation ceremony) to know how reliable the testimony of these persons is.

TESTIMONY OF MUBAHILA

When Christian scholars rejected the prophethood of Prophet Muhammad, the Almighty Allah revealed the verse of Mubahila and said:

فَمَنْ حَاجَّكَ فِيهِ مِنْ بَعْدِ مَا جَاءَكَ مِنَ الْعِلْمِ فَقُلْ تَعَالَوْا نَدْعُ أَبْنَاءَنَا وَأَبْنَاءَكُمْ وَنِسَاءَنَا وَنِسَاءَكُمْ وَأَنْفُسَنَا وَأَنْفُسَكُمْ ثُمَّ نَبْتَهِلْ فَنَجْعَلْ لَعْنَةَ اللَّهِ عَلَى الْكَاذِبِينَ.

But whoever disputes with you in this matter after what has come to you of knowledge, then say: Come let us call our sons and your sons and our women and your women and our near people and your near people, then let us be earnest in prayer, and pray for the curse of Allah on the liars.[1]

When this verse was revealed, the Prophet went to Imam 'Ali's house and covered Imam 'Ali, Fatima, Hasan and Husain with his cloak and prayed: "O Allah! These are my Ahl al-Bayt."

The Prophet set out for Mubahila along with these personalities only. When the Christian scholars saw their illuminated faces, they agreed to pay Jizyah Tax and kept away from Mubahila.

---

[1] Surah Aale Imran 3:61

This incident proves that these personalities are witnesses for entire Islam and even the Christians respected their testimony.

Sometime after the incident of Mubahila, these four personalities went to the Caliph. One of them was claimant while remaining four were witnesses.

The human mind would be surprised that the Caliph of Muslims rejected the testimony of those personalities whom Almighty Allah had made witnesses of truthfulness of entire religion of Islam.

Also it is enough to say regarding the Caliphate of these personalities that Allah has revealed the following verse for them:

(إِنَّمَا يُرِيدُ اللَّهُ لِيُذْهِبَ عَنْكُمُ الرِّجْسَ أَهْلَ الْبَيْتِ وَيُطَهِّرَكُمْ تَطْهِيراً.)

Allah only desires to keep away the uncleanness from you, O people of the House! And to purify you a (thorough) purifying.[1]

It was obligatory on Abu Bakr to accept the testimony of Lady Sayyada without any hassle because it is a well-known incident that a Bedouin had argued with the Prophet regarding a she-camel. Both of them said that the she-camel was their property. When the Bedouin asked the Prophet for a witness, Khuzayma ibn Thabit came forward and testified. Later on, Khuzayma was asked why he had testified without knowledge.

He replied: We also testify to the prophethood and revelation of Muhammad even though we have not seen archangel Jibraeel with our eyes. When we can testify to the prophethood without seeing it, why can't we testify in favor of the Prophet for a single she-camel? The Prophet declared the testimony of Khuzayma right and gave him the title of the owner of two testimonies (*Dhul Shahadatain*).

It would have been better for Abu Bakr if he had accepted the testimony of Lady Sayyada like the Bedouin had done. On the other hand, Lady Sayyada did not ask Abu Bakr for witness regarding his

---

[1] Surah Ahzaab 33:33

tradition of non-inheritance even though she had rejected this tradition.

It was not at all appropriate for Abu Bakr to reject the witness of the great truthful one (Siddiq Akbar) like Imam 'Ali (a). Umme Aiman was the Prophet's nurse, who served Islam and the Messenger of Islam all her life; then why was her testimony rejected?

INCONSISTENCY IN ACTIONS OF THE MUSLIM CALIPH

The stand of Abu Bakr regarding inheritance is really strange:

1. He let the Prophet's sword, slippers and turban remain with Imam 'Ali (a) and did not argue with him regarding these items.

2. Also the Prophet had handed over his sword and a ring to Imam 'Ali (a) in his last moments. Abu Bakr did not demand these things.

If the sword and ring were not taken by the Caliph because they were the gifts then Fadak was also a gift. Why was he so particular in confiscating Fadak only?

3. Lady Fatima had kept the dress of the Prophet, which he was wearing at the time of his demise. Abu Bakr did not ask for this dress also?

4. The wives of the Prophet also were not asked to vacate their houses.

5. The governor of Bahrain, Alla ibn Hadhrami sent some goods to the Caliph from Bahrain. Jabir Ibn Abdullah told the Caliph: "The Prophet had promised that he would give me a part from it. Now that the Prophet has passed away and you are the Caliph of Muslims, you should give that part to me." Abu Bakr did not demand any witness from him and granted the requested part of goods to him only by trusting his words.[1]

Wasn't the Chief of the ladies of Paradise as truthful as Jabir?

---

[1] *Sahih Bukhari,* Vol. 3, Pg. 180

6. When the goods from Bahrain were received by the Caliph, Abu Bashir al-Maazni came to him and said: "The Prophet had promised me a part of the goods from Bahrain." On hearing this, Abu Bakr handed him three handfuls of the wealth.

Students of History are amazed that when a common Companion of the Prophet demanded something, his testimony was accepted. On the other hand, when the daughter of Allah's Messenger demanded her right, she was asked to bring witnesses. The height of oppression is that the testimony of those witnesses was rejected. The Prophet's daughter who was the Chief of the ladies of Paradise was sent back empty-handed.

If the tradition of non-inheritance is accepted, many complications will arise. According to this tradition, it would not be legal to bury the Prophet in his own house because after the Prophet's passing away, all his property would be considered charity and the property of all Muslims. Now the Prophet will have no relation with his house. Then how could he be buried in a house, which is not his?

It is strange that Abu Bakr has himself narrated another tradition that prophets are buried at the same place where they pass away. When prophets pass away at a place, should that place be considered their property or charity?

If this property is considered charity, it will not be appropriate to bury prophets there. If it is appropriate to bury the prophet, it would be necessary to accept that whatever prophets leave behind is not charity.

Now another question arises here. Wasn't Abu Bakr aware of the conflict between these two traditions?

Further explaining it, we can say that Abu Bakr narrated the tradition: A prophet is buried at the place where he passes away.

Now a prophet can pass away only at one of the two places:

1. Either at his own property
2. Or at the property of someone else

If a prophet dies at his own property, it is not appropriate to bury him at that place because it has become charity.

If a prophet dies at the property of someone else, it would not be possible to bury him there at all because that place belongs to someone else.

Hence if the tradition of non-inheritance is considered correct, where would the prophet be buried?

The Place where the Prophet was buried belonged to him and it was turned into charity after he passed away. Then how did Abu Bakr get the right to make a will that he should be buried beside the Prophet? If we suppose that the room belonged to the Prophet and it was considered his property even after his demise, one should take the permission of owner before entering it. Did Abu Bakr take the permission from the Prophet in his life to get himself buried beside the Prophet's grave?

Or did the Prophet himself say that the first Caliph should be buried beside him?

All these problems arise if we accept the tradition of non-inheritance. It is strange that Ahl al-Sunnah commentators have tried their best to prove that the inheritance of prophets is regarding their knowledge only. Till today, we are not able to understand how knowledge and virtues could be inherited? If it is so, a son of a scholar must also be a scholar and a son of every illiterate person will be illiterate. It is wrong socially and psychologically that Abu Bakr acted upon a tradition whose only narrator was he himself.

While doing so he forgot the strong Islamic tradition whose authenticity was known to him also: that the Prophet had said, "Fatima is a part of me. Whoever hurts her has hurt me and whoever hurts me has hurt Allah."[1]

Abu Bakr should have remembered the incident of Abul Aas ibn Rubai while denying Lady Sayyada her right.

This Incident is narrated by historian Ibn Athir as follows: Abul Aas ibn Rubai ibn Abdul Aza ibn Abdul Shams was included among the prisoners of war in the battle of Badr. He was the husband of Zainab bint Khadija.

All prisoners of Mecca were released after paying compensation. Zainab bint Khadija sent a necklace as compensation for the release of her husband. This necklace was gifted by her mother, Lady Khadijatul Kubra. When the Prophet saw this necklace, he recollected the memories of Lady Khadija and was moved. He told the Muslims: If possible release the husband of Zainab and return the compensation also. Before the conquest of Mecca, once it so happened that Abul Aas was going to Syria carrying trade goods belonging to him as well as other people of Mecca. On the way he had a clash with Muslim army and the latter took all his goods away. He returned to his wife Zainab bint Khadija at night.

---

[1] The above mentioned tradition is discussed in *Sahih Bukhari*.

When Allah's Messenger was going to offer prayer at dawn, Zainab called out: "O people! I have given refuge to Abul Aas ibn Rubai."

The Prophet requested Muslims that they return the goods of Abu Aas if possible. He said that it was only desirable, so there would not be any punishment if the goods were not returned.

The people said: "O Messenger of Allah! We submit before your wish and we will return his goods." So the Muslims returned all the goods of Abul Aas including his walking stick.[1]

We have seen that Muslims returned the spoils of war to Abul Aas for the sake of the Prophet's foster-daughter, Zainab; even though they had the right to those goods. Even if Abu Bakr had thought that there was no inheritance for Lady Sayyada, keeping in mind the incident of Abul Aas, he should have preferred the pleasure of Lady Sayyada over everything.

Was this act of Abu Bakr in accordance to the Prophetic Practice (*Sunnah*)?

ANOTHER FACE OF THE SAQIFAH REGIME

Amirul Momineen (a) says:

"Beware! By Allah, the son of Abi Qahafa (Abu Bakr) dressed himself with it (the Caliphate) and he certainly knew that my position in relation to it was the same as the position of the axis in relation to the hand-mill. The flood water flows down from me and the bird cannot fly upto me. I put a curtain against the Caliphate and kept myself detached from it.

Then I began to think whether I should assault or endure calmly the blinding darkness of tribulations wherein the grown up are made

---
[1] Ibn Athir, *Al-Kamil fit Tarikh*, Vol. 2, Pg. 93-94

feeble and the young grow old and the true believer acts under strain till he meets Allah (on his death). I found that endurance thereon was wiser. So I adopted patience although there was pricking in the eye and suffocation (of mortification) in the throat. I watched the plundering of my inheritance till the first one went his way but handed over the Caliphate to Ibnul Khattab after himself."

Then he quoted al-Aasha's verse:

"My days are now passed on the camel's back (in difficulty) while there were days (of ease) when I enjoyed the company of Jabir's brother Hayyan."[1]

"It is strange that during his lifetime he wished to be released from Caliphate but he confirmed it for the other one after his death. No doubt these two shared its udders strictly among themselves."

The Caliphate which Abu Bakr had received due to the efforts of Umar was returned to the latter.

Before nominating Umar, Abu Bakr had called Uthman ibn Affan and Abdur Rahman ibn Auf. He discussed the matter of nominating Umar with them and asked for advice in this matter. Abdur Rahman ibn Auf said: "Whatever you think in this matter is much better." Abdur Rahman knew that even during the Caliphate of Abu Bakr, the central role was played by Umar only. Uthman ibn Affan replied: "His inner self is much better than his outer one and there is no one like him around us."

We know that Uthman was absolutely correct because the second Caliph has played a wonderful role in establishing the government of Saqifah.

We don't know whether both of them gave their advice from their hearts or just for the sake of respecting the Caliph's decision.

---

[1] *Nahjul Balagha,* Shiqshiqiya Sermon

WILL OF THE FIRST CALIPH REGARDING UMAR

Finally Abu Bakr asked Uthman to write down the nomination of Umar as Caliph.

Historians have recorded that Uthman was writing down as Abu Bakr dictated. Abu Bakr lost consciousness before mentioning the name of Umar. Uthman wrote Umar's name of his own. When Abu Bakr regained consciousness, Uthman said that he had written the name of Umar. Abu Bakr approved it and appreciated Uthman a lot.

1. We could not understand till date why Uthman himself wrote Umar's name in the will of some other person?

2. Will this act be included in his friendship?

3. If we suppose that Abu Bakr died in this state of unconsciousness, would the will of Abu Bakr be considered legal?

4. Why was the opinion of only two persons out of the entire Muslim Ummah taken regarding Umar's nomination?

5. What was so special about these two personalities?

6. It is said that Abu Bakr appointed his successor for the benefit of Muslim Ummah. Didn't the Prophet think of the benefit of Muslim Ummah like him?

7. Abu Bakr willed at his death-bed and it was accepted. However, when the Prophet had intended to do so, people said that he was talking rubbish.

8. After a few centuries later, if a person points out that Abu Bakr has willed at his death-bed in the state of illness and he was talking rubbish, will he be considered as a friend of Islam or its enemy? Muslim Ummah should also decide what that person should be called who used similar words for the Prophet.

9. Abu Bakr and Umar believed that the Prophet had not appointed anyone as his successor. Similarly, if Abu Bakr would not have

appointed his successor, wouldn't this act have been considered as per the Prophetic Practice (*Sunnah*)?

10. What was the problem in taking the views of Emigrants and Helpers regarding the Caliphate of Imam 'Ali (a)?

The simple and true answer to all these questions is that Umar played a central role in nomination of Abu Bakr as Caliph.

Hence Abu Bakr was obliged to nominate Umar after his death.

SHURA (CONSULTATION)

Till when the second went his way (of death) he put the matter (of Caliphate) in a group and regarded me to be one of them. But good Heavens! What had I to do with this "consultation"? Where was any doubt about me with regard to the first of them that I was now considered akin to these ones? But I remained low when they were low and flew high when they flew high. One of them turned against me because of his hatred and the other got inclined the other way due to his in-law relationship and this thing and that thing.[1]

Ibn Athir Umar ibn Maymun narrates the event of Shura as follows:

When Umar was fatally injured, people asked him to appoint a successor. He said: "Whom should I appoint? If Abu Ubaidah had been alive, I would have appointed him. I would then have told the Lord that I have appointed a person whom the Prophet had called trustworthy in his Ummah."

"If Saalim Huzaifah's freed slave had been alive, I would have appointed him as my successor and told the Lord that I have appointed such a person as my successor whom the Prophet called a great lover of Allah."[2]

We also accept that Umar would have indeed appointed Abu Ubaidah as Caliph if the latter were alive. He would have nominated

---

[1] *Nahjul Balagha*, Shiqshiqiya Sermon
[2] Ibn Athir, *Al-Kamil fit Tarikh*, Vol. 3, Pg. 34

Abu Ubaidah because the latter supported him in Saqifah and not because he was trustworthy. If it had been the case, the number of Rightly-guided Caliphs would have become five instead of four.

The student of History is astounded at this narration. People requested Umar not to leave them without a leader after his death. However it is strange that the same was not asked from the Prophet!

According to Ahl al-Sunnah point of view, the Prophet was not concerned about the future of Ummah, hence he left the selection of Caliph at the discretion of the Ummah. He did not care about the bloody battles resulting out of it and division of Ummah into numerous sects.

May Allah bless the two Shaykhs (Abu Bakr and Umar) who handled the situation in time and saved the Ummah from possible destruction. If Abu Ubaidah and Saalim were really capable why didn't Umar appoint them in Saqifah? He should have paid allegiance to Abu Ubaidah and then asked the people to follow him because the Prophet had called him trustworthy.

Or he should have sworn allegiance to Saalim and said that this person is a great lover of Allah.

The Prophet had called Abu Ubaidah a "trustworthy person of Ummah" and no such title was given to Abu Bakr. Then how could allegiance be paid by a more virtuous to a less virtuous one? If it was not possible to do so in Saqifah, Umar could have requested Abu Bakr when the latter was nominating the former to appoint Abu Ubaidah in his stead because he was a "trustworthy person of Ummah."

Also Umar had expressed his desire that he would have appointed Saalim as his successor if the latter were alive.

Abu Bakr had narrated a tradition in Saqifah because of which Helpers backed off: "The imams will be from Quraish."

Did Salim belong to Quraish?

If not, why Umar expressed his desire to appoint him as Caliph?

If Saalim did not belong to Quraish, the desire of Umar shows that it is not necessary for a Caliph to be from Quraish. If it is not necessary for a Caliph to be from Quraish, were the stands of both the caliphs contradicting each other? If that is so, which of them is correct?

Saalim was to be nominated as Caliph because he loved Allah very much.

It proves that the right to Caliphate is for one who loves Allah greatly.

Did the following tradition slip out of Umar's mind at that time? It is narrated in *Sahih Muslim* that the Prophet said: "Tomorrow I shall hand over the banner to a person who would be a real man. He loves Allah and His Messenger and they too love him. Allah will grant victory at his hands."[1]

The Prophet has depicted the virtue of Imam 'Ali (a) in this tradition that he loves Allah and His Messenger and they too love him. The tradition regarding Saalim was that he loves Allah but no tradition proves that he too is loved by Allah. Saalim loved Allah very much while Imam 'Ali (a) loved Allah and was also loved by Allah. Then why didn't Umar nominate Imam 'Ali (a) as his successor?

By the way, Umar selected a committee that included Imam 'Ali, Uthman, Saad ibn Abi Waqqas, Abdur Rahman ibn Auf, Zubair ibn Awwam and Talha ibn Ubaidullah. He told them: "After my death, you all take three days' time to decide who would be the Caliph. Suhaib would lead the prayers during this time. A Caliph must be appointed on the fourth day. My son, Abdullah ibn Umar would participate in the committee as an advisor but there is no place for him in Caliphate." Then Umar called Abu Talha Ansari and told him: "Bring along fifty men to keep a strict vigil on this committee till one of them is appointed as the leader."

---

[1] *Sahih Muslim*, Vol. 2, Pg. 224

Then he called Miqdad ibn Aswad and told him: "Gather these members at a place after my burial for election of a leader. If one of them rejects the appointment of a leader, cut off his head. If two persons disagree, kill both of them and if the committee is divided into two groups such that there are three persons on both sides, let my son, Abdullah ibn Umar take the decision. If they do not accept the decision of my son, you should support the decision of the side supported by Abdur Rahman ibn Auf and kill the other party."

Readers are requested to pause for a moment and note that Umar ordered that the Caliph should be appointed after his burial. Had the Caliph done the same at the time of the Prophet's demise?

According to Islamic history, the holy body of Allah's Messenger was still in the house when the activities of Saqifah started.

Umar considered election of a Caliph more important than the Prophet's burial. Then why didn't he consider appointment of Caliph more important at the time of his death?

It was a simple remark. Let us come back to history. When Umar died, Suhaib lead his funeral Prayer. When Umar was buried, Miqdad gathered the members of committee. Talha was not present in them.

SHURA PROCEDURE

The operations of Shura started. Abdur Rahman ibn Auf said: "Is there any of you who would back off from Caliphate and prefer someone else?" No one answered. Abdur Rahman said that he would back off. Uthman thanked him and others also showed their pleasure at this act. Imam 'Ali (a) was sitting quietly and watching everything. Abdur Rahman asked him: "O Abul Hasan! What is your opinion?" Imam 'Ali (a) said: "You should promise me that you would always prefer right, not succumb to your desires and instead work for complete benefit of Islam."

"Abdur Rahman promised Imam 'Ali (a) to do so."[1]

After a long discussion, Abdur Rahman ibn Auf told Imam 'Ali (a): "I pay allegiance to you on a condition that you will follow the book of Allah, The Prophetic Practice (*Sunnah*) and the practice of Abu Bakr and Umar."

Imam 'Ali (a) replied: "I will follow only the book of Allah, the Prophetic Practice (*Sunnah*) and my personal exertions (Ijtihaad)."

Then Abdur Rahman ibn Auf turned to Uthman and said: "I pay allegiance to you on a condition that you will follow the Book of Allah, the Prophetic Practice (*Sunnah*) and the practice of Abu Bakr and Umar." Uthman accepted all the three conditions.

Abdur Rahman ibn Auf made this offer to Imam 'Ali (a) three times but the latter refused to follow the practice of Abu Bakr and Umar every time.

When Abdur Rahman was assured that Imam 'Ali (a) would not follow the practice of Abu Bakr and Umar, he paid allegiance to Uthman and said: "Peace be upon you! O master of faithful!"

At this, Imam 'Ali (a) said: "I know why the responsibility of selecting a Caliph was handed to you and you have acted on the predetermined plan exactly."[2]

A FEW QUESTIONS

A few questions arise at this moment:

1. Did Abdur Rahman pay allegiance to Uthman unintentionally or it was planned in advance?

2. Was the purpose of including "practice of Abu Bakr and Umar" as a condition a way to prevent Imam 'Ali (a) from becoming a Caliph or something else was intended?

---

[1] Ibn Athir, *Al-Kamil fit Tarikh*, Vol. 3, Pg. 35-36
[2] Ibn Abil Hadid, *Sharh Nahjul Balagha*, Vol. 1, Pg. 50-67

Before considering these questions, it is necessary to discuss two important issues at Shura:

1. The historian, Tabari writes: When Umar was at his death-bed, he remembered Abu Ubaidah and Saalim very much. He expressed his desire again and again that if they were alive he would have appointed one of them as Caliph. A group of Companions had come to meet him. Imam 'Ali (a) was among them. Umar told the people: "I wanted to make such a person a leader who would show you the right path." Saying this he pointed to Imam 'Ali (a).

"Then I fell asleep and dreamt that a person has entered a garden and planted a few saplings in it. He plucked the flowers grown on plants. I interpreted this dream that Umar would die soon.

How can I carry your burden now alive or dead? Therefore appoint a Caliph after me from this group of people for whom the Prophet has given glad tidings of Paradise.

Saad ibn Zaid ibn Umar ibn Nufayl was also one of them. However I do not include him among the candidates for Caliphate. I feel that the rule should go to either Uthman or 'Ali.

If 'Ali becomes the ruler he would be humorous. However he is capable of restoring the rights of the people."[1]

2. Umar's Opinion about Shura Members

2. Another historian writes that once Umar summoned Talha, Zubair, Saad, Abdur Rahman, Uthman and 'Ali and said:

"O Zubair! What kind of person you are! One day you are a human being and another, a devil. O Talha! What kind of a person you are? The Prophet was angry with you because of your words till he passed away. It was because of you only the verse prohibiting marriage with the wives of the prophet was revealed."

---

[1] Tabari, *Tarikh al-Umam wal Muluk,* Vol. 2, Pg. 34-35

According to another tradition, Umar said: "O Talha! Aren't you the same person who said, 'I will marry the wives of Muhammad after his demise? Allah has not made Muhammad more rightful to the daughters of our uncles more than us.' Because of your audacity, Allah revealed this verse:

(وَمَا كَانَ لَكُمْ أَنْ تُؤْذُوا رَسُولَ اللَّهِ وَ؟ أَنْ تَنْكِحُوا أَزْوَاجَهُ مِنْ بَعْدِهِ أَبَداً.)

You should not give trouble to the Apostle of Allah, nor that you should marry his wives after him ever.[1]

Shaykh Abu Uthman says that if the character of those personalities was such, why Umar said on his death-bed that the Prophet was pleased with them all his life?

Then Umar turned to Saad ibn Abi Waqqas and said: "You are the leader of the group of persons who turn away. You are a hunter and play with bow and arrow. What is the relation of tribe of Zahra with Caliphate?"

Then he looked at Abdur Rahman ibn Auf and said: "A person is not eligible to Caliphate if he has weaknesses as much as you. By the way, what is the relation of Zahra with Caliphate?"

Turning to 'Ali he said: "If you had not been humorous, by Allah, you were most rightful to Caliphate. By Allah! If you become the ruler you will lead the people on the right path."

Looking at Uthman, he said: "I can see that the Quraish will make you the ruler. You will impose Bani Umayyah and Bani Muit over the people and hand over to them the Muslim public treasury."[2]

---

[1] Surah Ahzaab 33:53
[2] Ibn Abil Hadid, *Sharh Nahjul Balagha*, Vol. 3, Pg. 170

'ALI'S PROTEST IN SHURA MEETING

Imam 'Ali (a) raised his voice of protest before the members of Shura in order to prove his right to Caliphate. He said: "I hold witness Allah unto you, who is aware of your every truth and lie.

1. Is there anyone here except me whose brother has been granted two wings in Paradise by Allah?

2. Is there anyone here except me whose uncle is the chief of martyrs?

3. Is there anyone here except me whose wife is the chief of the ladies of the worlds?

4. The Prophet considered my sons as his own. Is there anyone here except me as such?

5. Is there anyone here except me whose sons are chiefs of the youth of Paradise?

6. Is there anyone here having more knowledge of the holy Qur'an than me?

7. Is there anyone here for whom the verse of purification was revealed?

8. Is there anyone here who has seen archangel Jibraeel?

9. Was the announcement of, "Of whomsoever I am the master..." made for anyone except me?

10. Was anyone, except me, made by the Prophet his brother?

11. Is there anyone who has conquered the Battle of the Ditch (*Khandaq*) except me?

12. Is there anyone who has been honored with the title of 'Haroon of Muhammad', except me?

13. Is there anyone except me who is called a believer by Allah in ten verses of holy Qur'an?

14. Is there anyone here except me who slept on the bed of the Prophet on the night of migration?

15. Is there anyone here except me such that angels stood by his side in the Battle of Uhad?

16. Is there anyone here except me such that the Prophet passed away in his lap?

17. Is there anyone here except me who has given the funeral bath to the Prophet after his demise; shrouded and buried him?

18. Is there anyone here except me who possesses the weapon, banner and ring of the Prophet?

19. Is there anyone here except me whom the Prophet had made to climb his shoulders to break the idols?

20. Did the voice from heaven call out for anyone except me: "If there is a sword, it is Zulfiqar; if there is a brave youth, it is 'Ali."?

21. Is there anyone here except me who has shared a roasted bird with the Prophet?

22. Is there anyone here except me for whom the Prophet said: "You are my standard-bearer in this world and the hereafter."?

23. Is there anyone here except me who has acted upon the verse of 'Najwa' (consultation)?[1]

24. Is there anyone here except me who has received the honor of being the Prophet's shoe-mender?

---

[1] *O you who believe! When you consult the Apostle, then offer something in charity before your consultation; that is better for you and purer; but if you do not find, then surely Allah is Forgiving, Merciful. (Surah Mujadila 58:12)*

25. Is there anyone here except me for whom the Prophet had said: "I love you more than the entire creation. You are most truthful after me?"

26. Is there anyone here except me who earned a hundred dates by pulling out a hundred buckets of water from well and then shared them with the Prophet?

27. Is there anyone here except me who was saluted by three thousand angels in Badr?

28. Is there anyone here except me who is the first Muslim?

29. Is there anyone here except me whose house was visited by the Prophet in the end while leaving the city and first when he came back?

30. Is there anyone here except me for whom the Prophet said: "You are my first testifier and first one to meet me at the cistern of Kauthar?"

31. Is there anyone here except me whose family members were taken along by the Prophet to Mubahila?

32. Is there anyone here except me who has paid Zakat in the state of Ruku (genuflection) and Allah has revealed the verse:

(إِنَّمَا وَلِيُّكُمُ اللَّهُ وَرَسُولُهُ وَالَّذِينَ آمَنُوا الَّذِينَ يُقِيمُونَ الصَّلَاةَ وَيُؤْتُونَ الزَّكَاةَ وَهُمْ رَاكِعُونَ.)

Only Allah is your Guardian and His Apostle and those who believe, those who keep up prayers and pay the poor-rate while they bow.[1]

33. Is there anyone here except me for whom Surah Dahr was revealed?

34. Is there anyone here except me for whom Allah has revealed the verse?

---

[1] Surah Maida 5:55

(أَجَعَلْتُمْ سِقَايَةَ الْحَاجِّ وَعِمَارَةَ الْمَسْجِدِ الْحَرَامِ كَمَنْ آمَنَ بِاللَّهِ وَالْيَوْمِ الْآخِرِ وَجَاهَدَ فِي سَبِيلِ اللَّهِ ۚ يَسْتَوُونَ عِنْدَ اللَّهِ ۗ)

What! do you make (one who undertakes) the giving of drink to the pilgrims and the guarding of the Sacred Mosque like him who believes in Allah and the latter day and strives hard in Allah's way? They are not equal with Allah.[1]

35. Is there anyone here except me who was taught a thousand such statements, of which each is the key to a thousand other statements?

36. Is there anyone here except me to whom the Prophet whispered and made the people quiet by saying: "I haven't whispered to him but Allah?"

37. Is there anyone here except me for whom the Prophet said: "You and your Shias will be successful on Judgment Day?"

38. Is there anyone here except me for whom the Prophet said: "One who thinks that he loves me and harbors malice for 'Ali is a liar?"

39. Is there anyone here except me for whom the Prophet said: "If a person loves my part he has loved me and a person who has loved me has loved Allah"? The Prophet was then asked who his part was. The Prophet replied: "They are 'Ali, Fatima, Hasan and Husain."

40. Is there anyone here except me to whom the Prophet said: "You are the best man after the prophets."

41. Is there anyone here except me whom the Prophet has made a criterion of right and wrong?

42. Is there anyone here except me whom the Prophet took under his cloak?

43. Is there anyone here except me who took the food of the Prophet to the cave of Hira?

---

[1] Surah Taubah 9:19

44. Is there anyone here except me for whom the Prophet said: "You are my brother, vizier and my companion from my family."

45. Is there anyone here except me for whom the Prophet said: "You preceded them in Islam, you are superior to them in actions and have more forbearance than them."

46. Is there anyone here except me who killed Marhab, the Jew?

47. Is there anyone here except me who uprooted the gate of Khaiber, which used to be handled by forty persons at a time?

48. Is there anyone here except me for whom the Prophet said: "Abusing him is abusing me?"

49. Is there anyone here except me for whom the Prophet said: "O 'Ali! Your destination, Paradise is linked with my destination, Paradise?"

50. Is there anyone here except me for whom the Prophet said: "You will be on the right side of the divine throne on Judgment Day and Allah will make you wear two clothes – one of them would be green and other red?"

51. Is there anyone here except me who offered prayer seven years before Muslims started to pray?

52. Is there anyone here except me whose love is considered as love of Prophet and whose enmity is considered as enmity of Prophet by the Prophet himself?

53. Is there anyone here except me the preaching of whose Wilayat (mastership) was made obligatory by Allah on the Prophet?

54. Is there anyone here except me whom the Prophet called 'Leader of believers' (Yasoobil Momineen)?

55. Is there anyone here except me for whom the Prophet said: "I will send to you one whom Allah has tested for faith."?

56. Is there anyone here except me whom the Prophet made to eat the pomegranate of Paradise?

57. Is there anyone here except me for whom the Prophet said: "I was granted what I asked from the Lord and whatever I ask from the Lord for myself, I ask it for you also."?

58. Is there anyone here except me for whom the Prophet said: "You will remain steadfast on the commandments of Allah, fulfill the promise of the Lord, be just in distribution of wealth and have a high rank near Allah."?

59. Is there anyone here except me for whom the Prophet said: "You are superior to this Ummah like a sun is to the moon and moon to all the stars."?

60. Is there anyone here, except me, whose friends are given tidings of Paradise and enemies are given tidings of hell?

61. Is there anyone here except me for whom the Prophet said: "People are from different trees and you and me are from a single tree."?

62. Is there anyone here except me whom the Prophet has called, 'Master of Arabs'?

63. Is there anyone here except me who has hosted archangel Jibraeel?

64. Is there anyone here except me who has preached Surah Baraat?

65. Is there anyone here except me who will distribute Paradise and Hell?

The committee members replied in negative to each question.

"When you know these virtues of mine, do not leave the right and follow the wrong."

A Probe into Saqifah

However, Abdur Rahman ibn Auf and his Companions deprived Imam 'Ali (a) of Caliphate.

ANALYSIS OF SHURA GATHERING

You have read the views of Umar regarding Shura and its members. He has expressed his views regarding all the members openly. Umar had selected a committee with a limited number of members while a committee with lots of members was required in order to find a solution of this crucial issue.

1. Umar had restricted the functioning of this committee. He had limited the freedom of thought in it.

2. The hands of this committee were tied up and the guards were ordered to kill whoever objected to the majority view immediately.

3. If the committee got divided into two equal sides, the side supported by Abdur Rahman ibn Auf was to be preferred. Why should the opinion of Abdur Rahman ibn Auf be given preference?

4. Was the opinion of Abdur Rahman ibn Auf considered as final verdict because he had supported Umar's nomination by Abu Bakr?

5. Is there any proof in holy Qur'an and traditions, which indicates that it is obligatory to kill one who opposes Abdur Rahman ibn Auf?

6. Allah says regarding killing of a believer:

(وَمَن يَقْتُلْ مُؤْمِنًا مُتَعَمِّدًا فَجَزَاؤُهُ جَهَنَّمُ خَالِدًا فِيهَا وَغَضِبَ اللَّهُ عَلَيْهِ وَلَعَنَهُ وَأَعَدَّ لَهُ عَذَابًا عَظِيمًا.)

And whoever kills a believer intentionally, his punishment is hell; he shall abide in it, and Allah will send His wrath on him and curse him and prepare for him a painful chastisement.[1]

If the chastisement of a common believer is such, what will be the punishment of killing a companion of the Prophet and those

---
[1] Surah Nisa 4:93

Companions with whom the Prophet was pleased till he passed away, as Umar himself admitted?

7. Ahl al-Sunnah often say that the Prophet said: "My Companions are like stars. You will be guided if you follow any of them."

Wasn't this tradition in the mind of Umar and that dispute between them was not harmful for Ummah? Why did he order killing of those stars who opposed?

8. Is it legal to kill a person if he has a different opinion in any religion or society of the world?

9. Was Abdur Rahman ibn Auf a criterion of right and wrong that it was made obligatory to severe the head of a person who opposed him?

10. Umar believed till the time of his death that appointment of Caliph was not Prophetic Practice (*Sunnah*) and that it was the practice of Abu Bakr to appoint a Caliph. Why did he leave the Prophetic Practice and follow the practice of Abu Bakr?

11. The Qur'an has ordered us to follow the Prophet and to keep away from deviating from his path. In spite of this, what were the reasons, because of which they did not follow the Prophet's way?

12. Why was Caliphate limited to six persons only, and why no capable person could be found in the entire Muslim Ummah?

13. It is said that the Prophet was pleased with all of them when he passed away. It is difficult to accept this statement as Umar himself said regarding Talha ibn Ubaidullah: "The Prophet remained angry with you for one of your statements till he passed away." When such people were included in the committee, how can it be said that they were selected because of the pleasure of the Prophet?

14. Even if we suppose that the Prophet was pleased with all of them, doesn't it mean that the Prophet was angry with the entire Ummah with the exception of these six?

15. If the answer is no, what can be the reason for limiting the Caliphate to six persons when the Prophet was pleased with thousands of people?

16. Umar accepted that Saeed ibn Amr ibn Nufayl was eligible for Caliphate. Then why wasn't he included in the committee?

17. The second Caliph remarked that 'Ali was humorous. Did anyone else also make such a remark?

18. Was Umar the only person to examine the life of Imam 'Ali (a)? Was the life of Imam 'Ali (a) away from the view of others?

If not, then why didn't others notice this flaw?

We should also remember these words of Ibn Abbas: "'Ali (a) so awe inspiring that we could not begin conversation with him out of fear."

19. Was the service to Islam done by all members of the committee equally? If not, why Umar made them stand in a single row?

20. Were not some members related to each other?

21. If yes, could they support their relative in an unfair manner or not?

22. Isn't it a fact that Talha was from Abu Bakr's tribe, Bani Tameem, which had sour relations with Imam 'Ali (a)?

23. Saad ibn Abi Waqqas and Abdur Rahman ibn Auf belonged to Bani Zahra and they had very close relations with Bani Umayyah. Hamna bint Sufyan was Saad ibn Abi Waqqas' mother and a close relative of Uthman. Could it then be expected that Saad ibn Abi Waqqas would leave his relatives and support 'Ali for Caliphate? Umme Kulthum bint Uqbah was the wife of Abdur Rahman ibn Auf. She was Uthman's sister. Could it be expected that Abdur Rahman ibn Auf would leave his brother-in-law and support someone else in this crucial matter?

24. Even if we consider the remarks of Umar regarding Imam 'Ali (a) correct, is it fair to deny Caliphate to a person only because of his humor?

25. We have read the narration of the historian, Tabari that Umar had said that 'Ali will guide people to the right path. If this statement is correct what was the reason for making the selection of 'Ali doubtful? Also the promptness shown in the meeting of Shura is also worth noticing.

26. Abdur Rahman showed his cunning and backed off from Caliphate so that no one can object to him. The point is whether this decision was a spontaneous or a preplanned one?

27. Didn't Abdur Rahman appoint his near relative after backing off?

28. Wasn't the appointment of Uthman because of family relations?

29. Abdur Rahman ibn Auf had put forward three conditions for Caliphate viz. following Qur'an, the Prophetic Practice and practice of the two Shaykhs (Abu Bakr and Umar). Why was the practice of two Shaykhs included as a condition in addition to Qur'an and Prophetic Practice?

30. If the practice of two Shaykhs is a part of holy Qur'an and Prophetic Practice (*Sunnah*) why was it mentioned separately?

31. If it is not a part of Qur'an and Prophetic Practice (*Sunnah*) why was it included as a condition for Caliphate?

32. There are numerous such incidents in books of History where the stand of Abu Bakr was different from that of Umar. Now if their successors were to follow their practice how would they decide the issues in which there was difference between the practices of the two? Whose practice should one prefer in such issues? There are numerous incidents where the practice of Umar was different from that of the Prophet.

SOME PERSONAL EXERTIONS OF UMAR

1. The Prophet and Abu Bakr used to give equal grants to all Muslims. Even Abu Bakr did not differentiate between those who were first in accepting Islam and common Muslims. However Umar did exactly opposite of this and stopped giving equal grants to all Muslims. He fixed different amounts for different people.[1]

Umar had a strange nature. At times he used to get angry with Islam and at other times he used to love abusive language. Hence his character was not at all fit for Caliphate. The pages of History are full of incidents depicting Umar's harsh nature.

1. A person came to him and said: "So and so person has done injustice to me. Please give me justice."

Umar whipped him hard and said: "When Umar is idle, you don't come. When he is busy with affairs of Muslims, you come here with your complains!"

The person went away groaning in pain. After sometime Umar summoned him again and handed him the whip and said: "Take revenge from me."

The person said: "I forgive you for the sake of Allah and for your sake."

Umar said: "Forgive me either for the sake of Allah or for my sake."

The person said: "I forgive you for the sake of Allah."

Umar said: "Now you can go."[2]

The justice of Farooq was affiliated to his harsh nature where petitioners sometimes had to bear punishment instead of getting justice.

---

[1] Abdul Fattah Abdul Maqsood, *Al-Imam 'Ali bin Abi Talib*, Vol. 2, Pg. 9-10
[2] Abdul Fattah Abdul Maqsood, *Al-Imam 'Ali bin Abi Talib*, Vol. 1, Pg. 200

2. Umar had made Noman ibn Adi ibn Nufaila the governor of Meesan province. A few days later, someone recited a poem to Umar praising Noman. Umar wrote to Noman saying that he has taken the post of latter back and asked him to return soon.

He came back and said: "By Allah! I never touched wine or women. It was just a poetic effect in those lines."

Umar said: "That is right, but you will not work for my government henceforth."

3. A person from Quraish was appointed as governor by Umar. Umar got to hear a stanza of a poem written in his praise as follows:

"Make me take a sip such that my bones become soaked and make Ibn Hisham have a cupful of it."

Umar summoned him after hearing these lines. The poet was very crafty. Umar asked whether he had written those lines.

He answered in affirmative and asked whether he had heard the lines following it. Umar replied in negative. Then the poet recited the lines:

"Make me drink honey mixed in rainwater for I do not like to drink wine."

Umar was impressed with his presence of mind and asked him to continue with his duties.

4. Umar asked a few questions from a governor regarding the holy Qur'an and Shariah. The governor gave satisfying answers and Umar asked him to continue with his duties. While returning he said: "I had a dream, please interpret it for me." Umar asked him to narrate his dream. He said: "I saw the sun and moon fighting each other. They had an army each." Umar asked: "From which side did you participate?" He said that he had participated from the side of moon.

Umar said: "I strip you of your post for Allah has said:

(وَجَعَلْنَا اللَّيْلَ وَالنَّهَارَ آيَتَيْنِ فَمَحَوْنَا آيَةَ اللَّيْلِ وَجَعَلْنَا آيَةَ النَّهَارِ مُبْصِرَةً.)

And We have made the night and the day two signs, then We have made the sign of the night to pass away and We have made the sign of the day manifest.[1]

5. A peace treaty was signed between the Prophet and Suhail ibn Amr at Hudaybiya. One of the conditions was: If a person from Mecca comes to Muslims, they would return him and if a person from Muslims comes to Mecca, he would not be returned.

Umar got angry when the Prophet accepted this condition. He went to Abu Bakr and protested there. Then he came and sat near the Prophet and told him: "Why do you want to disgrace us?"

The Prophet said that he was Allah's Messenger and would not disobey Allah.

Umar became infuriated and got up from there saying: "By Allah! If my supporters had been present I would not have borne this disgrace."[2]

Once Umar was walking in the city along with Abdur Rahman ibn Auf at night when he saw some people drinking wine. He told Abdur Rahman: "I know them." He summoned them in the morning and asked: "Why were you drinking wine at night?"

One of them asked: "Who told you?"

Umar said: "I saw you drinking wine at night." The person asked: "Didn't Allah order you to keep away from spying?" Umar forgave him.

---

[1] Ibn Abil Hadid, *Sharh Nahjul Balagha*, Vol. 3, Pg. 98, Surah Bani Israel 17:12
[2] Ibn Athir, *Al-Kamil fit Tarikh*, Vol. 3, Pg. 30

INCONSISTENCY BETWEEN THE PRACTICE OF THE PROPHET AND UMAR

We have already discussed the difference of opinion of Umar in distributing grants and at the time of the treaty of Hudaybiya. Only a handful of contradictions are mentioned here otherwise:

We need a ship to sail in this boundless sea.

1. The Prophet made an agreement with Jews of Khaiber after the battle that they would look after Khaiber orchards and have fifty percent share in the harvest. This practice continued during the Prophet's and Abu Bakr's time. Umar took away these orchards and land, and exiled all of them.

2. The Prophet had conquered the valley of Qura and had signed a similar agreement with Jews of that place.

Umar exiled all of them to Syria during the time of his Caliphate and grabbed all their lands.[1]

MUTUAL DIFFERENCES BETWEEN THE PRACTICE OF ABU BAKR AND UMAR

We have already discussed a few differences in previous sections. Some more contradictions are mentioned here as examples. We ask the scholars that when there were differences in the practice of Abu Bakr and Umar, how could one follow the practice of 'the two Shaykhs'? How could it be made a condition for Caliphate?

1. Uyyana ibn Husn and Iqra ibn Hubais went to Abu Bakr and said: "O Caliph of Prophet! We have barren land with us. It is not possible to cultivate it. If you give us fertile land we will work hard and benefit from it."[2]

---

[1] Balazari, *Futuhul Buldan*, Pg. 36
[2] These people belonged to the group of 'Muallafatul Quloobuhum', that is those who had some inclination to Islam, but had as yet not become Muslims. So the Holy

Abu Bakr asked the opinion of the people gathered there. The people approved the decision of giving them the land. Abu Bakr granted him the land and asked the witnesses to sign the papers. However Umar was not present at that time. Umar met them on the way and asked what those papers were? They said that they were papers of the land granted to them. Umar took the papers from them and tore them up saying: "The period during which the Prophet used to attract you was a disgrace for Islam. Today Islam has progressed by the grace of Allah and there is no need to win your hearts now!"

They came back to Abu Bakr and complained about Umar's behavior. By that time Umar had reached the place and he asked Abu Bakr angrily: "Is the land given to these people your personal property or that of all Muslims?"

Abu Bakr said: "It is the property of all Muslims." Umar asked: "Then why did you give it to them without the permission of the entire Muslim Ummah?" Abu Bakr said that he had taken the opinion of the people assembled there before granting them the land.

Umar asked: "Is every Muslim eligible to give the right advice?"[1]

2. The difference between the practice of Abu Bakr and Umar can be made explicit in the incident of Malik ibn Nuwairah

INCIDENT OF MALIK IBN NUWAIRAH

It is the saddest event in the history of Islam and Khalid ibn Walid committed many social and religious blunders in it.

1. Khalid ibn Walid attacked Malik ibn Nuwairah without the Caliph's permission.

2. The act of Khalid was wrong according to Shariah.

Prophet (s) had allotted to them a share from Islamic funds with the hope that they will eventually embrace the Faith.
[1] Ibn Abil Hadid, *Sharh Nahjul Balagha*, Vol. 3, Pg. 108, First Edition

3. Khalid ordered the killing of Malik in words which can be compared to 'treachery', which is strictly prohibited in Islam.

4. Khalid married Malik's widow even before his dead body was laid to rest. The law of chastity and Islamic Shariah do not permit this. However Abu Bakr forgave all his crimes. On the other hand, Umar disliked this act of Khalid. When he was appointed as Caliph, he dismissed Khalid. This incident can be summarized as follows:

Ibn Athir writes: When Khalid became free of fighting Fuzara, Asad and Bani Tai, he turned to Batah. Malik ibn Nuwairah and his clan lived in this area. Some followers of Khalid backed off and said that the Caliph had not ordered them to attack. They said that the Caliph had ordered them that when they were free from Buzakha; they should wait for the next order. Khalid told them: "I am your leader and Malik has been trapped by me. If you don't want to come I would take the army of Emigrants along with me."

Abu Bakr had advised his army to recite the call for prayer (*Adhan*) at any place they halt. If the opponents also do the same, do not trouble them. If they do not say Adhan they should be attacked. If they say Adhan they should be asked about Zakat. If they say that Zakat is obligatory, do not trouble them. If they say otherwise, attack them.

Khalid reached this place along with his army and recited the call for prayer (*Adhan*). The tribe of Malik also said the Adhan in reply. This was testified by Abu Qatadah, a soldier of Khalid.

Khalid's army attacked the Muslims, swords were unsheathed and battle began from both the sides. The people of Malik's tribe asked the attackers: "Who are you?" The attackers replied: "We are Muslims." The people of Malik's tribe said: "We are also Muslims. Then why should we fight?" Khalid's army asked them to put their weapons down and the people of Malik's tribe did so. Then Khalid ordered his army to arrest all the people of Malik's tribe and they were summoned. Malik ibn Nuwairah was also brought along. His wife came to meet him in Khalid's court. She was a beautiful woman and Khalid looked at her greedily. Malik told his wife: "If you hadn't come, we would have been saved. Now Khalid has seen you with his greedy eyes and I know that he would kill me in order to acquire you."

It was a cold and a dark night and the prisoners were shivering. Khalid signaled a caller and the latter called out loudly: "Warm up your prisoners!" but as translated according to the dictionary of Bani Kinana, it meant "Kill your prisoners." Khalid's soldiers got up and killed all the pious Muslims of that tribe.

The bodies of the martyred were still lying on the ground that Khalid married Malik's widow. On seeing this, Abu Qatadah came to Medina and informed Abu Bakr of this incident. Upon this, Umar said: "The sword of Khalid has become extravagant. He should be dismissed and punished severely."

Abu Bakr said: "He misinterpreted and committed a mistake. Khalid is 'the sword of Allah'. Do not object to Khalid." Khalid came to Medina after a few days and asked Abu Bakr to forgive him. Abu Bakr forgave him and legitimized his marriage.

Malik's brother, Mutammam ibn Nuwairah came to Abu Bakr and said: "My brother was martyred by Khalid and my people were brought to Medina unlawfully. I want Khalid to be punished as per Shariah and the prisoners should be released."

Abu Bakr released the prisoners immediately and gave compensation of Malik's death from Muslim treasury instead of punishing Khalid.

Mutammam ibn Nuwairah always recited elegies in the memory of his brother. His elegies have a great literary value in Arabic literature even today.[1]

---

[1] *Al-Kamil fit Tarikh*, Vol. 2, Pg. 242-243

ANALYSIS OF THE INCIDENT OF MALIK

1. The attack was carried out without the Caliph's permission.

2. The soldiers were ordered by Caliph that they should say Adhan and if the opponents also recited Adhan, they should not fight. Then they were supposed to ask regarding Zakat. If the opponents considered it obligatory, they should not be troubled.

Then what was the fault of Malik and his tribe? They said Adhan and offered prayer as witnessed by Abu Qatadah, a companion of Prophet. In spite of this, they were martyred. Why so?

3. Khalid had used an ambiguous statement to order their killing and it meant, "Warm up your prisoners", but according to the parlance of Bani Kinana, it meant: "Kill your prisoners!" Khalid thought that he would order the killing of prisoners by this statement. However if the Caliph gets angry he would say that he had ordered them to be warmed up to save himself. He could then say that he did not order killing of prisoners and that the soldiers misinterpreted his words. He could thus prove his innocence in the whole incident.

4. If Khalid had doubted their faith even after seeing them praying and saying Adhan he should have sent them to Medina to the Caliph. Who had given him the right to eliminate them?

5. The body of the husband lay while Khalid married the widow. This act of Khalid is worth condemnation at all costs. It is permitted neither by Islam nor by human nature!

6. Umar considered Khalid guilty and worthy of severe punishment. Then why did Abu Bakr forgive such a grave crime of Khalid?

7. Even Khalid had confessed his crime in front of the Caliph and asked for forgiveness, but the Caliph forgave him. Is there any clause in Islamic Shariah, which states that if a person confesses his guilt in front of the Caliph and pleads mercy, he should be exempted from legal penalty?

8. Is personal exertion (Ijtihaad) allowed in the presence of Express Text (*Nass*)?

This was the reason why Imam 'Ali (a) had refused to follow the practice of Abu Bakr and Umar.

9. The act of Abu Bakr also proves that Khalid was guilty because he immediately released the prisoners and paid compensation of Malik's death from Muslim treasury. We do not understand why the treasury of Muslims was made to bear the burden of Khalid's sin? After this incident, Abu Qatadah swore that he would not join Khalid's army. He returned to Medina after witnessing this oppression and related the entire incident to Abu Bakr. He said that he had stopped Khalid from killing Malik but Khalid did not heed his words. He accepted the suggestions of those Bedouins who had no other intention except to plunder.

After hearing Abu Qatadah, Umar also said that it is obligatory to punish Khalid.[1] When Khalid returned to Medina, Umar told him: "O enemy of your own life! You attacked a Muslim and killed him unlawfully and took his wife away. This is clear fornication. By Allah! We would stone you to death."

Historians have written that when Umar came to power, he gathered the surviving members of Malik's family and ordered Muslims to return their plundered belongings as soon as possible. He even returned those women who were sold as slave-girls and some of them were even pregnant. Those women were returned to their previous husbands.

Also Khalid is the same person who murdered Saad ibn Ubadah in Syria at night and then spread rumors that he was killed by Jinns.

Khalid had committed a similar blunder during the Prophet's lifetime. The Prophet prayed: "O Lord! I am aloof from this act of Khalid."

---

[1] Ibn Abil Hadid, *Sharh Nahjul Balagha*, Vol. 4, Pg. 184

Because of these feats, Khalid was dismissed by Umar from the post of commander.

Ibn Athir writes that as soon as Umar came to power, he wrote to his commander, Abu Ubaidah and ordered him to take charge of Khalid's army. He dismissed Khalid and ordered Abu Ubaidah to take the turban off Khalid's head and distribute his wealth.[1]

We can conclude from the above incidents that the practice of Abu Bakr and Umar was not consistent as regards religion and the world. Hence Imam 'Ali (a) had refused to follow it, because he knew that the basis of Islamic rule is Qur'an and Prophetic Sunnah and nothing else was required. 'Ali was not like the modern-day politician who is ready to accept any condition for the sake of gaining power.

On the other hand, Uthman accepted all conditions but History proves that he neither followed the Qur'an and Prophetic Practice (*Sunnah*) nor the practice of Two Shaykhs (Abu Bakr and Umar).

YET ANOTHER (THIRD) FACE OF SAQIFAH

UTHMAN IBN AFFAN

"Till the third man of these people stood up with heaving breasts between his dung and fodder. With him his children of his grandfather, (Umayyah) also stood up swallowing up Allah's wealth like a camel devouring the foliage of spring, till his rope broke down, his actions finished him and his gluttony brought him down prostrate.

At that moment, nothing took me by surprise, but the crowd of people rushing to me. It advanced towards me from every side like the mane of the hyena; so much so that Hasan and Husayn were getting crushed and both the ends of my shoulder garment were torn. They collected around me like the herd of sheep and goats. When I took up the reins of government, one party broke away and another

---

[1] *Al-Kamil fit Tarikh*, Vol. 3, Pg. 293

turned disobedient while the rest began acting wrongfully as if they had not heard the word of Allah saying:

(تِلْكَ الدَّارُ الْآخِرَةُ نَجْعَلُهَا لِلَّذِينَ لَا يُرِيدُونَ عُلُوًّا فِي الْأَرْضِ وَلَا فَسَادًا وَالْعَاقِبَةُ لِلْمُتَّقِينَ.)

"That abode in the hereafter, We assign it for those who intend not to exult themselves in the earth, nor (to make) mischief (therein); and the end is (best) for the pious ones."[1]

Yes, by Allah, they had heard it and understood it but the world appeared glittering in their eyes and its embellishments seduced them. Behold, by Him who split the grain (to grow) and created living beings, if people had not come to me and supporters had not exhausted the argument and if there had been no pledge of Allah with the learned to the effect that they should not acquiesce in the gluttony of the oppressor and the hunger of the oppressed, I would have cast the rope of Caliphate on its own shoulders, and would have given the last one the same treatment as to the first one. Then you would have seen that in my view this world of yours is no better than the sneezing of a goat."[2]

Uthman came to power after the death of Umar due to the special favor of Abdur Rahman ibn Auf.

As soon as he came to power, he appointed his relatives, Bani Umayyah and Bani Muit to crucial posts. Most of them had fought with the Prophet and Islam earlier. Their hearts were filled with the teachings of Umayyah ibn Abdus Shams, Harb, Abu Sufyan and Muawiyah instead of Islamic teachings.

Uthman took the services of the enemies of Islam like Marwan ibn Hakam etc. in Islamic government. In this way teachings of Islam were diluted.

---

[1] Surah Qasas 28:83
[2] *Nahjul Balagha*, Shiqshiqya Sermon

The Umayyad rule had sowed the seeds of crime and hypocrisy. People's greed for wealth increased during their rule. Mutual hatred and jealousy between different tribes and clans appeared in place of Islamic ideas of rewarding the right and punishing evil.

I do not want to discuss the abominable effects of Umayyad rule in Arabia. I would limit the discussion to the allegiance of Uthman to expose the favors done to Bani Umayyah and because of these favors, this unknown clan esteemed itself. I would like to discuss how they cleared their way for future? It is necessary to discuss in brief, Bani Umayyah's enmity with Islam.

BANI UMAYYAH'S ENMITY WITH ISLAM

BATTLE OF BADR

The Battle of Badr is a talking picture of Bani Umayyah's enmity with Islam. Hanzala ibn Abi Sufyan ibn Harb ibn Umayyah ibn Abdush Shams, the brother of Muawiyah was killed in this battle.

Among the near relatives of Uthman, present in Badr were Aas ibn Saeed ibn Aas, Ubaidah ibn Saeed ibn Aas, Walid ibn Uqbah ibn Rubai ibn Abdush Shams, the uncle of Muawiyah ibn Abi Sufyan and the brother of his mother, Hind. Shaybah ibn Rubai ibn Abdush Shams, Uqbah ibn Muit who was the step-father of Uthman. All these Umayyads were killed in the battle. Also many Umayyads were held captives. Abul Aas ibn Rubai ibn Abdul Uzza ibn Abdush Shams and Harth ibn Wajza ibn Abi Umar ibn Umayyah ibn Abdush Shams topped the list. Muawiyah's brother, Amr ibn Abi Sufyan, the son-in-law of Uqbah ibn Abi Muit was also one of the captives.

A companion of Abu Sufyan advised him to pay ransom for the release of his son. Abu Sufyan said: "Should the people of my household be killed and we pay ransom also? One of my sons, Hanzala is killed and now should I strengthen Muhammad economically by paying ransom for my second son? Never mind, I will not pay the ransom." A Muslim named Saad ibn Noman ibn Akala had come along with his son for Umrah. Abu Sufyan held them captive in place of his son. He said that he would pay the ransom of his son from the money he gets from Muslims for the release of this person. The couplets of Abu Sufyan are famous in this regard.

The maternal grandfather of Muawiyah was killed in the battle of Badr. His daughter, Muawiyah's mother, Hind used to sing the following elegy in the memory of her late father.

Today world is rotating against us and there is no way for us to control this rotation.

O Abu Sufyan! Take my message to the master. If I meet him some day I would condemn him.

Bani Umayyah had suffered huge losses of life and wealth in the Battle of Badr. As a result, the flames of hatred shot up in their hearts. They were always on a lookout to revenge Badr. Abu Sufyan was among the most deadly enemies of the Prophet. He mobilized infidels of Quraish for a new battle and appointed four representatives to join other Arabs with him. Amr ibn Aas was one of them. Abu Sufyan took an army of infidels with him for the Battle of Uhad. He had taken women along with him to cheer the soldiers. Muawiyah's mother, Hind, Khalid ibn Walid's sister, Fatima bint Walid and wife of Amr ibn Aas, Raita bint Munabbah were also included. These women cheered the soldiers by playing tambourine and they sang elegies for the dead.

When Hind passed by Wahshi, she told him: "O Abu Dusma! Calm down my emotions and I would set you free."

Khalid ibn Walid was leading a cavalry wing. Abu Sufyan was carrying the statues of Laat and Uzza. Hind followed him singing songs to the tune of tambourine. Some lines are quoted as follows:

We are the daughters of the stars. We walk on soft carpets. If you fight today we would hug you and spread the carpet for you. If you turn your backs today we would leave you and would not be related to you in any way.

Amr ibn Aas also sang martial songs in the Battle of Badr and cheered the infidels.

The tables turned in the Battle of Uhad because of the blunder of Muslim archers. Khalid ibn Walid attacked the Muslim army. Muslim soldiers stumbled, rows were torn apart and many brave Muslims were martyred. Amir Hamza, the Prophet's uncle was one of them.

After the battle, Muawiyah's mother misbehaved with the bodies of martyrs. She ordered the ears and nose of the martyrs to be cut off and wore a garland made of them. Still the fire of revenge in her heart did not calm down and she tore apart Hamza's chest and chewed at his liver. She climbed a mountain and said: "Today we have taken revenge of Badr. Today I have taken revenge of my father, brother and uncle."

Halis ibn Zuban narrates that he saw Abu Sufyan in Uhad. He was hitting the body of martyr Hamza and saying: "Enjoy the taste of my beatings."

While returning, Abu Sufyan announced: "Next year, we would fight with you at the place of Badr once again."

After this, Abu Sufyan tried to wipe out Islam and the Messenger of Islam by all possible means. As a result of Abu Sufyan's efforts, the Battle of the Ditch (Khandaq) was fought. Abu Sufyan conspired with the Jews of Medina to destroy the Muslim center of holy Medina.

Abu Sufyan was the one to send Amr ibn Aas and Abdullah ibn Abi Rubai as representatives to King Negus to get the migrants of Abyssinia expelled.

Finally when Umayyads failed to wipe out Islam by all means, they devised another plan to do so. They thought that they should become

Muslims and gain dual benefits. Firstly, they could save their lives and secondly they would become strong enough to hit Islam with a strong blow. According to their plan, if it was not possible to take revenge from Islam from outside they should try to harm Islam and the Messenger of Islam from inside. Accordingly they put their plan into action at the time of the conquest of Mecca.

FAITH OF THE UMAYYADS

The leader of Meccan infidels became a Muslim after the conquest of Mecca. The incident is narrated as when the Prophet reached the outskirts of Mecca with a huge army, Quraish was not prepared for the attack. Abu Sufyan petitioned Abbas, the Prophet's uncle, to take him to the Prophet. When Abbas took him to the Prophet, the latter said: "O Abu Sufyan! Hasn't the time come for you to testify to the oneness of Allah?"

Abu Sufyan replied: "May my parents be sacrificed for you! I have realized today that if these idols were gods, they would have helped us out." After that, the Prophet said: "Woe unto you! Hasn't the time come for you to testify to my prophethood?"

Abu Sufyan replied: "May my parents be sacrificed for you! You are such a respectful and kind person. I do not have a doubt regarding this in my heart." [1]

After accepting Islam, Abu Sufyan apparently controlled his emotions of infidelity. He stopped worshipping idols in public and accepted the new religion. However, at times, he used to express his hidden feelings unintentionally.

After the conquest of Mecca, a person named Harth ibn Hisham told Abu Sufyan: "If I had considered Muhammad a Messenger, I would have followed him sincerely." Abu Sufyan told him: "I don't want to

---

[1] *Tarikh Ibn Khaldun,* Vol. 2, Pg. 234

say anything because the walls also have ears. If I say anything now, this stone will also testify against me."[1]

The above discussion proves that Abu Sufyan was a hypocrite. If he were a true Muslim, he would have answered back the infidel.

Abu Sufyan's wife, Hind also accepted Islam under compulsion after the conquest of Mecca. When the Prophet took allegiance from women, he said: "Promise me that you would not kill your children." Upon this, Hind said: "We raised them and you killed them in Badr." The Prophet said: "Promise me that you won't commit fornication." Hind said: "Does a free woman commit fornication?" When the Prophet heard her instant replies, he looked at Abbas and smiled.

The like of Bani Umayyah, as regards enmity with Islam, is not found anywhere. Uthman was from Bani Umayyah and the members of this clan, young and old were filled with enmity of Islam. Marwan's father, Hakam used to make fun of the Prophet by mimicking him and he was exiled from Medina to Taif.

Balazari writes: Hakam ibn Umayyah was the uncle of Uthman. He was the Prophet's neighbor during the period of ignorance. He was the worst neighbor of the Prophet. He used to trouble the Prophet a lot even after accepting Islam and he made fun of the Prophet at his back by mimicking him.

Once the Prophet was sitting in the house of one of his wives. He saw that person mimicking him. He came out and said: "He and his children shall not live with me." The Prophet exiled him to Taif along with his children. When Uthman came to power, he called his uncle back to Medina.[2]

Ibn Abi Sarah was a trusted friend of Uthman. He initially acted as a scribe of revelation, but when he made distortions, the Prophet announced that he should be compulsorily killed. Walid ibn Abi

---

[1] *Sirah Ibn Hisham*, Vol. 4, Pg. 33
[2] Balazari, *Ansaab al-Ashraaf*, Vol. 5, Pg. 22

Muit, the step-brother of Uthman held a high status during Uthman's reign. He was sent to Bani Mustaliq to collect taxes. He went to this tribe and returned without meeting its members. He told the Prophet that those people wanted to kill him. He said: "Fortunately, I escaped alive from there."

The Prophet had intended to attack them.

During this time, a respectable person from this tribe came to the Prophet and said: "You representative had come to us. When we came to know of his arrival, we came forward to welcome him but he returned without meeting us."

Almighty Allah revealed the following verse:

(فَيَا أَيُّهَا الَّذِينَ آمَنُوا إِن جَاءَكُمْ فَاسِقٌ بِنَبَإٍ فَتَبَيَّنُوا أَن تُصِيبُوا قَوْمًا بِجَهَالَةٍ فَتُصْبِحُوا عَلَىٰ مَا فَعَلْتُمْ نَادِمِينَ.)

O you who believe! If an evil-doer comes to you with a report, look carefully into it, lest you harm a people in ignorance, then be sorry for what you have done.[1]

Almighty Allah has called the step-brother of Uthman a 'hypocrite' in holy Qur'an.

Abu Sufyan and his followers were called 'Tulqa' (freed slaves) by other Muslims. Muslims used to say regarding Muawiyah: "He is the son of the leader of infidels, Abu Sufyan and a dear one of Hind, the liver-eater."[2]

Zubair ibn Bakr narrates from Mughaira ibn Shoba: "One day Umar asked me: Have you ever seen something with a single eye?" I said: "No."

---

[1] Surah Hujurat 49:6
[2] Dr. Taha Husayn, *'Ali wa Banuh*, Pg. 155

Umar said: "By Allah! Bani Umayyah would make Islam one-eyed like you. Then they would make Islam completely blind. No one would know from where Islam came and where it went away."

Bukhari writes in *Sahih:* A person asked the Prophet: "Would we be asked about the acts we performed during the period of ignorance?"

The Prophet said: A person who has performed good deeds after accepting Islam will not be asked about his previous deeds. If a person commits bad deeds even after accepting Islam, he will be asked about his previous as well as new deeds.[1] The policy of Uthman was purely based on nepotism. He had opened the treasury of Muslims to Bani Umayyah.

FAVORS GRANTED TO BANI UMAYYAH

Uthman gave two hundred thousand dinars to Marwan ibn Hakam. He had given two hundred thousand dinars to Ayesha, the daughter of Marwan as wedding gift. Also he bestowed many properties to Marwan.

The situation worsened so much that the treasurer of Muslim treasury resigned. The above mentioned grant was one of the smallest. As soon as he came to power, he granted a hundred thousand dirhams to Abu Sufyan.[2]

He gave a slip of a hefty amount to one of his relatives and sent him to the treasurer. The treasurer was an honest man. He refused to withdraw such a huge amount. Uthman asked the treasurer again and again to grant the amount to that person but the treasurer refused to budge.

Uthman condemned him saying: "What is your status here? You are just a treasurer." He replied: "I am the treasurer of the wealth of

---

[1] *Sahih Bukhari* Vol. 8, Pg. 49
[2] Dr. Taha Husayn, *Al-Fitnah Al-Kubra, 'Ali wa Banuh*, Pg. 94

Muslims and not your personal treasurer." Then he brought the keys of the treasury and placed them on the Prophet's pulpit.[1]

Balazari narrates this incident in detail as follows: Abdullah ibn Arqam was the treasurer of the Muslim treasury. Uthman wanted to withdraw an amount of a hundred thousand dirhams. Abdullah ibn Usaid ibn Abil Aas came to Uthman from Mecca at that moment. Uthman granted Abdullah three hundred thousand dirhams and a hundred thousand dirhams to each of his Companions.

The treasurer refused to grant the said amount. Uthman said: "You are the treasurer of our treasury. You don't have any right to refuse."

The treasurer said: "I am the treasurer of the wealth of Muslims and not your personal treasurer. I submit my resignation now." He took the keys of treasury and placed them on the pulpit of the Prophet and resigned from his job.

Uthman granted him three hundred thousand dirhams in order to please him, but the latter rejected it.

Incidents of Uthman's generosity became public and people developed hatred against him as a result of it. After some days, a rumor circulated that an expensive necklace present in the Muslim treasury was gifted to a relative by Uthman. People felt bad and protested against Uthman much. Uthman became angry at this protest and announced: "We would meet our expenses from Muslim treasury only and don't care about any person's jealousy." Ammar ibn Yasir said: "By Allah, I am not pleased with this act."

Uthman said: "O immoral man! How dare you challenge me?" Then he ordered the police to arrest him.

Ammar was arrested and beaten up so badly that he fell down unconscious. He was taken to the room of Lady Umme Salma. He laid there unconscious for the entire day and missed his Zuhr, Asr and Maghrib prayers. When he regained consciousness, he

---

[1] Abdul Fattah Abdul Maqsood, *Al-Imam 'Ali bin Abi Talib*, Vol. 2, Pg. 20-21

performed ablutions and offered prayer and said: "Praise be to Allah! For the first time in my life, I have been beaten up for the sake of Allah's religion."

Lady Umme Salma or Ayesha took out the dress and slipper of the Prophet and told the people in the mosque: "O People! These are the dress and slippers of the Prophet. This dress has not even become old and you have changed his practice (*Sunnah*)."

Uthman had to bear shame as a result of this incident and he could not afford a reply.[1]

If this incident is authentic, it means that Uthman has committed two mistakes:

1. Bani Umayyah was granted the wealth of Muslims in an unlawful manner.

2. A great companion of the Prophet was made to face severe atrocities.

Uthman's generosity was beyond compare. He permitted Marwan ibn Hakam to use all the Khums money collected from Africa region and granted three hundred thousand dirhams to his son, Harith.

He gave three hundred thousand dirhams to Abdullah ibn Khalid ibn Usaid Amawi and gave a hundred thousand dirhams to each person present in his delegation.

He allotted six hundred thousand dirhams to Zubair ibn Awwam.

He bestowed a hundred thousand dirhams to Talha ibn Ubaidullah.

He gifted a hundred thousand dirhams to Saeed ibn Aas.

Saeed ibn Aas married off his four daughters. Each daughter was granted a hundred thousand dirhams from Muslim treasury. Balazari

---

[1] Dr. Taha Husayn, *Al-Fitnah al-Kubra 'Uthman bin Affan*; Balazari, *Ansaab al-Ashraaf*, Vol. 5, Pg. 48

writes about these incidents in the following words: Muslim army conquered Africa in 27 A.H. and got a lot of wealth as war booty. The Khums (one-fifth part) of this wealth was given to Marwan ibn Hakam. Also Africa was conquered under the leadership of Abdullah ibn Saad ibn Abi Sarah who was a foster-brother of Uthman. The commander bought all the Khums in return of a hundred thousand dirhams. Later on, he requested Uthman to write off this debt and the latter obliged him.

The camels of Zakat were brought to Medina. Uthman gave all the camels to Harith ibn Hakam ibn Abil Aas.

Uthman appointed Hakam ibn Aas to collect Zakat from Bani Qazaya. He collected three hundred thousand from them. This entire amount was given to Hakam.

Harith ibn Hakam ibn Abil Aas was given three hundred thousand dirhams.

Zaid ibn Thabit Ansari was given a hundred thousand dirhams.

Abu Zar could not bear to see this and he recited the following verse of holy Qur'an in public:

(وَالَّذِينَ يَكْنِزُونَ الذَّهَبَ وَالْفِضَّةَ وَلَا يُنْفِقُونَهَا فِي سَبِيلِ اللَّهِ فَبَشِّرْهُمْ بِعَذَابٍ أَلِيمٍ. يَوْمَ يُحْمَىٰ عَلَيْهَا فِي نَارِ جَهَنَّمَ فَتُكْوَىٰ بِهَا جِبَاهُهُمْ وَجُنُوبُهُمْ وَظُهُورُهُمْ هَٰذَا مَا كَنَزْتُمْ لِأَنْفُسِكُمْ فَذُوقُوا مَا كُنْتُمْ تَكْنِزُونَ.)

(As for) those who hoard up gold and silver and do not spend it in Allah's way, announce to them a painful chastisement, On the day when it shall be heated in the fire of hell, then their foreheads and their sides and their backs shall be branded with it; this is what you hoarded up for yourselves, therefore taste what you hoarded.[1]

Marwan complained to Uthman about this act of Abu Zar. Uthman ordered Abu Zar to desist from that act.

---

[1] Surah Taubah 9:34

Abu Zar said: "Does Uthman want me to desist from reciting the Book of Allah? By Allah! I can bear the displeasure of Uthman for the sake of Allah."

You have seen the economic policy of Uthman. Pause for a moment here, then read about the economic policy of Imam 'Ali (a) as opposed to this.

Monetary Policy of Imam 'Ali

The Incident of Aqeel is sufficient to prove the justice of Imam 'Ali (a).

This incident was narrated by Aqeel himself in the court of Muawiyah ibn Abi Sufyan when he reached there after running away from Imam 'Ali's justice. He said: "I was involved in severe debts. So I took my children to my brother, 'Ali. The poverty was visible on the faces of my children and their faces had become red with hunger.

My brother, 'Ali asked me to come in the evening. I came to him in the evening along with my son. He kept the child away from me and called me near him. I thought that he would give me a bag full of wealth but he caught my hand and kept it over red hot iron. I fell down on my back like a bull is thrown on the ground by the butcher."[1]

This incident is narrated by Imam 'Ali (a) himself in one of his sermons:

"By Allah, I certainly saw (my brother) Aqeel fallen in destitution and he asked me a saa (about three kilograms in weight) out of your (share of) wheat, and I also saw his children with disheveled hair and a dusty countenance due to starvation, as though their faces had been blackened by indigo. He came to me several times and repeated his request to me again and again. I heard him, and he thought I would sell my faith to him and follow his tread leaving my own way.

---

[1] Ibn Abil Hadid, *Sharh Nahjul Balagha*

Then I (just) heated a piece of iron and took it near his body so that he might take a lesson from it, then he cried as a person in protracted illness cries with pain and he was about to get burnt with its branding. Then I said to him, 'Moaning women may moan over you, O' Aqeel. Do you cry on account of this (heated) iron which has been made by a man for fun while you are driving me towards the fire which Allah, the Powerful, has prepared for (a manifestation of) His wrath? Should you cry from pain, but I should not cry from the flames?'"[1]

The life of Imam 'Ali (a) is a perfect example of truthfulness and respect of human life.

We know that Imam 'Ali (a) hated Khawarij very much. He considered them misguided. Then also his behavior with them is described as good. It is described in the words of Dr. Taha Husayn in the following incident:

Harith ibn Rashid Sami Khariji came to Imam 'Ali (a) and said: "By Allah! I would neither obey you nor offer prayer behind you." Imam 'Ali (a) neither showed his displeasure nor did he punish him. Imam 'Ali (a) offered him to debate with him and said: "Discuss the matter with me so that truth becomes manifest." The person promised to come the next day and Imam 'Ali (a) accepted it.[2]

Have a look at the behavior of Imam 'Ali (a) with a Khariji and the behavior of Uthman with Ammar. You can see for yourself the difference between 'Ali and Uthman?

Uthman showered Muslim wealth not only on his relatives but also famous persons of that time. Uthman gave six hundred thousand to Zubair ibn Awwam and a hundred thousand dirhams to Talha ibn Ubaidullah and freed him of all of his debts.

---

[1] *Nahjul Balagha*, Sermon no. 221
[2] Al-Fitnah al-Kubra *'Ali wa Banuh*, Pg. 125

He continued to favor his relatives much. On the other hand, common Muslims died of hunger and severe poverty as most of the wealth of Muslim treasury was given to Bani Umayyah and their relatives and the real destitute were deprived of it.

WEALTH OF SOME FAMOUS PERSONS

Masoodi has narrated a picture of the wealth of the upper class during Uthman's time as follows:

A group of Companions had become extremely rich during this time. They bought immense property and constructed majestic palaces on it. Zubair ibn Awwam constructed a palace for himself in Basra, which remained in the same condition in 332 A.H. also. Traders and rich persons used to stay over here.

He had also constructed magnificent palaces in Egypt, Kufa and Alexandria and scholars are aware of his other properties.

Fifty thousand dinars cash was recovered from the house of Zubair after his death. He had also left behind a thousand horses and a thousand slave-girls.

Talha ibn Ubaidullah had also constructed splendid palaces in Kufa. He used to earn a thousand dinars daily from the sale of his crops. Other historians have narrated a higher figure. He used to earn much more than this from other parts of Iraq. He had constructed a unique palace in Medina using teak.

Abdur Rahman ibn Auf Zuhri had also constructed a tall and vast palace. His stable always had a thousand horses. He had a thousand camels and ten thousand goats. He had four wives at the time of his death and each of them inherited 84000 dinars.[1]

You have seen a slight image of these 'people of Paradise'. When the ruler himself is extravagant in spending the Muslim wealth, how can we expect the subject to be patient? How can we expect the

---

[1] Masoodi, *Murujuz Zahab*, Vol. 2, Pg. 222

governors of that time to keep away from washing hands in this flowing water?

Uthman not only gave cash to Bani Umayyah but also gave them huge properties. It is possible that the followers of Uthman i.e. Ahl al-Sunnah and Motazela would say that he had granted those lands to make them inhabited.

Shias say that this reason is wrong because it was not even employed by Uthman. It is a case where the defendant is passive and the witness is active. Shias can also ask why those properties were given only to Bani Umayyah? Were they specialist in this matter?[1]

After this description by Dr. Taha Husayn, it would be absolutely correct to say that there were two consequences of the economic policy of Uthman, each worse than the other:

1. Wealth of Muslims was spent in an unlawful manner

2. As a result, a new class of rich came into being whose only intention was to usurp the rights of others and increase their wealth. This class was ready to obey the worst ruler for the sake of wealth. They also had another peculiarity that it was ready to welcome all rulers who are hazardous to Muslims but beneficial to them in order to protect their wealth.

This class of people was on the forefront in opposing Imam 'Ali (a) during the time of his Caliphate. They did so in order to protect their wealth.

You have seen the basis of the economic policy of Uthman. Let us have a look at some of his other governmental policies.

GOVERNMENTAL POLICIES OF UTHMAN

As far as other governmental policies of Uthman are concerned, it can be said that none of his personal policies were in order. He

---

[1] Dr. Taha Husayn, *Al-Fitnah al-Kubra Uthman bin Affan*, Pg. 193-194

always relied on Bani Umayyah and gave importance to what his in-laws and other relatives said.

Marwan ibn Hakam held a special honor in Uthman's time. Uthman always relied on Marwan's suggestions and preferred Bani Umayyah over Muslims.

As soon as Bani Umayyah came to power, they increased injustice and oppression on Muslim Ummah and it became a target of severe atrocities because of them. However, despotic rulers continued to plunder Muslims and did not care about them because the Muslim Caliph was pleased with them. They had no qualms about the displeasure of other Muslims.

The worst part of Uthman's personality is that he was strict to other Companions and common Muslims as much as he was generous to Bani Umayyah. He misbehaved with even great Companions like Abdullah ibn Masood, Abu Zar Ghiffari and Ammar ibn Yasir. These Companions became victims of oppression under his order. Abu Zar was not only oppressed but also exiled to Rabaza. He was left there alone without food and water. The only mistake of these great Companions was that they wanted to put an end to the plundering of Bani Umayyah.

Balazari writes regarding this: Uthman appointed as governors those persons of Bani Umayyah who never accompanied the Prophet nor did they have any status in Islam. Uthman used to turn a deaf ear to complaints of common people and he appointed his cousin as governor, six years prior to his death.

Abdullah ibn Saad ibn Abi Sarah was appointed as governor of Egypt during this time. He lived in Egypt for a number of years. People of Egypt complained to Uthman about his injustice. Uthman wrote to him advising him to keep away from evil. However he did not heed Uthman's words and inflicted severe atrocities on the complainants, as a result of which one of them died on the spot.

After that, another representative of the Egyptian folks came to Medina to complain about Ibn Abi Sarah. He met the Companions during prayer times and narrated the atrocities inflicted on them. Consequently, Talha came to Uthman and protested against him harshly. Ayesha also sent him a message demanding justice for the people of Egypt.

The great Companions including Imam 'Ali (a), Miqdad, Talha and Zubair sent a letter to Uthman reporting the injustice of his governors. They also condemned Uthman saying that if he did not improve, it would not be rightful for him to be a Caliph.

Ammar took that letter to Uthman. Uthman got angry on reading a single line. He told Ammar: "How dare you bring this letter to me?"

Ammar replied: "I did so because I care about you."

Uthman said: "O son of Sumayya! You are a liar."

Ammar said: "By Allah, I am the son of the first martyrs of Islam, Sumayya and Yasir."

Uthman ordered his slaves to tie up Ammar. The slaves caught him and tied him up. Uthman kicked Ammar so hard that he fell down unconscious.[1] After analyzing the history of Uthman, it becomes clear that the only aim of his financial and governmental policies was to play with the destiny of Muslim Ummah, weaken the supporters of Islam and to pave way for the rule of the enemies of Islam, especially Bani Umayyah.

The policy of Uthman was not only different from holy Qur'an and Prophetic Practice (*Sunnah*) but also different from the practice of Abu Bakr and Umar.

Waqidi narrates: People protested strongly when Uthman gave a hundred thousand dirhams to Saeed ibn Aas. Imam 'Ali (a) and other Companions discussed this matter. Uthman said: "He is my close

---

[1] Balazari, *Ansaab al-Ashraaf*, Vol. 5, Pg. 25-26

relative." The Companions asked: "Didn't Abu Bakr and Umar have relatives in this world?"

Uthman said: "They used to be happy after depriving their relatives while I feel happy after giving wealth to my relatives."

This practice of Uthman was not similar to the practice of Abu Bakr and Umar. It had nothing to do with the spirit of Islam.

PRACTICE OF UTHMAN'S GOVERNORS

Let us have a look at the practice of Uthman's governors:

There is no doubt that Uthman relied on his relatives for government. We are not so narrow-minded that we would object to someone only because of his relations. It is an old practice of the rulers to appoint their reliable relatives in government posts. There is no harm if the relatives are capable, but were the relatives upon whom Uthman relied capable and reliable?

Uthman also appointed such relatives to important posts about whose mischief, justice and hypocrisy Allah has testified in holy Qur'an.

The character of some of them is presented below as example for readers. If we discuss the evil acts of Uthman's governors, a separate book would be required for it.

WALID IBN UQBAH

To begin with, let us consider the real face of Walid ibn Uqbah ibn Abi Muit who was appointed as the governor of Kufa.

A brief account of this star of Bani Umayyah is that he was sent to Bani Mustaliq to recover taxes on behalf of the Prophet, but he went to this tribe and returned without meeting its members and told the Prophet that they wanted to kill him. "Fortunately, I escaped alive from the place." The Prophet intended to attack them.

During this time, a respectable man from this tribe came to the Prophet and said: "Your representative had come to us, but when we came to know of his arrival and we came forward to welcome him, he returned without meeting us."

Almighty Allah revealed the following verse:

$$\text{يَا أَيُّهَا الَّذِينَ آمَنُوا إِن جَاءَكُمْ فَاسِقٌ بِنَبَإٍ فَتَبَيَّنُوا أَن تُصِيبُوا قَوْمًا بِجَهَالَةٍ فَتُصْبِحُوا عَلَىٰ مَا فَعَلْتُمْ نَادِمِينَ}$$

O you who believe, if an evil-doer comes to you with a report, look carefully into it, lest you harm a people in ignorance, then be sorry for what you have done.[1]

Once Walid's wife came to the Prophet and complained that her husband beats her without any excuse. The Prophet told her: "Go and tell him that you are under the protection of Allah's Messenger."

She returned and conveyed the Prophet's message but came back the next day and said: "O Messenger of Allah! He beat me on hearing your message."

The Prophet tore up a part of her dress and said: "Go and tell him that the Prophet has torn it as a sign and tell him not to beat you." She came back after some time, crying and said: "O Messenger of Allah! When I gave your message and showed your sign, he beat me more."[2]

WALID DRINKS WINE IN KUFA

Uthman had appointed this Walid as governor of Kufa. He used to drink wine the whole night with his friends. Once he went to lead the Morning Prayer completely drunk. He offered four units (rakats) instead of the prescribed two and turned to the congregation and asked: "If you want, I can offer more."

Some narrators report that he used to recite in prostration: "Drink and make me also drink."

---

[1] Surah Hujurat 49:6
[2] Ibn Abil Hadid, *Sharh Nahjul Balagha*, Vol. 4, Pg. 195

A person standing in the first row said: "I am not surprised at you. I am astonished at the person who appointed you as our ruler." Once Walid delivered a sermon and the people stoned him. He was taken aback and went inside his palace.

Walid was a fornicator and he used to drink wine. Once he entered the mosque to lead prayers while drunk and he vomited in the Prayer Niche (*Mihraab*). The color of wine was distinct in vomited liquid. Then he recited these lines:

"My heart became attached to Rabab when both of us reached the age of adolescence."

The people of Kufa came to Uthman with complaints and asked him to take legal action. Uthman appointed a person to punish Walid. When that person came to Walid with a whip, Walid told Uthman: "I beg forgiveness from you for the sake of Allah and our relation." Uthman forgave him. Then he thought that the people would say that he has shunned a religious commandment. So he got up and whipped him three or four times.

When the people of Kufa came to Uthman again with their complaints, he got really angry with them and said: "Whenever you are angry with a ruler, you start picking out his faults."

The people came to Ayesha to seek help. When Uthman saw that they were under the protection of the Mother of faithful, he said: "Only the house of Ayesha will provide shelter to the hypocrites of Iraq." When Ayesha heard these words, she came out with a slipper of the Prophet in her hand and said: "You have left the Practice (*Sunnah*) of the owner of this slipper."[1]

---

[1] Masoodi, *Murujuz Zahab* Vol. 2, Pg. 224

Why Walid was Appointed as a Governor of Kufa?

The story of Walid's appointment as governor of Kufa is also strange. Narrator says that there was space for only one more person to sit on the throne that Uthman occupied.

Only four persons used to sit with Uthman viz. Abbas ibn Abdul Muttalib, Abu Sufyan ibn Harb, Hakam ibn Aas and Walid ibn Uqbah.

Once Walid was sitting with Uthman and Hakam ibn Abil Aas arrived. Uthman signaled Walid to get up in order to make Hakam sit near him. Walid said: "You gave preference to your uncle over your cousin. I hereby quote two lines."

It should be clear that Marwan's father Hakam was Uthman's uncle and a senior member of Bani Umayyah, while Walid was a maternal cousin of Marwan.

Uthman asked him to recite those lines:

I have seen that people respect their uncles more than their brothers, which was not customary earlier. May your sons Umar and Khalid live long so that they address me as uncle one day.

Uthman appreciated him for these lines and said: "I make you the governor of Kufa."

This Walid is same whom Qur'an has called a hypocrite. He is the same who did not obey the Prophet's command.

He took his appointment letter to Saad, the governor of Kufa. Saad asked him: "You have come here for a vacation or to rule?"

Walid replied: "I have come here as a ruler." Saad said: "By Allah, I don't know whether I have gone crazy or you have become wise."

Walid said: "Neither you have gone crazy nor I have become wise. It is the decision of one who rules."[1]

Books of history are full of descriptions of other governors of Uthman. Even though many experienced and elder Companions were present at that time, Uthman appointed Abdullah ibn Aamir as the governor of Basra, who was 25 years old at that time.

Abdullah ibn Saad ibn Abi Sarah was appointed as the governor of Egypt. He is the one whose killing was made obligatory by Allah and His Messenger. It was announced at the time of conquest of Mecca that everyone is safe except Abdullah ibn Saad ibn Abi Sarah. He should be killed even if he is found clinging to the covering of holy Kaaba.[2]

UTHMAN'S BEHAVIOR WITH COMPANIONS

The Injustice done by despotic rulers of Bani Umayyah to Muslims is one part of history. However, Uthman's personal behavior with the great Companions was unsound.

Readers of History are well-aware of the fact that Umayyad governors did not misbehave with Muslim Ummah as much as Uthman misbehaved with senior Companions.

When the selected Companions complained to Uthman, that despotic governors should be dismissed, he targeted them with oppression instead of behaving with them in a nice manner.

Abdullah ibn Masood was one of those who had to bear oppression. When he had conflict with Uthman regarding compilation of holy Qur'an, Uthman ordered his slaves to whip him instead of settling the matter. The slaves hit him badly and he was thrown down flat, as a result of which his ribs were broken. As if this was not enough, Uthman stopped his pension. He misbehaved with Abu Zar Ghiffari more than this.

---

[1] Dr. Taha Husayn, *Al-Fitnah al-Kubra 'Uthman bin Affan*, Pg. 187
[2] Abdul Fattah Abdul Maqsood, *Al-Imam 'Ali bin Abi Talib* Vol. 2, Pg. 33

Abu Zar Ghiffari was an honorable Companion of the Prophet, about whom the Prophet had said: "Paradise is waiting for Abu Zar." The Prophet has compared Abu Zar's piety with that of Prophet Isa's. The following tradition is very famous: "There is no one under the sky or over the earth more truthful than Abu Zar."

Capitalism and stockpiling had increased during the time of Uthman to a great extent and Abu Zar decided to fight against it. He used to go out in the markets protesting and he used to recite the following verse of Surah Taubah:

(وَالَّذِينَ يَكْنِزُونَ الذَّهَبَ وَالْفِضَّةَ وَلَا يُنْفِقُونَهَا فِي سَبِيلِ اللَّهِ فَبَشِّرْهُمْ بِعَذَابٍ أَلِيمٍ يَوْمَ يُحْمَى عَلَيْهَا فِي نَارِ جَهَنَّمَ فَتُكْوَىٰ بِهَا جِبَاهُهُمْ وَجُنُوبُهُمْ وَظُهُورُهُمْ هَٰذَا مَا كَنَزْتُمْ لِأَنْفُسِكُمْ فَذُوقُوا مَا كُنْتُمْ تَكْنِزُونَ.)

(As for) those who hoard up gold and silver and do not spend it in Allah's way, announce to them a painful chastisement, On the day when it shall be heated in the fire of hell, then their foreheads and their sides and their backs shall be branded with it; this is what you hoarded up for yourselves, therefore taste what you hoarded.[1]

When Uthman realized that the lower class people of Medina were becoming aware due to Abu Zar's protests, he was exiled to Syria and Muawiyah, the governor of Syria was ordered to keep a close watch on him.

Abu Zar continued his practice in Syria also. Muawiyah sent him to Medina on a fierce camel, but Uthman did not allow him to live in Medina. He was instead exiled to a desert called Rabaza. His son Zar passed away over there and his daughter was left alone. He also passed away in this state after a few days. When a caravan of Iraqis passed by, they shrouded and buried this great Companion of the Prophet.

---

[1] Surah Taubah 9:34-35

Balazari narrates that when the Caliph got the news of Abu Zar's demise, he said: "May Allah's mercy be on him."

Ammar asked: "What is your opinion regarding a person who exiled him?" Uthman promptly replied: "Do you think that I feel ashamed after exiling Abu Zar?"

Then he ordered that Ammar should also be exiled and told him: "You also go to the desert of Rabaza."

Ammar had made all the preparations for his exile. The people of his tribe, Bani Makhzoom came to Imam 'Ali (a) to redress their grievance. Imam 'Ali (a) went to Uthman and said: "Fear Allah, you had exiled a virtuous believer earlier who passed away as a result of it. Now you want to repeat that with someone else." Both had a bitter argument and Uthman told Imam 'Ali (a): "You are more rightful of being exiled as compared to Ammar."

Imam 'Ali (a) said: "If you have courage, try to exile me." After that, Emigrants gathered around the Caliph and said: "Whenever someone argued with you, you have exiled him. This is not a good practice."[1]

He was compelled to cancel the order of Ammar's exile. A great companion like Ammar was made the target of severe atrocities, the detailed description of which is narrated as follows in the words of Allamah Abul Fatah Abul Maqsood: "Many Companions came forward and wrote a letter complaining about the injustice of Uthman's governors. Ammar took this letter to Uthman but when he reached Uthman's court, Marwan said to Uthman: "This black slave is trying to instigate people against you. You would remain safe from harm in future if you kill him now."

Uthman followed Marwan's advice and began to hit Ammar with a stick, non-stop. The Caliph's men left no stone unturned in beating Ammar.

---

[1] *Ansaab al-Ashraaf,* Vol. 5, Pg. 54-55

As a result of this beating Ammar got hernia. The servants of Caliph threw him on the road, in rain and cold weather.[1] This was the time when justice disappeared and clouds of oppression hovered on the Muslim Ummah.

Dr. Taha Husayn has correctly said: Ahl al-Sunnah and Motazela will not only have to justify the deeds of Uthman's governors but also the deeds of Uthman himself. His behavior with great Companions like Abdullah ibn Masood and Ammar ibn Yasir was not at all appropriate.

Ammar was beaten up so badly that he suffered from hernia. Abdullah ibn Masood was disgraced before being thrown out of the mosque and his ribs were crushed.

Such behavior of Uthman to these great Companions was on the advice of his governors.

Both of these personalities were not tried in court nor were the testimonies taken from witnesses. They were made to suffer without any solid proof.

Surely, Uthman had no legal right to do so. Take the example of Abu Zar. His only crime was that he had criticized Uthman for favoring his relatives i.e. Bani Umayyah which was the basis of his economic policy; therefore he had to exile Abu Zar from Medina.

Not only this, he had given complete right to all his governors to exile whomever they wished. After getting this right, his governors used to exile all those who opposed them from Kufa to Syria or from Syria to Basra or from Basra to Egypt. Saeed used to exile people and send them to Muawiyah and vice versa. He also used to exile people and send them to Abdur Rahman ibn Khalid. There was no one to hear the pleas of oppressed persons nor could they appeal to some court.[2]

---

[1] Abdul Fattah Abdul Maqsood, *Al-Imam 'Ali bin Abi Talib*, Vol. 2, Pg. 34
[2] Dr. Taha Husayn, *Al-Fitnah al-Kubra 'Uthman bin Affan*, Pg. 198-199

STORY OF ABDULLAH IBN MASOOD'S VICTIMIZATION

The story of Abdullah ibn Masood's oppression has a great lesson. His sufferings started when Walid ibn Uqbah, the maternal cousin of Uthman became governor of Kufa. Abdullah ibn Masood was the treasurer of Muslim treasury at Kufa during that time.

Walid withdrew a huge amount from the treasury and Abdullah permitted him to do so. After a few days, Walid ordered another huge withdrawal, but this time Abdullah refused. Walid wrote to Uthman and complained about the behavior of the treasurer.

Uthman wrote to Abdullah ibn Masood saying that he was their treasurer and must obey Walid's orders.

After reading this letter, Abdullah ibn Masood threw the keys away and said: "I considered myself a treasurer of Muslim wealth. If you want me to be your personal treasurer, I am resigning."

He lived in Kufa even after resigning.

Walid wrote to Uthman narrating the whole incident. Uthman ordered that he should be sent to Medina. Ibn Masood left Kufa and the people of Kufa bade farewell to him. He advised the people to fear Allah and adhere to the holy Qur'an. The people told him: "May Allah reward you. You have taught the illiterate among us and made our scholars steadfast. You have taught us Qur'an and religion."

When Ibn Masood arrived in Medina, Uthman was delivering a sermon from the Prophet's pulpit. When he saw Ibn Masood, he said: "Look there, the worm of evil comes to you."

Ibn Masood said: "I am not as such; I am a companion of the Prophet." Uthman ordered his courtiers to disgrace him and take him out of the mosque. Abdullah ibn Zamna lifted him up and threw him flat on the ground with full force. As a result, his ribs broke.

Abdullah ibn Masood lived in Medina and Uthman did not allow him to go out of the town. He passed away two years before Uthman's murder. Uthman had come to see him a few days before his death and they had the following conversation:

Uthman: What disease are you suffering from?

Ibn Masood: My sins

Uthman: Should I call a doctor?

Ibn Masood: The doctor has given this disease to me.

Uthman: What do you want?

Ibn Masood: My Lord's mercy.

Uthman: Should I continue your pension?

Ibn Masood: When I needed it, you did not grant me. What will I do with it at my death-bed?

Uthman: Your children will live a happy life with pension.

Ibn Masood: Allah is their sustainer.

Uthman: O father of Abdur Rahman! Pray for my forgiveness.

Ibn Masood: I pray to Allah that he take back my right from you.

Ibn Masood willed that Uthman should not attend his funeral.[1]

People objected to Uthman's behavior and some objections were due to incidents, which were not at all in accordance with the soul of Islam, the Prophetic Practice (*Sunnah*) and the practice of Abu Bakr and Umar.

The Companions also objected to other acts of Uthman's extravagance. Some were against holy Qur'an and Prophetic Practice (*Sunnah*). All these objections can be concluded in the words of Dr. Taha Husayn as follows:

---

[1] Balazari, *Ansaab al-Ashraaf*, Vol. 4, Pg. 27

ALLEGATIONS OF UTHMAN'S RIVALS

Uthman's opponents used to accuse him that he broke the laws of Shariah immediately after coming to power.

1. He did not punish Umar's son, Abdullah even though he killed Hurmuzan, Jufaina and daughter of Abu Lulu in retaliation of his father's murder. He should have filed a case of his father's murder and the court would have delivered a verdict. He took the law in his hands instead of approaching the court. Hurmuzan was a Muslim, while Jufaina and Abu Lulu's daughter were citizens accorded protection by Muslim State and Islam is responsible for the safety of its Zimmis (non-Muslim subjects) in its jurisdiction.

A group of Companions demanded from Uthman that it was obligatory to punish Umar's son and that this Islamic ruling should not be ignored in any way. Uthman took no action against him and said: "Yesterday his father was killed, do you want me to kill him today?" He forgave Umar's son. Muslims protested severely at this and said: "Taking no action against him is against Qur'an and Prophetic Practice (*Sunnah*). It is also against practice of Abu Bakr and Umar.

2. He offered complete prayer in Mina while the Prophet, and Abu Bakr and Umar used to offer shortened (*Qasr*) prayer. Even Uthman had offered the shortened prayer at that place many times.

Companions were taken aback seeing this because they considered it against Prophetic Practice (*Sunnah*). The Emigrants in particular considered it very harmful because when the Prophet migrated from Mecca to Medina, he considered Medina his home and Mecca a distant location. Therefore whenever the Prophet or his Companions used to come to Mecca, they used to offer shortened prayers so that everyone should come to know that Mecca is no longer a home for the Prophet and he does not intend to shift there in future. The Prophet did not like that a Companion should die in Mecca after migration.

3. The Companions also objected to Uthman because he used to levy Zakat on horses also. The Prophet had not included horses in Zakat and nothing of this sort existed during the time of Abu Bakr and Umar also.

4. Uthman had acquired the possession of some pastures. The Companions objected to it because the Prophet had made water, air and pastures free to all.

5. Zakat was also spent in wars during Uthman's time. Many Companions objected to it saying that Almighty Allah has fixed the ways of spending Zakat and any expenditure other than those mentioned is incorrect.

6. A group of Companions objected during the compilation of holy Qur'an. They objected that the committee elected for compilation was limited to a handful of persons. While such reciters and memorizers were present during that time that had more knowledge than the selected members of the committee.

Personalities like Abdullah ibn Masood and Imam 'Ali (a) were not included in the committee. It should be remembered that Abdullah ibn Masood was a great reciter of holy Qur'an. He used to say: "I learnt the verses and Surahs of holy Qur'an from the Prophet while Zaid ibn Thabit had not even reached puberty." Imam 'Ali (a) is an elevated personality about whom Allah says: "One who has the knowledge of the book." Sidelining these great personalities to appoint Zaid ibn Thabit and his friends in the committee was not appropriate.

7. It was not right to burn the remaining copies of holy Qur'an.

8. Uthman was also blamed for recalling his uncle Hakam and his cousin, Marwan, to Medina. Earlier they were banished from Medina by the Prophet.

9. Hakam ibn Abil Aas lived near the Prophet's house before the advent of Islam. He was the worst neighbor of the Prophet. He used to trouble the Prophet very much.

He had accepted Islam after the conquest of Mecca in order to save his life. However he had not changed his ways even after migrating to Medina. He used to make fun of the Prophet in his absence by mimicking him. Once the Prophet saw him doing so and said: "Hakam and his children cannot live with me in the same town." Then he was exiled to Taif where he remained during the times of Abu Bakr and Umar also. Uthman recalled him to Medina as soon as he came to power. The Companions used to say that Uthman should not have hurt the Prophet by recalling the person whose face was disliked by the Prophet.

10. Uthman not only allowed his exiled uncle to return but also gifted him a hundred thousands dinars. Was this gift given to hurt the Prophet or for some other purpose?

11. Marwan, the son of Hakam was appointed as his special advisor. Wasn't any virtuous person left at that time?

12. Harith ibn Hakam was made in-charge of activities in Medina. His practice was not at all in accordance with the demands of trustworthiness and honesty. He was favored with wealth instead of being interrogated for his corrupt activities.[1]

DISLOYALTY OF RELATIVES

"Leaves that were relied upon began to fly away."

Downfall of Uthman's Caliphate began when his supporters started ignoring him. Excessive wealth and bloated bellies had showed him this day when his own relatives, supporters and those who appointed him as Caliph, began to oppose him.

---

[1] Dr. Taha Husayn, *Al-Fitnah al-Kubra 'Uthman bin Affan*, Pg. 175-176

The example of Muhammad ibn Abi Huzaifah is explicit. He complained that Uthman favors his relatives more than him. He asked the soldiers coming back from the battle of Rome: "Are you returning from Jihad?"

They replied in affirmative. Then he pointed to Hijaz and said: "At this time, we need to do Jihad against Uthman."

Then this person went to Egypt to spread more hatred. He organized the opponents of Uthman telling them: "O Egyptians! If you want to do Jihad, go to Medina and perform Jihad against Uthman."

Uthman sent him thirty thousand dirhams and a royal robe in order to placate him, but he brought those things to the mosque and said: "People! Bear witness that Uthman wants to buy my religion but I am not going to be sold."

This incident led to severe opposition against Uthman in Egypt.

REPENTANCE OF A PERSON WHO REPENTED SOON

Seeing the nepotism of Uthman and his abnormal practice, even Abdur Rahman ibn Auf who had appointed him as Caliph started to oppose him and he used to say: "If I had brought the next one before, even my shoe lace would not have appointed Uthman as Caliph."

Abdur Rahman was murmuring in his death-bed: "Keep him away. Hasten to stop his rule before it becomes strong."[1]

Balazari narrates: After the sorrowful demise of Abu Zar, Imam 'Ali (a) came to Abdur Rahman ibn Auf and said: "You are responsible for all this. You made him the ruler and because of that he inflicted several atrocities on an innocent companion. You are the real criminal."

---

[1] Abdul Fattah Abdul Maqsood, *Al-Imam 'Ali bin Abi Talib*, Vol. 2, Pg. 72

Abdur Rahman said: "If you want, I would unsheathe my sword and you also do so. We both will fight against him. He did not care about the vows he had taken."

Abdur Rahman ibn Auf willed at his death-bed that Uthman should not be allowed to attend his funeral.

AMR IBN AL-AAS AND UTHMAN

Uthman dismissed Amr ibn al-Aas from the post of governor of Egypt, hence Amr ibn al-Aas had also become his rival. He also started spreading hatred against Uthman among the people. Once he dared to say before Uthman: "You did injustice to people and we participated in it. Therefore seek repentance and we will also do so."

When Amr ibn al-Aas saw that conditions are out of Uthman's control, he returned to his property in Palestine and waited there for news from Medina.

He lived in Palestine with his two sons where he got the news of Uthman's murder after some time. He told his son Abdullah: "Abdullah! I am your father. You must draw blood from the wound I have scratched till date."

This statement shows that he paved the way for Uthman's murder and it happened.[1]

Amr ibn Aas narrates: "I created Uthman's hatred in the hearts of people. I also instigated the shepherds against him."[2]

In the first siege of Uthman by the rebels Amr ibn al-Aas came to meet Uthman and told him: "You have done a lot of injustice to people. Fear Allah and seek repentance."

Uthman replied: "O son of Nabigha! You played a great role instigating people against me because I dismissed you from the charge of Egypt.

---

[1] Dr. Taha Husayn, *Al-Fitnah al-Kubra 'Ali wa Banuh,* Pg. 67-68
[2] Abbas Mahmood al-Aqqad, *Abqariyat al-Imam 'Ali,* Pg. 83

After that, Amr ibn al-Aas came to Palestine and instigated people against Uthman. When he got the news of Uthman's murder, he remarked: "I am Abdullah's father. Whichever wound I have scratched till date, has invariably bled."[1]

UTHMAN AND MOTHER OF BELIEVERS, AYESHA

Out of all Mothers of faithful, Ayesha opposed Uthman the most. When Uthman insulted the great companion, Abdullah ibn Masood, Ayesha scolded Uthman from behind the veil. She used to criticize Uthman and his governors openly. The people used to consider her as the greatest opponent of Uthman.[2]

Once Ayesha brought a shirt of the Prophet to the mosque and raising it said: "People! Look at this. The Prophet's shirt has not become old but Uthman has made his Practice (*Sunnah*) old. Slay Nathal, may Allah kill Nathal."[3]

Ayesha instigated people against Uthman and ordered them to kill Uthman on numerous occasions. When the oppressed people laid siege to Uthman, she went to Mecca on the pretext of performing Hajj and Umrah and she did not try to extinguish the flames of sedition lit by her. Although she resided in Mecca she was always waiting for news of Medina.

Once she heard a rumor that Uthman has killed the protestors and the agitation has come to an end. Ayesha was enraged on hearing this. She said: "This is very bad! People seeking justice and opposing injustice were killed!"[4]

Once there was a bitter argument between Ayesha and Uthman. Uthman said: "What have you got to do with the affairs of government? Allah has ordered you to sit in your house."

---

[1] Balazari, *Ansaab al-Ashraaf*, Vol. 5, Pg. 74
[2] Dr. Taha Husayn, *Al-Fitnah al-Kubra 'Ali wa Banuh*, Pg. 29
[3] *Sharh Nahjul Balagha*, Ibn Abil Hadid Mutazali, Vol. 4, Pg. 408
[4] Abdul Fattah Abdul Maqsood, *Al-Imam 'Ali bin Abi Talib*, Vol. 2, Pg. 276-277

She became furious on hearing this. She took out a few hair, a dress and a slipper of the Prophet and said: "The hair, dress and slipper of the Prophet have not become old and you have left his practice (*Sunnah*)!"[1]

The wave of agitation reached the entire Muslim community because of protests from the Mother of faithful and some great Companions. The agitation was more severe in Hijaz, Egypt and Iraq as compared to other parts of the Muslim world. It is strange that Uthman was completely unaware of this wave of discontent. He did not heed the humble advice of great Companions but always accorded importance to the advice of Marwan ibn Hakam and other governors, who were responsible for all the problems.

BANI UMAYYAH CONFERENCE

When Uthman was surrounded by agitation from all sides, he called a meeting of his cabinet comprising of Muawiyah ibn Abi Sufyan, Abdullah ibn Abi Sarah, Abdullah ibn Aamir and Saeed ibn Aas.

Uthman addressed the trusted persons in this meeting: "Every king has a vizier and you all are my viziers. You all are aware of current agitation and I need your advice to put it down."

Muawiyah suggested that all governors should be sent to their respective states and should be given all powers to handle people who create mischief. And that the governors should not allow any agitator to go to Medina.

Saeed ibn al-Aas suggested: "The leaders of this agitation should be eliminated." Abdullah ibn Abi Sarah suggested: "In this way, our government will be dishonored more. We should silence the leaders by bribing them with huge amounts. Abdullah ibn Aamir suggested that people should be involved in Jihad and sent to the border."[2]

---

[1] Balazari, *Ansaab al-Ashraaf*, Pg. 48-49
[2] Dr. Taha Husayn, *Al-Fitnah al-Kubra 'Uthman bin Affan*, Pg. 206-207

The above mentioned advices show that the advisors had overlooked reality and they could not come to a conclusion. They were planning to involve people in external battles instead of putting an end to nepotism and misuse of public funds. Even Uthman could not put forward any suggestion in this meeting. He had no temporary or permanent solution to end the troubles.

We are surprised to know that some Companions gave him humble advice, however Uthman told them: "Every Ummah has some calamity and the calamity of this Ummah is criticism against me."

"O Emigrants and Helpers! What kind of people you are! You objected to those of my acts which were also done by Umar ibn Khattab. You did not object to him and now you criticize me. You did not object to Umar because the migrants were ready with bridles pulled. You should know that the family of Ibn Khattab was small, while mine is large."

This discourse of Uthman shows that the Companions wanted him to rule according to holy Qur'an, the Prophetic Practice (*Sunnah*) and the practice of Abu Bakr and Umar. However, this legal and natural demand of the Companions was considered greedy and harmful by Uthman. He should have justified himself and his governors and justified the expenditure on Bani Umayyah. Instead, he taunted them saying that Umar also did so but they did not object to it. The Caliph ended his discourse with a threat.

It was because of these policies that this spark of hatred which entered the army, gradually turned into a huge flame.

When Abdullah ibn Aamir was returning after defeating the Romans, Muhammad ibn Abu Huzaifah had instigated his army against him. Muhammad ibn Abu Huzaifah used to tell his men: "We should do Jihad against Uthman in Medina because Uthman is not acting according to the Book of Allah, Prophetic Practice (*Sunnah*) and practice of Abu Bakr and Umar. He has stripped the Companions of the Prophet off important posts and appointed hypocrite and dishonest relatives in their place. The example of your leader is explicit. Holy Qur'an has testified to his hypocrisy and the Prophet had made it obligatory to kill him. In spite of all these, Uthman appointed him as your leader because he is the step-brother of Uthman.[1]

Such a front opened up against Uthman that reports were released about him openly and circulated among all the people but no one knew their true origin.

When Uthman expanded the area of the Prophet's Mosque, people used to say: "The Prophet's mosque is being expanded but his practice (*Sunnah*) is being distorted."

A number of pigeons had increased during the time of Uthman. The roofs of the Prophet's Mosque and houses of Medina were inhabited by a large number of pigeons. Uthman ordered that the pigeons should be exterminated. At this, People said: "The pigeons who were seeking shelter were killed and the person who was exiled by the Prophet i.e. Hakam ibn Abi al-Aas and his son Marwan were recalled and given shelter."[2]

Balazari has narrated the following tradition from Saeed ibn Musayyab: "When Uthman ordered the slaughter of pigeons, people said: 'Innocent pigeons are being killed and those who were exiled by the Prophet are given shelter in Medina.'"[3]

AN IMPORTANT QUESTION THAT MUST BE ANSWERED

Here an important question arises. It is extremely necessary to find the answer to it. The question is: From where did the agitation against Uthman start? Did it start from Medina, the center of Caliphate? Or did it start from other cities and covered Medina also?

---

[1] Dr. Taha Husayn, *Al-Fitnah al-Kubra 'Uthman bin Affan*, Pg. 168
[2] Ibid.
[3] *Ansaab al-Ashraaf*, Vol. 5, Pg. 77

This question can be answered explicitly in the following words: Did the wave of agitation against Uthman start from Emigrants and Helpers and then spread to all cities? Or did it start from the army and then traveled to Medina and reached Emigrants and Helpers?

We know that it is very difficult to answer this question for those who have blind-faith.

If we assume the first case, it means that the Caliphate of Uthman was first opposed by Emigrants and Helpers Companions and after that others followed them.

If we assume the second case, considering it less harmful, it would mean that seeing the political disparities of Uthman his loyal army began the opposition and Companions followed the opponents. But along with this, we would also have to consider if great Companions were prone to accept the statements of common people and could they allow themselves to be manipulated by them?

We believe that the agitation against Uthman started from Medina and it was the source from which the agitation spread to other cities.[1]

We have the practice of senior Companions as proof of our assumption. We know what Uthman did to Abu Zar. We also know how much Uthman oppressed Abdullah ibn Masood and Ammar ibn Yasir. There are numerous examples of such behavior of Uthman. Hence the Companions had also started to protest against him.

Let us have a look at the discourse of Jaballa ibn Amr al-Saadi as narrated by Balazari: During the days when opposition of Uthman had become common, Uthman passed by the house of Jaballa ibn Amr al-Saadi who was standing at his doorstep. He told Uthman: "O Nathal! By Allah, I will kill you or I will exile you and make you mount a fierce camel. You have appointed Harith ibn Hakam in-

---

[1] Dr. Taha Husayn, *Al-Fitnah al-Kubra 'Uthman bin Affan*, Pg. 136

charge of the market and you have done such and such wrong things."¹

It should be clear that Harith ibn Hakam was Marwan's brother who had tyrannized the entire market of Medina. Hence Jaballa ibn Amr ibn al-Saadi objected to it. Someone told Jaballa: "You should not oppose Uthman in this matter." He replied: "I have to present myself in front of Allah tomorrow and I do not want to say:

(اِنَّا أَطَعْنَا سَادَتَنَا وَكُبَرَاءَنَا فَأَضَلُّونَا السَّبِيلَا؟.)

*Surely we obeyed our leaders and our great men, so they led us astray from the path.*²

UTHMAN'S MURDER

Uthman's relatives had created havoc in the Islamic government. The poor people sent delegations to Medina with hope that conditions would improve but Marwan ibn Hakam always gave advices to Uthman and the members of delegations returned to their homelands in despair.

A Great tragedy occurred during the last days of Uthman. The people of Egypt came to Uthman complaining about their governor. They demanded that he must be dismissed and some worthy person be appointed in his place.

After a long debate, Uthman accepted their demand and a new governor was appointed; while the current governor was dismissed.

The people of Egypt were returning to their homeland satisfied. They had reached a place called Kinana where they saw a rider on a she-camel, going on an unknown way. They doubted that person and caught him after a good chase. They checked all this belongings and recovered a letter enclosed in wax in his water-bag. This letter was written by Uthman to the governor of Egypt. He had ordered his

---

¹ Balazari, *Ansaab al-Ashraaf*, Vol. 5, Pg. 47
² Surah Ahzaab 33:67

governor to kill the leader of this agitating group and punish the remaining members severely.

The People arrested that black slave and confiscated the she-camel. This was the slave of Uthman and the she-camel was a part of Muslim treasury. The original seal of Uthman was present on the letter.

The people came back to Medina along with the she-camel and that slave and asked the Caliph: "Why did you do this?" The Caliph swore and denied writing any such letter.

The people asked: "Do you know this negro?" Uthman replied: "Of course, he is my slave."

The people then asked: "Do you know this she-camel?"

He replied: "Yes, and this seal is also mine."

The people said: "Then how is it possible that the she-camel, slave and the seal belong to you and you have not written the letter?"

Uthman said: "I have not written the letter. This is the work of Marwan." The people requested him: "We accept your words and consider you innocent. All blame goes to Marwan; so please hand him over to us. After that we would not trouble you in any way."

Uthman flatly refused to fulfill their demand. The people besieged Uthman's palace and this siege continued for a month. None of Uthman's relatives helped him during this time nor did any companion from Medina come forward to speak in his favor.

After this long siege, the people entered his house and murdered him.[1]

---

[1] Refer Pg.400-406 of *Al-Isabah fi Tamiz al-Sahaba* for the detailed explanation of this incident. I have written this incident briefly. Apart from this, this incident is mentioned in all books of History.

CONSPIRACIES OF BANI UMAYYAH AFTER UTHMAN'S MURDER

I would like to describe the conspiracies of Muawiyah and Marwan before discussing about Imam 'Ali (a). After Uthman's death, Bani Umayyah began to hatch conspiracies to end Imam 'Ali's rule.

They wrote to different persons in order to launch an armed agitation against Imam 'Ali (a). I would like to present some of those letters to the readers:

Marwan ibn Hakam wrote to Muawiyah ibn Abi Sufyan after Uthman's murder:

"I write this letter to you after Uthman's murder. The traitors attacked him and killed him unjustly. They have spread all over like clouds and went to 'Ali ibn Abi Talib like a swarm of locusts.

Therefore gather Bani Umayyah around you and take up the central position as one of the exalted stars. You are most appropriate to take revenge for Uthman's death."

When this letter reached Muawiyah, he gathered the people and gave an emotional speech. Muawiyah's speech had such an effect that even women offered to participate in the war.

After that, Muawiyah wrote to Talha ibn Ubaidullah, Zubair ibn Awwam, Saeed ibn al-Aas, Ubaidullah ibn Aamir, Walid ibn Uqbah and Yaala ibn Ameeya.

Muawiyah wrote the following letter to Talha:

"You hold a high rank among Quraish because of the beauty of your face and your generosity. You have the honor of accepting Islam during its early days. You are of those who were given glad-tidings of Paradise. You earned a special honor in the Battle of Uhad. You should accept whatever post is given to you by the people. Allah will be pleased with you if you do so. I would make the situation beneficial for you as much as possible. Zubair does not have more excellence than you. It would be appropriate for one of you to become an Imam and other to become his heir-apparent."

Muawiyah wrote the following letter to Zubair:

"Zubair! You are the son of the Prophet's paternal aunt. You are the Companion of the Prophet, son-in-law of Abu Bakr and a leader of Muslims. You should know that the subjects have become like wild beasts. There is no one to control them. You should save their lives. I want to turn the matter of Caliphate in favor of you and your companion. One of you should become the master and the other should be the vizier."

Then Muawiyah wrote to Marwan ibn al-Hakam:

"I have received your letter. I got the news of the state of Amirul Momineen through your letter. You should become active like a cheetah after you receive this letter. Hunt your prey by deceiving them and remain careful like a fox. Tread the path carefully and hide yourself in these conditions, in the same way as a porcupine hides her head on sensing danger. You should become humble and wretched at this moment like a person who has become hopeless after serving the community. You must leave Hijaz for Syria soon."

Muawiyah wrote the following letter to Saeed ibn al-Aas:

"O Bani Umayyah! The days of disgrace have come for you. You will have to travel long distances to earn a simple living. Your acquaintances will also feign ignorance. Your relatives will cut off ties from you. I see that in future, Bani Umayyah will roam in the valleys hiding their faces. You will be concerned about your sustenance.

People got angry with Amirul Momineen only because of you. He was killed only because of you. Why did you not help him? Why have you become lazy in taking revenge of his blood?

You are the near relatives of the deceased and you are his heirs. You have kept yourselves busy with simple matters of this world. You have gathered all this wealth and goods only through Amirul Momineen. All this would be snatched away from you soon."

Muawiyah wrote to Abdullah ibn Aamir:

"O Bani Umayyah! I see that you will be exiled in future and made to sit on the backs of camels. Try to control the mischief of the opponents. You should take as much precautions as possible. Use the weapon of persuasion quickly. Keep your eyes away from one-eyed opponents. Avoid people who love to fight. Shower your love on people who stay away and encourage your Companions."

Then he wrote to Walid ibn Uqbah:

"If the rule goes into the hands of your opponent you will run hiding your face in sand like an ostrich. You will have to drink muddy water and wear the clothes of fear."

He wrote the following letter to Yaala ibn Umayyah:

"Of all the allegations put on the deceased Caliph, your appointment as the governor of Yemen and remaining in power for such a long time is the first target. People got angry with the Caliph only because of you. He was killed in spite of the fact that he used to offer prayer, observe fast and keep himself occupied in the recitation of holy Qur'an.

You know that the iron-collar of allegiance of the deceased Caliph is around our necks. It is our duty to revenge his murder. You make preparations to enter Iraq. I have strengthened my rule in Syria. You should not worry about Syria. I have written to Talha ibn Ubaidullah and told him to meet you in Mecca. I want you both to prepare a possible plan to revenge this unlawful murder. I have also written to Abdullah ibn Aamir to prepare the land of Iraq for you. You should also know that soon people will take away your wealth from you."

Marwan wrote to Muawiyah in reply:

"The protector of the community and guardian of honors, Muawiyah should know that I would remain firm on my intention and sanctity of our relations. My blood is also boiling like yours but I do not have a say before your word or actions.

You are the son of Harb. You are rebellious and self-sufficient. I would change my color like a chameleon who is troubled because of hot sun and who is keeping a close watch on the conditions. My condition is like a beast that has somehow saved itself from the clutches of the hunter and now it fears its own voice.

I am keenly awaiting your order and would surely obey it."

Abdullah ibn Aamir replied to Muawiyah:

"No doubt Amirul Momineen was like a wing shading us and small children used to take shelter under it. Alas when people attacked this shelter, we ran away like ostriches. I want to make you aware of the fact that nine out of ten persons are with you in this agitation and one of them is against you.

By Allah, it is better to die respectfully than to live the life of disgrace. You are the son of Harb. You are a warrior of battles. You are the guardian of the honor of Bani Abdush Shams. All agitations are related to your personality at this moment. You are responsible for granting honor to the tribe. All hopes of Bani Umayyah are reposed in you after the death of Uthman. I wait for your order."

Walid ibn Uqbah replied to Muawiyah:

"According to intellect, you are the lion of Quraish. You are unique as far as understanding and reasoning is concerned. You have the wealth of beautiful character and etiquette of ruling because whenever you come down for a battle, you prove yourself wise and successful. Whenever you leave a battle, it is because of your wisdom and foresight.

There is no point in being kind. Disgrace is a defect and a weakness. I have prepared myself for death and shackled my conscience in chains like a camel. Now I would get killed like Uthman or eliminate his killer.

Also I would act as per your orders. We are always with you and follow your footsteps."

Yaala ibn Umayyah wrote to Muawiyah in reply:

"We, the people of Bani Umayyah are like a stone, which cannot be kept on another without kneaded clay. We are sword-holders. My father should cry at my death if I keep away from taking revenge of Uthman. I feel that life has become bitter after Uthman's death."

The reply of Saeed ibn al-Aas was different from those mentioned above.[1]

---

[1] Ibn Abil Hadid, *Sharh Nahjul Balagha*, Vol. 8, Pg. 83

CALIPHATE OF AMIRUL MOMINEEN (A)

Praise be to Allah for His favor. The right returned to its owner. (Imam 'Ali ibn Abi Talib)

Imam 'Ali (a) was supported by divine help. He remained patient in spite of troubles. Even though he saw his right being usurped, he did not turn away from working for the benefit of Muslims. He did not fight the three caliphs keeping in mind the well-being of Islam. He used to give his precious advices in the interest of Islam wherever required.

It was natural that after Uthman's murder, Imam 'Ali (a) should have presented himself for Caliphate and have tried all possible means for it. However Imam 'Ali (a) was such an elevated personality that he did not try to gain Caliphate in such a situation also even though Islamic Ummah was forcing him to take charge. Imam 'Ali (a) did not require Caliphate, instead the Caliphate required Imam 'Ali (a).

Tabari narrates the story of Caliphate of 'Ali as follows: Emigrants and Helpers gathered after Uthman's murder. Talha and Zubair were also among them. All of them came to Imam 'Ali (a) and told him: "We want to pay allegiance to you."

He replied: "I don't want your kingdom and I don't care whom you appoint."

They said: "We would not appoint anyone, except you."

Imam 'Ali (a) rejected their offer. After that, Emigrants and Helpers came to Imam 'Ali (a) a number of times and requested him to take charge.

On 18th Zilhajj, Imam 'Ali (a) had gone to the market. People surrounded him and requested him to take the charge of Caliphate.

Imam 'Ali (a) broke himself away from them and went to the orchard of Bani Amr ibn Mabdhool. There was a high wall surrounding this orchard. Imam 'Ali (a) ordered Abi Amr ibn Umar ibn Mohsin to shut the gate. The people had gathered outside the gate and they were knocking it.

When the door opened, the crowd of Emigrants and Helpers surged in. Talha and Zubair again requested Imam 'Ali (a) to take Caliphate and requested him to stretch his hands so that they could pay allegiance to him.

One of Talha's hands was paralyzed and when he paid allegiance, Habib ibn Zuaib said: "The allegiance began with a paralyzed hand!"[1]

After taking allegiance from the people, Imam 'Ali (a) delivered a sermon explaining the features of his rule as follows:

Almighty Allah has revealed the book of guidance. He has narrated good and evil in it. You should accept the good and shun evil and fulfill your duties.

"O servants of God! Fear Allah for His servants and cities. You will be interrogated regarding them. You will be asked about your animals also."[2]

This sermon of Imam 'Ali (a) has a few statements but he explained all the rights and duties of the subjects. History proves that Imam 'Ali (a) did not have any greed for power. He rejected the offer to take the charge of government. When the insistence of people increased, he said:

"Leave me and seek someone else. We are facing a matter which has (several) faces and colors, which neither hearts can stand nor intelligence can accept. Clouds are hovering over the sky, and faces are not discernible. You should know that if I respond to you, I

---

[1] *Tarikh al-Umam wal Muluk*, Vol. 5, Pg. 152-153
[2] Ibn Abil Hadid, *Sharh Nahjul Balagha*, Vol. 3, Pg. 157

would lead you as I know and would not care about whatever one may say or abuse."[1]

In spite of this, when people continued to insist, Imam 'Ali (a) accepted this religious duty and shocked the people by saying: "I am responsible for every statement of mine. Piety does not allow those who have learnt a lesson to have a doubt. Bear it in mind that your test has begun from today in the same way as it was during the early days of Islam.

I swear by one who appointed the Prophet, you will have to face severe tests and you will be sieved using a filter of examination. The whip of death will overpower you, till the mean ones among you become elevated and the elevated among you become mean. Those who are left behind move ahead and those who move ahead will be left behind."[2]

Imam said the above because he knew that people had stopped respecting truth and started worshipping wealth. Hence they would not be able to bear a just government and would cease to benefit as a result. They would then oppose him but will not be able to dismiss him by writing a letter.

Imam had depicted the picture of people's insistence and his rejection in the following words: "You drew out my hand towards you for allegiance, but I held it back and you stretched it but I contracted it. Then you crowded over me as thirsty camels crowd at the watering holes, so much so that shoes were torn, shoulder-cloths fell away and the weak got trampled"[3]

This is also explained in another sermon by him as follows:

"At that moment, nothing took me by surprise, but the crowd of people rushing to me. It advanced towards me from every side like the mane of the hyena; so much so that Hasan and Husain were

---

[1] Ibn Abil Hadid, *Sharh Nahjul Balagha*, Vol. 2, Pg. 170
[2] Ibn Abil Hadid, *Sharh Nahjul Balagha*, Vol. 1, Pg. 90
[3] Ibn Abil Hadid, *Sharh Nahjul Balagha*, Vol. 3, Pg. 181

getting crushed and both ends of my cloak were torn. They collected around me like a herd of sheep and goats. When I took up the reins of government, one party broke away and another turned disobedient while the rest began acting wrongfully."[1]

---

[1] Ibn Abil Hadid, *Sharh Nahjul Balagha,* Vol. 1, Pg. 67

THE ALLEGIANCE BREAKERS (NAKITHEEN)

No doubt, it is a fact that the Mother of faithful, Ayesha and Talha and Zubair had instigated people against Uthman and developed such a state that people went to the extent of murdering him.

Zubair ibn Awwam was on the forefront among those opponents while Talha ibn Ubaidullah was just behind him.

Once Uthman had said regarding Talha: "I am really sad about Talha. I had given him so much gold and now he wants to kill me. O Lord! Do not let him enjoy that wealth. Make him suffer for his betrayal."[1]

After Uthman's murder, the above mentioned three persons took up the pretext of his death because they were on the forefront in his murder.

Uthman was besieged in his house. One day Imam 'Ali (a) told Talha: "For the sake of Allah, send these rioters away from Uthman." Upon this, Talha replied: "By Allah, I would not do so until Bani Umayyah returns the wealth of Muslim Ummah that it has usurped."

Tabari writes: Uthman had given a loan of fifty thousand dirhams to Talha. Once when Uthman was going to the mosque, he met Talha on the way; Talha said: "I have saved the loan amount. You may take it from me whenever you want." Uthman said: "O Abu Sehr! I exempt you from repayment of this loan." When Uthman was besieged, he used to say: "He has repaid me as a thief repays a person."

Madaini writes in *Murder of Uthman:* "Talha did not allow Uthman's body to be buried for three days. When Hakim ibn Hazm

---

[1] Dr. Taha Husayn, *Al-Fitnah al-Kubra 'Ali wa Banuh*, Pg. 8

and Jubair ibn Mutim were taking his body away, Talha appointed a few persons on the way to stone it."[1]

Dr. Taha Husayn writes: "Talha's love for the rioters was not hidden. His continued his efforts in enraging them. Uthman used to complain about this habit of Talha in private and public."

Reliable narrators say: Once Uthman requested Imam 'Ali (a) to dispel the rioters somehow. Imam 'Ali (a) came to Talha and saw a large number of rioters with him. He said: "Send all of them back." However Talha refused to do so.[2]

The role of Ayesha in Uthman's murder is as clear as daylight. She had shown the Prophet's shirt a number of times to Uthman and said: "Even the Prophet's shirt is not worn out and you have ignored his practice (*Sunnah*)." She stood behind the veil a number of times and said: "Kill Nathal!"

It is a fact that the Mother of faithful was the greatest enemy of Uthman. You have read the narration in previous pages that when someone informed Ayesha in Mecca that Uthman has killed the rioters and the agitation has come to an end, she said: "What kind of justice is this? People seeking justice are being killed! The oppressed people are put at the mercy of swords instead of being provided with justice!"

As soon as Imam 'Ali (a) came to power, Ayesha stood up to revenge Uthman's death. She began preparations for Basra on advice of Talha and Zubair. During this period, Saeed ibn al-Aas came to the Mother of faithful and asked: "What do you want?" She replied: "I want to go to Basra." Saeed asked: "Why do you want to go there?" She replied: "I want to revenge Uthman's murder."

---

[1] Ibn Abil Hadid, *Sharh Nahjul Balagha*, Vol. 2, Pg. 5-6, Egypt
[2] *Al-Fitnah al-Kubra, Ali wa Banuh*, Pg. 8

Saeed ibn al-Aas said: "O Mother of faithful! Uthman's killers are your allies."[1]

On the basis of historical facts, we can say that those who initiated the Battle of Jamal were the greatest enemies of Uthman, having Uthman's blood on their hands. The majority of Muslims of that time was well-aware of Uthman's killers.

After having a look at this historical fact, an interesting question arises: When the heroes of the Battle of Jamal were real killers of Uthman, why did they want to revenge Uthman's murder? Why did they instigate people against Imam 'Ali (a)?

Were some hidden factors active at that time, which were taken as pretext to oppose the government?

Why did Talha and Zubair pay allegiance to Imam 'Ali (a) then?

If the revenge of Uthman's murder was important, was betraying the government the only way to do so? Did Uthman pass away without leaving an heir behind? All know that Amr, the son of Uthman, was present at that time.

Which law granted to the Mother of faithful, Talha and Zubair, the right to punish Uthman's killers?

Why was Basra chosen for punishing Uthman's killers? Why wasn't Egypt chosen for this 'virtuous deed' in spite of the fact that majority of rioters was from Egypt only?

AYESHA'S AGE-OLD HATRED TO 'ALI (A)

It is not a concealed fact for students of History that Ayesha was jealous of Imam 'Ali (a) since the Prophet's lifetime. The hatred of Imam 'Ali (a) was in her veins. There were two reasons for his jealousy:

---

[1] Abdul Fattah Abdul Maqsood, *Al-Imam 'Ali bin Abi Talib*, Vol. 3, Pg. 427

1. Ayesha was taunted during the Battle of Bani Mustaliq and Imam 'Ali (a) did not take her side.

2. Ayesha was jealous of Imam 'Ali (a) because of her barren status. She knew that the Prophet's progeny would continue through Lady Fatima. Ayesha did not bear any children. Hence, at times, Ayesha used to talk ill about the dearest wife of the Prophet, Lady Khadija. She had also hurt Lady Fatima many times by talking ill about her late mother.

The Mother of faithful narrates the incident of Ifk as follows: "Whenever the Prophet intended to go for a journey, he used to draw the names of his wives and take along one whose name was selected. I was selected in the draw at the time of the Battle of Bani Mustaliq and the Prophet took me along.

On our return, we halted at a place near Medina. I came out to answer nature's call. I was wearing a necklace at that time. After I was done, my necklace was lost. I began to search it. Meanwhile, departure was announced.

People began to depart but I continued to search the necklace. At last, I found it but when I returned to the camp, all had departed. I lay there after covering myself with a sheet.

In the meantime, Safwan ibn Muattal Salmi who was left behind because of some work, happened to come there. He recognized me because he had seen me before the revelation of the verse of veiling (*Hijab*).

He brought his camel to me and made me mount it. Then he moved his camel swiftly and we reached Medina. People of Medina began to point fingers at me. These talks reached the ears of the Prophet and my parents.

Then I observed a change in the Prophet's behavior. His love for me had decreased. I asked him that if he permitted, I would go to the house of my parents. "I am not feeling well and my mother will take care of me over there."

The Prophet permitted me and I went to the house of my parents.

The Prophet called 'Ali and took his advice in this matter. 'Ali said: "O Messenger of Allah! There is no dearth of women for you. You can marry anyone else in her stead. You can ask the slave-girl and she would guide you in this matter."

The Prophet called Buraira but 'Ali ordered her to speak to the Prophet nothing but the truth...

By Allah, the Prophet had not even got up from this meeting that he received revelation from Allah. After some time he got up wiping his forehead and said: "O Ayesha! Congratulations! Allah has revealed your acquittal." After that Mustah ibn Athatha, Hissan ibn Thabit, Hamna ibn Jahash and their companions were punished for *Qazaf* (accusing a chste woman of unchastity)."[1]

The above narration gives rise to the following issues:

1. The Mother of faithful, Ayesha had accompanied the Prophet to the Battle of Bani Mustaliq.

2. When the army had halted at a place on their return, she went out to answer nature's call without informing anyone.

3. When she returned to the camp, she realized that her necklace was missing.

4. She went to that place once again in search of her necklace. She found her necklace but everybody had departed by the time she returned.

5. She lost all hopes and went to sleep after covering herself with a sheet. Fortunately Safwan was passing by on his camel and he

---

[1] Tabari, *Tarikh al-Umam wal Muluk*, Vol. 3, Pg. 76-77

recognized her because he had seen her before the revelation of the verse of veiling.

6. Safwan's eyesight was so sharp that he recognized her from over the sheet in the dark night.

7. Safwan made her mount his camel and brought her to Medina. Some people including Hissan ibn Thabit taunted the Mother of faithful.

8. The Prophet took the advice of Imam 'Ali (a) in this matter, who advised him to divorce the Mother of faithful.

Bukhari has also narrated this tradition in detail: Ayesha narrates: Whenever Allah's Apostle intended to go on a journey he used to draw lots amongst his wives, and take with him one whose name was drawn. He drew lots during one of the battles which he fought and the lot fell on me; so I proceeded with Allah's Apostle after Allah's order of veiling (the women) had been revealed. I was carried (on the back of a camel) in my litter and carried down while still in it (when we came to a halt). So we went on till Allah's Apostle had finished from that battle of his and returned.

The Muslim army camped at a place near Medina. When they announced departure the next day, I had gone to answer nature's call and I far away from the camp. When returned to my litter, I touched my chest and found that my necklace of *Zifar* beads[1] was missing. So I returned to look for my necklace and my search for it detained me.

In the meanwhile, people who used to lift my litter to the camel came and took my litter and put it on camel back, on which I used to ride, as they considered that I was in it. In those days women were light in weight for they did not get fat, and flesh did not cover their bodies in abundance as they used to eat only a little food. Those people therefore, disregarded the lightness of the litter while lifting and carrying it; and at that time I was still a young girl. They made the

---

[1] Yemenite beads partly black and partly white

camel rise and all of them left (along with it). I found my necklace after the caravan had gone. Then I returned to the camp to find no one there. I sat there for some time and then sleep overcame me.

Safwan ibn Muattal As-Salmi Adh-Dhakwani was behind the army. When he reached my place, he saw the figure of a sleeping person and he recognized me as he had seen me before the order of veiling. So I woke up when he recited the *Istirja* (i.e. We belong to Allah and to Him we shall return).Then he made me mount his camel and brought me to Medina.[1]

The following points can be concluded from the narration of Bukhari:

1. The Mother of faithful left the camp when the departure was announced.

2. She did not feel it right to inform anyone before going.

3. Nobody in the entire army saw her going.

4. Even the people carrying the litter did not realize it because all women of that time used to be light in weight as Ayesha.

5. The weight of Ayesha was negligible because of malnutrition hence the people handling the litter lifted it and put it on the camel back.

6. When the mother of faithful saw the ground empty, she slept there covering herself with a sheet.

7. Safwan was left behind the army. He recognized a sleeping person from far away because he had seen her before the revelation of the verse of veiling.

8. Safwan made the Mother of faithful mount his camel and brought her to Medina.

---

[1] *Sahih Bukhari*, Vol. 3, Pg. 154-156

The incident of Ifk is one of the causes of hatred between the Mother of faithful and Imam 'Ali (a). Also there are other factors because of which she was jealous of the Prophet's daughter and 'Ali al-Murtada.

Ayesha wanted to become a beloved one of the Prophet. She had such ego that she criticized the late beloved wife of the Prophet in his presence. She had tried to prove to the Prophet that Lady Khadija was an old woman whose teeth had fallen; while Allah has given him a young wife in her stead.

The Prophet had scolded Ayesha for this and said: "Khadija testified to me when people were opposing me. She sacrificed all her wealth for my sake when people had deprived me. The greatest virtue of her is that she is the mother of my progeny and this virtue is not shared by anyone else."

Ayesha and Hafasa are the wives of the Prophet for whom Surah Tahrim was revealed and they are addressed by Almighty Allah as follows:

(إِنْ تَتُوبَا إِلَى اللَّهِ فَقَدْ صَغَتْ قُلُوبُكُمَا وَإِنْ تَظَاهَرَا عَلَيْهِ فَإِنَّ اللَّهَ هُوَ مَوْلَاهُ وَجِبْرِيلُ وَصَالِحُ الْمُؤْمِنِينَ وَالْمَلَائِكَةُ بَعْدَ ذَلِكَ ظَهِيرٌ.)

If you both turn to Allah, then indeed your hearts are already inclined (to this); and if you back up each other against him, then surely Allah it is Who is his Guardian, and Jibreel and the believers that do good, and the angels after that are the aiders.[1]

This verse proves that these two wives had certainly hatched some plot behind the Prophet, as a result of which Allah has mentioned about His help and that of Jibraeel, other believers and angels.

If someone claims that there was no conspiracy, he should be asked: If the conditions were all right, why Allah mentioned about such a

---

[1] Surah Tahrim 66:4

large army? Why did he threaten them with divorce? Why did he consider them deviated from the right path?

Almighty Allah had deprived Ayesha of bearing children, so when she used to look at Lady Sayyada, the Prophet's daughter, she used to be extremely jealous of her.

REASON OF TALHA AND ZUBAIR'S OPPOSITION

The reason behind the opposition of Talha and Zubair is also obvious, as they were aspiring for Caliphate, and were also included in the Shura committee appointed by Umar. However they could not get Caliphate through this committee and Uthman was selected; but in any case they derived a lot of benefits during Uthman's Caliphate.

When they saw the tide turning, they also turned their directions and thought that if they played a good part in opposing Uthman they would get Caliphate after him. But, their efforts were in vain as no one considered them worthy of Caliphate after Uthman's murder and Imam 'Ali (a) got Caliphate.

They became furious at this and continued their practice, demanding the governorships of Kufa and Basra, but they were denied it by the Imam.

Also the financial policy of Imam 'Ali (a) was completely different from that of the three caliphs and Imam 'Ali (a) was never influenced by anyone's personality. Neither did he believe in making friends with famous personalities by offering them wealth. On the other hand, both of them (Talha and Zubair) had got into the habit of accepting huge properties as gifts.

You have already read in details the wealth they had taken from Muslim treasury and the wealth they acquired during the time of Abu Bakr and Umar is described briefly by Balazari as follows:

Hisham ibn Urwah narrates from his father that Abu Bakr allotted all the property of Jarf and Qanaat to Zubair.

Madaini told me that Umar was allotting properties to people. When he reached the valley of Aqiq, he said: "Where are the seekers of this land? I have not seen a better land than this." Zubair said: "Please allot this land to me." Umar allotted the entire property to him.[1]

This narration shows that these personalities did not have the habit of supporting anyone free of cost. They had demanded maximum compensation for their support in every age.

However, a just Imam like 'Ali could not give them anything because he had not given anything more than required even to his brother.

Some historians have recorded an incident which clearly shows the reason why Talha and Zubair were angry with 'Ali.

Before rising up in revolt, Talha and Zubair sent Muhammad ibn Talha to Imam 'Ali (a) with the following message:

"We paved the way for you. We instigated people against Uthman until they killed him. When we saw that people wanted to pay allegiance to you, we led them to you. We were the first to pay allegiance to you. We have subdued the Arabs for you. Emigrants and Helpers paid allegiance to you because of us. However, we are sad that you turned away from us after becoming the ruler and disgraced us like slaves."

Imam 'Ali (a) got the message through Muhammad ibn Talha, and told him to go and ask them what they wanted.

He returned to 'Ali and said: "They demand from you that one of them should be made the governor of Basra and another, governor of Kufa." Upon this Imam 'Ali (a) said: "If I do so, mischief would increase and they would make it difficult for me to govern other places also. I am not at peace while they are in Medina, so if I make them governors of important regions, the chances of evil conspiracies would increase."

---

[1] Balazari, *Futuhul Buldan*, Pg. 26

Both became hopeless at this reply of Imam 'Ali (a) and they saw all their aspirations fail. So they went to Imam 'Ali (a) and said: "Please permit us to go to Mecca for Umrah." Imam 'Ali (a) said: "Promise me that you will not break my allegiance and will not betray me. You must not harm Muslim unity and come home directly after the Umrah."

Talha and Zubair accepted these conditions and Imam 'Ali (a) permitted them to go for Umrah. After that, they did what they wanted to do.[1]

When they were leaving for Mecca, Imam 'Ali (a) asked them: "Have I ever deprived you of your right? Have I ever decreased the amount of your pension? Have you ever seen me negligent in providing justice to an oppressed one?

By Allah, I never desired for Caliphate and kingdom. You invited me to this kingdom and I accepted it. After coming to power, I sought guidance from holy Qur'an. It has taught me the rights and duties of a ruler and subjects. I have made the commandments of holy Qur'an as principles of my government and have followed the Prophetic Practice (*Sunnah*).

I neither needed your advice in this leadership nor that of anyone else. Till today, I have not received a case for which I need your advice."

Imam 'Ali (a) describes the mischief of Talha and Zubair in the following words: "By Allah, they cannot put any blame on me. They did not do justice with me. They were demanding a right they had left and seeking revenge of a murder for which they themselves were responsible.[2]

---

[1] Ibn Abil Hadid, *Sharh Nahjul Balagha*, Vol. 3, Pg. 4 to 9, Egypt
[2] Ibn Abil Hadid, *Sharh Nahjul Balagha,* Vol. 2, Pg. 405

INSTIGATORS OF THE BATTLE OF JAMAL IN BASRA

Talha and Zubair departed for Basra along with the Mother of faithful, Ayesha seeking the revenge of Uthman's murder, although their claim was wrong both according to religion and reason.

1. According to religion, they had no right to it because Uthman did not die heirless and his son, Amr had the right to file a case of murder with the Muslim Caliph and the Caliph was supposed to find the culprits and punish them.

Therefore Talha, Zubair and Ayesha had no right to seek the revenge of Uthman's murder in the presence of his son.

2. Those who rose up to take revenge, committed many crimes: They killed a number of innocent persons. They robbed the Muslim treasury of Basra and tortured Muslims in general and the governor in particular, which is not permissible according to human nature or as per legal ruling.

3. Why did the evokers of Jamal go to Basra in search of the murderers instead of going to Egypt?

4. The Mother of faithful had no right to come out of her house because Almighty Allah had ordered her to remain in the house in the verse of:

"And stay in your houses…" (Surah Ahzaab 33:33).

She disobeyed Allah's order by coming out to the battlefield.

5. Does Islamic law permit one to initiate a larger sedition in order to end a mischief? Especially when the rioters were aware of the fact that Imam 'Ali (a) was not at all involved in Uthman's murder and he had not even granted official posts to the murderers. The evokers of Jamal were angry with Uthman first and then they got angry with Imam 'Ali (a). However the reason of their anger was completely different.

They were angry with Uthman because of his unjust economic policies; on the other hand, they were angry with Imam 'Ali (a) because his economic policy was just and fair.

Imam 'Ali (a) did not appoint any wealth-lover to an official post, therefore, his policy seemed more harmful than Uthman's.

In present political terminology, it would be appropriate to say that Imam 'Ali (a) came to power after an agitation in which he had not participated. The fruit of this revolution fell in Imam 'Ali's (a) favor and the agitators did not get even a part of it.

Also Talha, Zubair and the Mother of faithful feared that if Imam's government becomes powerful, he would charge them for Uthman's murder and they would face punishment for this crime.

Keeping this danger in mind, Talha and Zubair broke their oath of allegiance and set out for Basra along with the Mother of faithful. They passed by a spring on the way and some dogs surrounded Ayesha's mount and started barking at it. As a result of which the camel became wild and the person controlling it said: "May Allah curse the dogs of Hawwab. There are so many dogs here."

When Ayesha heard this, she said: "Turn back the camel as I don't want to go ahead, because I heard the Prophet say: I see that dogs of Hawwab are barking at one of my wives. Then he told me: I don't want you to be that woman." Upon this, Zubair said that they have already crossed Hawwab. They bribed fifty Arabs to testify to Ayesha that the fountain was not Hawwab. This was the first false mass testimony in the history of Islam.

Imam 'Ali (a) wrote to the governor of Basra, Uthman ibn Hunayf: "The traitors have broken the oath they gave to Allah. When they come to you, invite them to Allah's obedience. If they accept, it would be nice for them."

On reading this letter, the governor of Basra sent Abul Aswad Duali and Amr ibn Haseen Khuzai to the rebels. Both these honorable personalities of Basra went to the Mother of faithful and advised her as instructed but she told them to go to Talha and Zubair.

So they came to Zubair and asked: "Why have you come to Basra?" Zubair replied: "To take the revenge of Uthman's murder."

They told him: "Uthman was not murdered in Basra. You know the killers of Uthman very well. You both and the Mother of faithful were the deadliest enemies of Uthman and you instigated people against him; now that he is murdered, you arose to revenge his death. Also you paid allegiance to Imam 'Ali (a) a few days ago at your free will, now you have broken the oath and want to fight against him.

Upon this, Zubair told them to meet Talha and the peace-makers proceeded there, but after holding a discussion with him, they concluded that Talha wanted to wage a war at any cost.

Meanwhile another dignified person of Basra, Abdullah ibn Hakeem Tamimi came to Talha and Zubair with a bunch of letters and asked: "Were these letters not sent by you?" Talha and Zubair replied in affirmative.

Abdullah ibn Hakeem Tamimi said: "Then fear Allah. Till yesterday you were instigating us to depose Uthman and if that was not possible to kill him; but now that he is murdered, you want to revenge his death."

The governor of Basra, Uthman ibn Hunayf came to Talha and Zubair and reminded them for the sake of Allah and His Messenger that they had already given allegiance to Imam 'Ali (a), hence they should desist from rebelling against him. But they said: "We have come to revenge Uthman's death."

Uthman ibn Hunayf said: "What have you got to do with Uthman's murder? The right to revenge rests with his heir, because he did not die heirless."

The governor signed an agreement with Talha and Zubair and this agreement was written down on a sheet of paper. According to it, both parties would wait for the arrival of the Caliph of Muslims and would not fight in any way.

There was peace in Basra for a few days because of this agreement. After that, Talha and Zubair wrote to the chiefs of different tribes and made them join their side. Bani Azd, Qais ibn Ghailan, Bani Amr ibn Tameem, Bani Hanzala and Bani Darim were deceived by their words and paid allegiance to them. However some religious persons of Bani Majash strictly opposed them.

Talha and Zubair betrayed in one more way. One night they armed their followers and made them wear armors inside their clothes so that no one could suspect them. It was a stormy night and it was raining heavily. They entered the mosque in such weather along with their followers. As soon as the governor, Uthman ibn Hunayf moved ahead to lead the prayer congregation, the armed followers of Talha and Zubair pulled him back at once and sent Zubair ahead. The security guards came forward and pulled Zubair back and moved Uthman ibn Hunayf ahead.

Meanwhile some more armed followers of Talha and Zubair reached the mosque and fought with the security guards of the government fiercely. They defeated the guards and handed over the leadership of congregation to Zubair. As a result of this, the time of sunrise was nearing and the congregation shouted: "The time of prayer will lapse." In the end, Zubair snatched the leadership somehow and led the congregational prayer. After completing the prayer, Zubair ordered his followers to take Uthman ibn Hunayf into their custody and punish him severely. They caught hold of the governor and punished him by pulling out the hair of his face and head. They also arrested the security guards and plundered the Muslim treasury.

The guards and the governor of Basra were brought to the Mother of faithful and the 'merciful' mother ordered all of them to be killed.[1]

---

[1] *Tarikh Tabari and Sharh Ibn Abil Hadid,* Vol. 2, Pg. 497-501

I would like to quote one more narration to complete the discussion of the allegiance-breakers (*Nakitheen*). Ibn Athir writes:

The Mother of faithful had gone to Mecca when Uthman was besieged and she was returning to Medina after completing Hajj, when she reached a place called Sarf and a person from Bani Laith named Ubaidullah ibn Abi Salma met her.

Ayesha enquired about the going-ons in Medina and he informed her that Uthman was killed. She asked him as to who succeeded to Caliphate and he told her that the government had gone into the hands of Imam 'Ali (a).

The Mother of faithful became furious and said: "The sky should have crashed to the earth." She ordered to be taken back to Mecca saying: "The innocent Uthman is dead!"

Ubaidullah ibn Abi Salama said: "O lady! What are you saying? You were instigating us to kill the Nathal for he had become a polytheist."

Then he quoted the following lines: You were the source. The dust has originated from you only. Storm and heavy rainfall is from you only. You ordered us to kill the Caliph and used to say that he was a disbeliever. We obeyed you and killed him. According to us, the real killer is one who ordered the killing.

The Mother of faithful then came to Mecca and gathered people around her, saying that Uthman's murder was unlawful. Uthman was better than all the inhabitants of the earth. Abdullah ibn Aamir brought a lot of wealth and gave it to the Mother of faithful. Similarly, Yaala ibn Umayyah brought a great deal of wealth from Yemen and gave it to her and suggested to her to proceed to Basra.

The other wives of the Prophet were also present in Mecca at that time. Ayesha insisted them to accompany her. Lady Umme Salma opposed her strongly and told her: "Fear Allah for He has ordered us to stay in our houses and not to lead the army in war." Hafasa bint

Umar was prepared to leave, but her brother, Abdullah ibn Umar advised her against it.

The Mother of faithful set out with Talha and Zubair. Marwan asked: "Who would become the Imam from these two?"

Abdullah ibn Zubair said that his father would be the Imam and Muhammad ibn Talha said that his father would be the Imam. When Ayesha got the news of this argument, she sent a message to Marwan: "Why are you creating dissension between us? My nephew, Abdullah ibn Umar will lead the congregational prayer."

A person from this group named Maaz ibn Abdullah says: "Thank God, we were defeated. If we had won, Zubair and Talha would have fought for Caliphate and we would have destroyed ourselves."

When this group of traitors was proceeding to Basra, Saeed ibn al-Aas met Marwan and said: "The people from whom we have to take revenge are with you. In order to implement this operation in real sense, you should kill those instigators and return home."

Talha and Zubair narrated a remorseful story of Uthman's death to people on reaching Basra and expressed their desire to avenge his death. The Mother of faithful also addressed the people on several occasions.

At this, Jariya ibn Qudama Saadi stood up and said: "O Mother of faithful! The pain would not have been as severe at the death of a hundred such Uthmans as it is because of your public appearance. Allah granted you honor and respect because you are the Prophet's wife, but you torn all curtains of this honor and came to the battlefield."

Another youth from Bani Saad stood up and addressed Talha and Zubair: "Have you both brought your wives in the battlefield? If not, then shame on you. You have kept your wives in veil and have brought the Prophet's wife out." After that he also quoted a few poetic lines in this regard.

Then they came to Basra and arrested Uthman ibn Hunayf after betraying them, pulled out his beard and hair and whipped him forty times. The Mother of faithful wrote to Zaid ibn Sauhan from Basra: "This is from the beloved wife of the Prophet, Ayesha, to her son Zaid ibn Sauhan! You should come and join our side and if you cannot, instigate people to hate 'Ali as much as possible."

Zaid ibn Sauhan replied: "I am your son only if you return and sit at home, otherwise I am your greatest enemy."

Then Zaid addressed the people and said: "I feel pity for the Mother of faithful. She was ordered to stay in her house and we were ordered to fight in battles. She disobeyed that order and is doing what we were commanded."

Once Talha and Zubair were addressing the public when a person from Bani Qais stood up and said: "O Emigrants! Please listen to us. When the Prophet passed away, you paid allegiance to a person and we accepted it. When that person died, he appointed his successor without consulting us. We accepted him also as our leader. When the death of this leader approached, he selected a committee of six persons without consulting us.

One of the members was elected as Caliph from that committee and we accepted him also. Then you pointed his defects and killed him without taking advice from us. Then you paid allegiance to 'Ali without involving us. Now, what is wrong with 'Ali? Why do you want to fight against him? Has he given the wealth of Muslims to a person not worthy of it? Has he left the right path and is going astray? What crime has 'Ali committed that you want to fight against him?"

At this, some people ordered that person to be killed but the people of his tribe protected him and that day passed away somehow. On the next day, the traitors attacked the house of that person and killed him and other persons of his tribe.

Imam 'Ali (a) started for Basra to put an end to this mischief. On the way he fought a fierce battle, in which Imam 'Ali (a) was victorious and Talha and Zubair died.

The Mother of faithful took shelter in the house of Abdullah ibn Khalaf. Amirul Momineen (a) ordered his army not to kill injured persons and women or entering any house or to plunder the belongings.

Amirul Momineen (a) arranged to send the Prophet's wife to Medina, accompanied by forty women. He sent along Muhammad ibn Abu Bakr, Ayesha's brother for extra protection. At the time of departure, Ayesha said: "There should be no misunderstanding between us. The conflict between me and 'Ali is like that of a woman with her brother-in-law."

CRIMES OF JAMAL INSTIGATORS

You have gone through the deeds of the allegiance-breakers, how they committed a number of crimes in this entire mayhem.

1. Talha and Zubair bribed fifty persons to testify falsely that the name of that spring was not Hawwab. This was the first case of mass false testimony in the history of Islam.

Refer to this tradition of *Sahih Bukhari* to understand what a great sin, false testimony is:

The Prophet has said that the greatest sin is to join others in worship with Allah, to be undutiful to one's parents and to testify falsely. He kept on repeating that warning till we thought he would not stop.

2. We think that the Mother of faithful would not have returned to her house on hearing the name of Hawwab because the witnesses were saying that they had just passed by Hawwab. If she had given even an iota of importance to the Prophet's words, she would have returned home.

3. Talha and Zubair paid allegiance to Imam 'Ali (a) and then broke the oath. They also broke the promise made to Uthman ibn Hunayf.

4. They did not care about the sanctity of mosque and prayer. Even though Holy Qur'an has promised severe punishment for killing a believer, they killed the guards unlawfully.

5. The instigators of the Battle of Jamal pulled out the hair of Uthman ibn Hunayf's face and head. Let us consider it in the light of the teachings of the Prophet:

Umar told the Prophet: "Suhail ibn Amr is a polytheist orator, and he always instigates the disbelievers through his speeches. If you permit me, I will break two of his lower teeth. After that, his speeches will not have much effect and he won't be able to instigate people against Islam."

The Prophet strictly forbade him from doing this and said: "I don't want to disfigure anyone's face, or Allah will disfigure mine even though I am a prophet."[1]

You can see how the Prophet did not permit disfiguring the face of even the worst disbeliever, however, Talha and Zubair went against the teachings of Islam and disfigured the face of a trustworthy believer. Does Islam permit this evil act?

6. What is the relation between Uthman's murder and plundering Basra?

7. If the behavior of the rebels with Uthman was not right, was the behavior of Talha and Zubair with Uthman ibn Hunayf according to Islamic teachings?

8. Islam has emphasized honoring a promise and called breaking of oath a sign of hypocrisy as narrated in the tradition of the Prophet by Imam Muslim:

---

[1] *Tarikh Tabari*, Vol. 2 Pg. 289

The Prophet said: "A person having the following four signs is a real hypocrite and if a person has even one sign, he is a hypocrite till he gets rids of it viz. 1) lying 2) dishonoring the terms of an agreement 3) breaking promises 4) resorting to abuse during a quarrel."[1]

I would like to leave it to the just readers to search for these signs in the group of the allegiance-breakers (*Nakitheen*) and request the readers to compare this with the practices of Imam 'Ali (a).

I hope that the just readers would conclude that the difference between the practices of Imam 'Ali (a) and his rivals was like that of the heaven and the earth or between light and darkness.

---

[1] *Sahih Muslim*, Vol. 1, Pg. 42

THE UNJUST GROUP (QASITEEN)

The Prophet said: "I feel pity for you, O Ammar! A group of traitors will kill you. You will invite them to Allah and they would try to pull you to hell."

"The people brought down my honor to an extent that they used to say: ''Ali and Muawiyah'." (Imam 'Ali ibn Abi Talib)

We reviewed the activities of allegiance-breakers in the previous part and there is no doubt that this group had sown the seeds of betrayal and fraud in the Muslim world. The result of these activities came to light in the form of a battle between right and wrong.

The spirits of Muawiyah and his followers were boosted due to the Battle of Jamal and they dared to launch an armed attack on the Islamic government. Muawiyah had got enough time to gather mischievous and evil powers because of the Battle of Jamal and he unfurled the flag of betrayal against the immaculate religion. All those who feared that Imam 'Ali (a) would try them legally gathered under Muawiyah's banner, the best example being Ubaidullah ibn Umar ibn Khattab.

When Abu Lulu attacked Umar fatally, his (Umar's) son Ubaidullah ibn Umar took up the sword and killed Abu Lulu and also killed a Persian named Mazan and an apostate called Jufaina.

As soon as Uthman was appointed as Caliph, Imam 'Ali (a) told him that Ubaidullah had broken the rule of the Prophet's Shariah and that he should be punished for it. But Uthman did not pay any heed and said: "His father was just killed yesterday. Do you want me to kill him today?"

Uthman gave full immunity to the criminal and did not interrogate him. As soon as Imam 'Ali (a) came to power, Ubaidullah feared for his life and he ran away from the justice of Imam 'Ali (a) arriving in Syria to a warm welcome by Muawiyah.[1]

Similarly, Musqala ibn Hubaira Shibani had bought five hundred survivors of war from Khirriyat ibn Rashid Usami Kharji and freed them. When Ubaidullah ibn Abbas asked for the payment, he said: "If I had asked for this amount from Uthman, he would have granted it without any hesitation." He went to Muawiyah in Syria instead of paying the amount and Muawiyah made him the governor of Tabristan. Later on, he advised his brother Naeem ibn Hubaira also to come to Muawiyah.[2]

The son of the liver-eater mother had become a shelter for the rivals of Imam 'Ali (a) and those who wanted to seek protection against his justice. He sowed the seeds of violence in the Muslim community. He left the commandments of religion and boosted the spirits of people against Islam. The effects of Muawiyah's character were not limited to his life; the Muslim Ummah is still suffering from its ill-effects.

Muawiyah rejected the necessary things of religion on pretext of avenging Uthman's murder. The greatest catastrophe on the honor of humanity is that Muawiyah was considered better than Imam 'Ali (a), whose father was Abu Talib, the guardian of the Prophet and the father of Muawiyah was Abu Sufyan who always waged war against Islam and the Messenger of Islam.

'Ali's mother was Fatima bint Asad who is considered as a mother by the Prophet whereas Muawiyah's mother was Hind, who had chewed a human-liver.

Maisoona, Muawiyah's wife was the daughter of a Christian whereas the wife of 'Ali was Lady Fatima Zahra, the beloved daughter of the Prophet. The Prophet used to stand up in her respect and used to remember her with the title of the chief of the women of the worlds.

---

[1] Masoodi, *Murujuz Zahab*, Vol. 2, Pg. 261
[2] Dr. Taha Husayn, *Al-Fitnah al-Kubra 'Ali wa Banuh*, Pg. 127

The result of the teachings of Muawiyah and Maisoona was Yazid, the accursed. The children born and brought up under the care of Imam 'Ali (a) and Zahra were Hasan and Husain, chiefs of the youth of Paradise. Abu Sufyan, Muawiyah's father and Hind, his mother had accepted Islam after the conquest of Mecca because they had no other option to save their lives and wealth.

If Muawiyah had a pure intention to avenge the death of Uthman he should have paid allegiance to Imam 'Ali (a), then he should have taken Uthman's son along with him, filed a case and waited for justice.

However, it is a fact that Muawiyah had only intended to seek his vested interests. He had no interest in avenging Uthman's murder. The historical proof of this is the fact that Muawiyah took no interest in avenging Uthman's murder even after coming to power and did not interrogate any murderer of Uthman.

Muawiyah sought wealth and was successful in forming a party of enemies of Imam 'Ali (a) on pretext of avenging Uthman's murder. Eventually Muawiyah got everything except the revenge of Uthman's murder.

It is a fact that Muawiyah had always thought that Uthman should be killed in one way or the other so that he could succeed him. Uthman remained besieged in his house for a long period, during which period Muawiyah could have saved him by sending an army but he purposely kept quiet so that the circumstances result as expected and after that Muawiyah can become the hero of Bani Umayyah.

Muawiyah had once lectured Abu al-Tufayl and said: "I feel pity for you that you did not help Uthman."

Abu al-Tufayl said: "At that time, I remained quiet like other Emigrants and Helpers but you had a province like Syria. Why didn't you help him in spite of it?"

Muawiyah replied: "I am helping him by raising the slogan of the revenge of his death." Upon this, Abu al-Tufayl laughed and said: "Your case can be compared to the couplet which says:

I see you crying for me after my death while you did not help me in any way when I was alive."

Muawiyah had appointed the opponents of Uthman to key posts.

We have already discussed in previous pages that Uthman had dismissed Amr ibn al-Aas, so after that Amr instigated people against Uthman, and said that if he met even a shepherd, he used to incite him against Uthman. After Uthman was killed, he addressed his son, Abdullah: "O Abdullah! I am your father. You should draw blood from the wound I have scratched till date."[1]

This enemy of Uthman was befriended by Muawiyah and he became Muawiyah's chief advisor. Appointing such a great enemy of Uthman to this important post is a clear proof that Muawiyah had no interest in avenging Uthman's death. He only desired to come to power and he made Uthman's murder a pretext to fulfill his ambition. Ibn Hajar Asqalani narrates the stand of Imam 'Ali (a) in his own words thus:

"First of all, Muawiyah and his followers should leave the wrong path and pay allegiance to me. After that, the heir of Uthman ibn Affan should file a case in my court. Then I will proceed with legal rulings and give a proper judgment."[2]

A letter sent by Imam 'Ali (a) to the people of various provinces, giving them the causes of the Battle of Siffeen said:

"It began in this way: We and the Syrians faced each other, while we had common faith in one Allah, in the same Prophet (s) and on the same principles and canons of religion. So far as faith in Allah and the Prophet (s) was concerned we never wanted them (the Syrians) to

---

[1] Dr. Taha Husayn, *Al-Fitnah al-Kubra Uthman bin Affan*
[2] *Al-Isabah fi Tamiz al-Sahaba*, Vol. 2, Pg. 501-502

believe in anything over and above or other than what they believed in, and they did not want us to change our faith. Both of us were united on these principles. The point of contention between us was the question of Uthman's murder and it had created the split. They wanted to lay the murder at my door while I am actually innocent of it.

I advised them that this problem cannot be solved by excitement. Let the excitement subside, let us cool down; let us do away with sedition and revolt; let the country settle down into a peaceful atmosphere and when once a stable regime is formed and the right authority is accepted, then let this question be dealt with on principles of equity and justice because only then will the authority have enough power to find the criminals and bring them to justice. They refused to accept my advice and said that they wanted to decide the issue on the point of the sword."[1]

This venture of Muawiyah is denotative of the hereditary enmity of his tribe with Bani Hashim. Bani Umayyah and Bani Hashim were perpetual enemies of each other even before the advent of Islam.

There was a Jew slave of Abdul Muttalib who was engaged in trade, and this could not be tolerated by Muawiyah's grandfather. Therefore Harb ibn Umayyah instigated a few youths of Quraish to kill that slave and rob his goods. People like Aamir ibn Abde Manaf, Sakhar ibn Harb ibn Amr ibn Kaab al-Tamimi, grandfather of Abu Bakr complied with Harb's orders and killed that slave and robbed his goods.[2]

BATTLE OF SIFFEEN

Imam 'Ali (a) came to Kufa after the Battle of Jamal and sent Jurair ibn Abdullah Bajali as his messenger to Muawiyah with a message inviting him to accept his Caliphate.

---
[1] *Nahjul Balagha*, Letter no. 58, Vol. 2
[2] Ibn Athir, *Al-Kamil fit Tarikh*, Vol. 2, Pg. 9

Jurair went to Muawiyah with Imam 'Ali's message but Muawiyah did not meet him for many days. He asked Amr ibn al-Aas to give him the best suggestion in this matter.

Amr ibn al-Aas advised him to gather a large number of Syrians and accuse 'Ali of Uthman's murder and then present a circular with regard to revenge of his blood. During this time, Noman ibn Bashir reached Damascus from Medina with a blood stained shirt of Uthman.

Muawiyah displayed that shirt from the pulpit and delivered an emotional speech. The people promised Muawiyah that they would not go near their wives or sleep on a soft bed until they avenge Uthman's death. Jurair returned from Damascus and narrated the story of the betrayal of Syrians and their preparations for battle.

Imam 'Ali (a) also embarked with his army and halted at a place called Nukhaila. He made Malik Ashtar the commander of the vanguard battalion and sent him with the advice:

"Don't begin hostilities and do not go so near to the enemy that he may think you are going to attack him. Also do not remain so far that they think that you have accepted defeat and ran away from them. You must wait for my arrival and do not fight till I come."

Muawiyah's army captured the route to river Euphrates and cut off Imam 'Ali's access to water. When Imam 'Ali (a) arrived at the spot, he was informed of thirst by the army. Imam 'Ali (a) sent Sasaa ibn Sauhan to Muawiyah who said to Muawiyah: "We don't want to fight with you without any reason but you have cut off the water supply and we are forced to fight you. Every living being has right to get water. Please order your army to vacate the path so that all of us can have access to water.

Muawiyah did not agree and Imam 'Ali (a) ordered his army to throw away the enemies from there. The Imam's army attacked Muawiyah and pushed them far away and captured the route. Although the soldiers of the Imam suggested cutting off water supply to Muawiyah, Imam 'Ali (a) was so kind-hearted that he ordered his army: "No one should be stopped from water. If Muawiyah does not allow others to take water and 'Ali does the same, what will be the difference between them?"

Imam 'Ali (a) called Abu Amr, Bashir ibn Mohsin al-Ansari, Saeed ibn Qais al-Hamadani and Shabth ibn Rabi al-Tamimi and told them: "Go to Muawiyah and invite him to my obedience."

These persons went to Muawiyah. Bashir ibn Mohsin al-Ansari said: "O Muawiyah! For God's sake, keep away from betrayal and desist from deviating from the path of Islam." Muawiyah said: "Should we desist from avenging the death of Uthman? By God, I would never let this happen."

Shabth ibn Rabi al-Tamimi said: "O Muawiyah! We are well-aware of your intentions. You raised the slogan that you are avenging the murder only to mislead people and call them to you so that you can establish your power.

We know it very well that you did not help Uthman and you delayed in helping him on purpose. You actually wanted him to be killed, so that you could use his murder for political gain.

O Muawiyah! Fear Allah and obey the Caliph of the Muslims."

Muawiyah told them: "Go away from here, only the sword will decide the rightful one among us."

Towards the end of 36 A.H., the Syrian army started the skirmishes and in the beginning of 37 A.H., a temporary battle took place between Imam 'Ali (a) and Muawiyah. Then they came to an agreement that they would keep away from war to preserve the sanctity of the month of Mohurrum.

Muawiyah benefited from this temporary war and began to expand his army. During this time, Imam 'Ali (a) sent a number of letters to Muawiyah advising him to desist from war. However Muawiyah rejected all of them and as a result of it the battle started. Imam 'Ali (a) delivered the following sermon to his army before the battle:

"Do not initiate hostilities as you are on proof and argument and not initiating war is another proof for you. After the enemy is defeated, do not chase anyone who flees. You should neither kill any injured person nor destroy the bodies of the dead. Do not unveil anyone and do not enter the house of anyone. Do not touch any woman even if she abuses you or your government."

Following conclusions can be derived from the above mentioned incidents:

1. The Imam invited Muawiyah to unite with him and the central government in all possible ways.

2. He tried all means to keep Muawiyah away from misguiding the Muslims.

3. He advised Uthman's heirs to file a petition of his murder in Islamic court and assured that the convicts would get severe punishment.

4. Muawiyah displayed Uthman's blood-stained shirt and betrayed the government.

5. He instigated the Syrian army against the central government.

6. They captured the path to the river and cut off Imam's water supply, which is indicative of the inhuman behavior of Muawiyah.

7. The Imam's army recaptured the path and the kind nature of Imam 'Ali (a) was obvious when he did not stop anyone from using the water.

8. The cutting off of the water supply in Kerbala was continuity of Muawiyah's character.

9. Imam 'Ali (a) did not give up advising Muawiyah in spite of his hopelessness and continued to send representatives asking him to desist from war.

10. Muawiyah rekindled the enmity of the days of ignorance between two representatives of Imam 'Ali (a) viz. Saeed and Shabth.

11. Darkness suffered defeat at the hands of light in the Battle of Siffeen between the right and the wrong. When Muawiyah saw death approaching, he ordered pages of Qur'an to be lifted on points of spears and asked the people of Iraq to stop fighting. He said that they would decide right and wrong according to holy Qur'an.

12. This deceit of Muawiyah proved successful and the Imam's army got divided. Khawarij came into being and the holy Imam was martyred later on.

Keeping the above points in mind, we again say that the war between Imam 'Ali (a) and Muawiyah was between two persons who were exactly opposites of each other.

Muawiyah's nature was that he did not care about lawful and unlawful in fulfilling his ambition and tried all ways in this pursuit. He killed his opponents by poison and broke all types of promises. An illegitimate person was made the son of Abu Sufyan. He martyred great Companions like Ammar ibn Yasir, Owais Qarni, Khuzayma ibn Thabit Dhul Shahadatain, Hujr ibn Adi and their friends. Muawiyah had no respect for a good character.

He had the weapon of temptation while Imam 'Ali (a) had the weapon of Islamic power. Muawiyah had a long and clear way for his mission because he did not care about lawful and unlawful. He cared for nothing except his mission. The way was not as smooth for Imam 'Ali (a) as he had to work within the limits of Islam.

There was a lot of difference between persons joining Muawiyah and those joining 'Ali (a).

The result of befriending Muawiyah was to receive enormous wealth and the result of joining Imam 'Ali (a) was to follow the teachings of Islam.

Muawiyah's friends included persons like Amr ibn al-Aas and Busr ibn Artat. The Companions of Imam 'Ali (a) included Ammar ibn Yasir, Owais Qarni and Hujr ibn Adi who used to pray all night and fast during the day.

There was difference between their followers also. Muawiyah's followers included those who could not distinguish between a male and a female camel. On the other hand, most followers of Imam 'Ali (a) were jurists and narrators of traditions.

However, Muawiyah had one advantage and it was that his men obeyed him blindly, whereas the army of Imam 'Ali (a) had a number of people having unwanted inquisitiveness.

The followers of Muawiyah followed him so blindly that once he led Friday prayer congregation on a Wednesday and no one objected to it.[1] Muawiyah had spread ignorance among his subjects and the Syrians were kept illiterate for a long period of time.

Masoodi has quoted an interesting incident: A scholar told me that a group of scholars were discussing about Abu Bakr, Umar, 'Ali and Muawiyah. An intelligent and foresighted person said: "Why are you comparing 'Ali and Muawiyah?"

A scholar asked him: "Do you know 'Ali?"

The Syrian replied: "Why not? 'Ali was martyred with the Prophet in the Battle of Hunain."

Here is another example of the ignorance of Syrian people: Abdullah ibn 'Ali came to Damascus along with his army in search of Marwan al-Himar. He sent a few senior persons from Damascus to Abul Abbas Saffah who swore before him and said: "They (Bani

---

[1] Masoodi, *Murujuz Zahab*, Vol. 2, Pg. 334

Umayyah) had completely assured us that only they were the relatives of the Prophet till you came here."[1]

Muawiyah spread ignorance among the people in order to remain in power. He resorted to fabrication of traditions as a weapon to develop narrow-mindedness in Muslim Ummah. Thousands of traditions praising the three caliphs were innovated on his order. Abu Huraira and persons like him worked day and night fabricating new traditions and this emerged as a new industry and thousands of people washed their hands in this flowing river.

Muawiyah liked to kill his opponents through poisoning. He poisoned Malik Ashtar, Imam 'Ali's (a) governor of Egypt, through a landlord. He promised the landlord to exempt him from payment of tributes and he was instigated by his words. He mixed poison in honey and administered it to Malik Ashtar.

After that, Muawiyah and Amr ibn al-Aas used to laugh and say: "Allah has an army of honey."

He poisoned Imam Hasan al-Mujtaba through Judah bint Ashath, the wife of Imam Hasan.

At times, Muawiyah used to handle his enemies through flattering and pleasing them. At other times, he attacked them openly with his army.

Once Muawiyah sent his close companion, Busr ibn Artat with a huge army and advised him to cause havoc in the area under the rule of Imam 'Ali (a).

Busr demolished the area very badly and plundered the goods of Muslims. He terrorized the people of Medina and forced them to pay allegiance to Muawiyah. Then that malicious person went to Yemen and the governor of Yemen fled on hearing the news of his arrival. As a result, Busr killed people openly and the Yemenis also paid allegiance to Muawiyah.

---

[1] Masoodi, *Murujuz Zahab*, Vol. 2, Pg. 51

He martyred two young sons of Ubaidullah ibn Abbas. When Imam 'Ali (a) got the news of these incidents, he appointed Jariya ibn Quddam to fight Busr. When that accursed one got the news that Imam 'Ali (a) has sent an army, he fled to Syria.

Jariya invited the Yemenis to pay allegiance to Imam 'Ali (a) and they accepted it whole heartedly. When Jariya returned, he got the news that the protector of Islam, Imam 'Ali (a) was martyred.[1]

The above mentioned conditions prove that Muawiyah had more beastly instincts than human nature. His beastliness changed with conditions. He used to tear apart weak people like a wolf and used to flatter the powerful ones.

Conversely, the life of Imam 'Ali (a) included fear of Allah, love for humans and following the commandments of religion. Imam 'Ali (a) liked justice and brotherhood.

To sum up, their lives can be described in the following words:

Imam 'Ali (a) had as many virtues as Muawiyah had flaws. Imam 'Ali (a) had as much justice as Muawiyah had injustice. Imam 'Ali (a) knew it well that Bani Umayyah would become the masters of Islamic government. He had predicted this in the following words:

"I swear by the Lord under Whose control is my life, these people want to conquer you. They would not conquer you because they are on the right path. They would conquer you because they are consistent in following evil. You are very lazy in spite of being on the right path.

Normally subjects are afraid of their ruler but today I am afraid of my subjects.

I praise Allah for whatever He ordained and whatever He destined and for my trial with you, O group of people who do not obey when I order and do not respond when I call you. If you are at ease, you

---

[1] Dr. Taha Husayn, *Al-Fitnah al-Kubra 'Ali wa Banuh*, Pg. 150

engage in (conceited) conversation, but if you are faced with battle, you show weakness. If people agree on one Imam, you taunt each other.

If you are faced with an arduous matter you turn away from it. May others have no father (woe to your enemy!) what are you waiting for in the matter of your assistance and for fighting for your rights? For you, there is either death or disgrace. By Allah, if my day (of death) comes. And it is sure to come; it will cause separation between me and you although I am sick of your company and feel lonely with you.

May Allah deal with you! Is there no religion which may unite you or sense of shamefulness that may sharpen you? Is it not strange that Muawiyah calls out to some rude low people and they follow him without any support or grant, but when I call you, although you are successors of Islam and the (worthy) survivors of people, with support and distributed grants, you scatter away from me and oppose me?

Truly, there is nothing between me and you, which I like and you also like it, or with which I am angry and you may also unite against it. What I love most is death. I have taught you the Qur'an, clarified to you arguments, apprised you of what you were ignorant of and made you swallow what you were spitting out. Even a blind man would have been able to see, and he who was sleeping would have been awakened. How ignorant of Allah is the community whose leader is Muawiyah!"

On another occasion, he said:

"You have not paid allegiance to me suddenly. Relationship between us is not same. I love you for the sake of Allah and you love me for the sake of yourselves.

O people! Help me even if it is against your wish. By Allah, I would give justice to the oppressed ones and drag the oppressor holding his locks to the valley of truth even if he dislikes it."

ARBITRATION - APOSTATES (MARIQEEN) - IMAM'S MARTYRDOM

Imam 'Ali (a) tried all possible ways to avoid war but Muawiyah wanted nothing but war and at last, a battle was fought between the two parties. When Muawiyah sensed that his army was going to be defeated, he told Amr ibn al-Aas: "Can you think of some way to unite our men and divide the enemy?" Amr ibn al-Aas said: "Yes." Muawiyah said: "Tell me so that we may be saved."

Amr ibn al-Aas said: "The idea is to lift pages of Qur'an on points of spears and ask the people of Iraq to stop fighting. We would ask them to settle our dispute through Qur'an and the enemy's army would get divided. In this way, the Syrian army would become dominant."

Finally, the Syrian army raised Qur'an on points of spears and said: "O people of Iraq! Stop fighting and settle the dispute through the Book of Allah."

When the army of Imam 'Ali (a) saw this, they said: "We are beckoned by the Book of Allah." 'Ali (a) said: "O servants of God! Be steadfast on your path and keep on fighting for your right. Muawiyah, Amr ibn al-Aas and Ibn Abi Muit are neither religious nor people of Qur'an. I know them much better than you do. I have known them through their childhood, puberty and youth, till now. They raised the Qur'an only for the sake of deceiving you."

The majority said: "It is inappropriate to decline if the enemy is inviting us to Qur'an."

Imam 'Ali (a) said: "I am also fighting them so that they accept the verdicts of Qur'an. These people have disobeyed Allah."

However, the people of Iraq put their weapons down and refused to fight. At last Imam 'Ali (a) had to stop the fighting.

It was decided that both parties should select their representatives and together decide the proceedings.

Amr ibn al-Aas was the representative from Muawiyah's side and the people of Iraq insisted Abu Moosa Ashari to be their representative. Imam 'Ali (a) said: "You disobeyed me once when you refused to continue the battle. I don't want you to do it again. I don't trust Abu Moosa Ashari. My son, Hasan, will be my representative."

The people of Iraq objected saying: "He being your son is also a party." Imam 'Ali (a) said: "If you don't accept him, I appoint Abdullah ibn Abbas as my representative."

However, the people of Iraq were great fools and they said: "He is your cousin and Abu Moosa is not your relative in any way."

Imam 'Ali (a) said: "Abu Moosa is not trustworthy. He had always been on the forefront in opposing me and has separated people from me." But the people of Iraq were bent on appointing Abu Moosa. At last Imam 'Ali (a) said: "Do whatever you want."

After that an agreement was written down for the rulers. Some of its conditions are as follows:

This is an agreement between 'Ali ibn Abi Talib and Muawiyah ibn Abi Sufyan.

1. We shall obey the commands of Allah

2. We shall abide by the Book of Allah

3. The rulers shall ponder over the book of Allah and settle the dispute through it.

4. If they don't find a solution from Qur'an they shall look for it in Prophetic Practice (*Sunnah*) common to us.

Then the opposing parties should guarantee the protection of the lives and properties of each other.[1] Senior persons from both sides signed the agreement and it was decided that the two rulers would meet each other in a place called Domastul Jindal and announce the verdict.

Imam 'Ali (a) came back to Kufa with his army and Muawiyah started for Damascus. When the delegates met on the said date at the place called Domastul Jindal, Amr ibn al-Aas told Abu Moosa Ashari: "Why don't you hand over the Caliphate to Muawiyah?" Abu Moosa replied: "Muawiyah is not worthy of Caliphate."

Amr ibn al-Aas said: "Don't you know that Uthman was killed while he was innocent?" Abu Moosa Ashari replied in affirmative. Amr ibn al-Aas said: "Muawiyah wants to avenge Uthman's death." Abu Moosa Ashari said: "Amr, the son of Uthman is alive and Muawiyah cannot be his heir in the presence of his son."

Amr ibn al-Aas said: "If you follow my words the practice of Umar ibn Khattab would be enlivened. Let my son, Abdullah become the Caliph."

Abu Moosa Ashari said: "Why shouldn't I appoint Abdullah ibn Umar instead of your son?"

Amr ibn al-Aas said: "Abdullah ibn Umar is not worthy of Caliphate. We require a person for Caliphate who has two molars; he should eat with one and enable the people to eat with the other."

Abu Moosa Ashari said: "I want to dismiss both 'Ali and Muawiyah and give choice to Muslims to select their Caliph."

Amr ibn al-Aas said: "I liked your decision. It would be better if we go and declare this in public."

---

[1] Ibn Athir, *Al-Kamil fit Tarikh*, Vol. 3, Pg. 160-168

The delegates came to public and started their speech saying: "Finally, we have come to a conclusion which is purely for the benefit of the Ummah."

Amr ibn al-Aas said: "Sure, you are right."

Abdullah ibn Abbas told Abu Moosa Ashari: "Hold on! If you have come to a conclusion, ask Amr ibn al-Aas to come and speak to the public first. Probably you don't know that you are dealing with a liar. Therefore avoid speaking first."

Abu Moosa asked Amr ibn al-Aas to come forward make declaration. However, this cunning one said: "You are a great Companion of the Prophet. I cannot dare to precede you. You must declare in public."

Abu Moosa Ashari was deceived by his words and announced: "O servants of God! We held a long discussion on this matter and came to a conclusion that we would dismiss both 'Ali and Muawiyah. After that, it is up to the people to appoint whoever they want."

Saying this Abu Moosa Ashari stepped away and Amr ibn al-Aas came forward and said: "O people! You heard what Abu Moosa Ashari said. He has dismissed 'Ali, his companion and I accept it. Now I appoint Muawiyah to Caliphate because he is the heir of Uthman ibn Affan and an avenger of Uthman's murder. He is the only person capable of Caliphate."

Abu Moosa Ashari said: "O Amr ibn al-Aas! May God destroy you! You acted against the agreement. You are like a dog, which goes on barking."

Amr ibn al-Aas said: "You are like a donkey loaded with books." Syrians intended to punish Abu Moosa because he spoke much. People were on lookout for him but he hid somewhere. Later on, he went to Mecca.

This conclusion of the delegates was not in accordance with justice. Truth was killed by this decision. Abu Moosa expressed his enmity with Imam 'Ali (a) by taking this decision. Amr ibn al-Aas deceived him because of his ignorance and simplicity. That is why Imam 'Ali (a) had said when pages of Qur'an were raised: "This is a trick of enemy. Don't get deceived by his words. Muawiyah, Amr ibn al-Aas and Ibn Abi Muit had no relation with holy Qur'an or religion."

CHARACTER OF AMR IBN AL-AAS

We would like to describe the character of Amr ibn al-Aas before discussing about Arbitration so that readers get more information about the 'right hand of Muawiyah'. The father of Amr, Aas al-Sahmi, was one of those who mimicked the Prophet and regarding him the Almighty Allah has said in Surah Kauthar:

(إِنَّ شَانِئَكَ هُوَ الْأَبْتَرُ.)

Surely your enemy is the one who shall be without posterity.[1]

Ibn Khaldun writes thus about those who ridiculed the Prophet (*Mustahzi'een*): Quraish saw that the Prophet's uncle was helping him openly and he would not allow anyone to touch him. They made it a practice to immediately meet visitors of Mecca and tell them that they have a magician in Mecca who is a poet and he is also crazy. They used to ask the visitors to keep away from him. They had formed an entire group in order to hurt the Prophet. Rabi's two sons viz. Utbah and Shaybah, Uqbah ibn Abil Muit, Abu Sufyan, Hakam ibn Umayyah, Aas ibn wail and his two cousins viz. Nabia and Munabbah were the members of this group.

They used to ridicule the Prophet at every place. If they got an opportunity they used to hurt the Prophet physically also. The mother of Amr ibn al-Aas was known for her bad character and was notorious for sleeping with rich strangers. She also had a flag atop her house announcing her services as was a custom at that time.

---

[1] Ibn Athir, *Al-Kamil fit Tarikh*, Vol. 2, Pg. 49-50

When Amr was born, both Aas and Abu Sufyan began to claim that the child belonged to them. When the conflict increased, they decided to go to the mother and ask her. She said that he was the son of Aas.

On being asked why she mentioned Aas instead of Abu Sufyan, she said that Abu Sufyan was a miser and Aas used to spend more on her.

Mother's lap is the first school for a child and the mother's character affects the child. Amr had grown up on the milk of such a mother and under the care of a father who was a great enemy of the Prophet. When parents have such manners, how can the child be noble?[1]

Amr ibn al-Aas was one of the worst enemies of Islam during his youth he had participated from the side of disbelievers of Mecca in the Battle of Uhad. The poetic verses recited by him regarding the Battle of Uhad are very famous. When Amr saw that the Prophet was getting an upper hand in every place, he thought that his future was dark. He took to hypocrisy instead of being an open enemy.

Ibn Hisham has recorded the following words of Amr: "After we returned from the Battle of Confederates (*Ahzaab*) defeated, I gathered the people of Quraish who used to listen to me. I told them: I see that Muhammad's power is increasing day by day. I think that we should go to King Negus. Muhammad will dominate our community soon. Therefore it is better for us to be under the rule of Negus than to be slaves of Muhammad. If our community dominates Muhammad, we would return."[2]

Amr ibn al-Aas was the same who stopped Uthman ibn Affan from punishing Ubaidullah ibn Amr. He told him: "It is not obligatory on

---

[1] Ibn Khaldun, *Kitabul Abru Diwan al-Mubtada wal Khabar*, Vol. 2, Pg. 177; Abdul Fattah Abdul Maqsood, *Al-Imam 'Ali bin Abi Talib,* Vol. 2, Pg. 270
[2] *Sirah Ibn Hisham*, Vol. 2, Pg. 177

you to avenge the death of Hurmuzan and Jufaina because you were not the ruler when they were killed by Ubaidullah."[1]

We are surprised at Amr ibn al-Aas how he considered that it was not the responsibility of Uthman to avenge the death of Hurmuzan and Jufaina because he was not the ruler when they were killed, but this same person was on the forefront in avenging the death of Uthman from Imam 'Ali (a), even though Imam 'Ali's (a) government was not established when Uthman was murdered?

AMR IBN AL-AAS WITH MUAWIYAH

We have seen in the previous pages how Amr ibn al-Aas was a one of the bitterest enemies of Uthman and that he used to instigate everyone he met against Uthman. As per his own admission: "I instigated every shepherd I met against Uthman."

Amr had not supported Muawiyah for free. He had taken a huge amount for this purpose. Amr ibn al-Aas was the governor of Egypt during the time of the third Caliph. However, Uthman dismissed him and appointed Ibn Abi Sarah in his place. Amr ibn al-Aas was enraged at this and he quarreled with Uthman. Then he returned to his property in Palestine and lived there along with two sons. He used to instigate the locals against Uthman. Finally, a time came for which he had waited for. He got the news that Uthman was killed, 'Ali (a) had become the Caliph of the Muslims and Muawiyah has hoisted the flag of betrayal against the central government.

Muawiyah invited him to be his ally, and he asked Muawiyah to give in writing that he would make him the governor of Egypt. Muawiyah complied with his request and gave in writing that if he conquers Egypt, he would hand over its charge to him.

Amr discussed his future political life with his two sons. Abdullah said: "If you want to take a part any way, join 'Ali."

---

[1] Abdul Fattah Abdul Maqsood, *Al-Imam 'Ali bin Abi Tali*b, Vol. 4, Pg. 83

Amr told him: "If I join 'Ali, I would get no benefit from him. 'Ali would treat me like a common Muslim. On the other hand, if I go to Muawiyah he would give me lots of respect and would make me his chief advisor. He would hand over the charge of Egypt to me as promised."

His second son, Muhammad, advised him to join Muawiyah. Amr ibn al-Aas told Abdullah: "You have advised me to better my hereafter and Muhammad advised me to better my worldly life. The hereafter is credit and worldly life is cash. An intelligent person should leave credit and take cash."

Amr ibn al-Aas came to Muawiyah and told him: "It is a fact that we are not better than 'Ali. We are opposing him for the sake of gaining this world."[1]

Amr ibn al-Aas was Muawiyah's representative in Arbitration.

The representative of Imam 'Ali (a) was Abu Moosa Ashari who used to stop people from helping the Imam during his tenure as the governor of Kufa. At last, Imam 'Ali (a) was forced to dismiss him.

ARBITRATION AND THE STAND OF 'ALI (A)

It is necessary to know the reality of this Arbitration before understanding the stand of Imam 'Ali (a) in this matter.

It is common belief of the entire Islamic Ummah that one should take guidance from Book of Allah and Prophetic Practice (*Sunnah*) in event of dispute and this is what Imam 'Ali (a) proposed from the day one.

The foundation of the Imam's government was laid on Qur'an and he behaved with his relatives and common people as prescribed by it. He held onto Qur'an tightly and followed its justice strictly. As a result, many people left him and joined his rivals, however, he always preferred the justice of Qur'an.

---

[1] Abbas Mahmood al-Aqqad, *Muawiyah bin Abi Sufyan*, Pg. 53-55

Imam 'Ali (a) always supported the verdict of Qur'an and opposed Arbitration in the Battle of Siffeen because he knew that the enemy had raised Qur'an only for the sake of their own benefit.

The invitation for Arbitration was given by those who had always fought Qur'an and people of Qur'an. They had never followed Qur'an in their individual and collective lives.

Amr ibn al-Aas had not advised raising of Qur'an because he wanted to follow it but because he wanted to save himself from defeat.

The whole plan of raising holy Qur'an was made at night. A copy from Egypt was divided into five parts and they were raised on five different spears. Apart from this, all copies of Qur'an present in Muawiyah's army were gathered at one place and each was raised on a spear.

The Syrians came to the Iraqi army at dawn lifting holy Qur'an on spears and the Iraqis were completely unaware of what the Syrians were carrying before light spread.

As soon as morning light spread everywhere, a Syrian commander, Abul Aawar al-Salmi mounted a horse and moved forward. He had kept the Qur'an on his head and he announced: "O people of Iraq! The Book of Allah shall decide between us."

Upon this, Imam 'Ali (a) said: "O servants of God! I am the first to accept the Book of Allah. However remember that these people only want to deceive you through Qur'an. They are weary of war and would be defeated in a few moments. They have raised Qur'an only because they want to save themselves from death.

Even after knowing all these facts, I consider the book of Allah as supreme authority. I have come to fight Syrians in order to make them accept the commandments of Qur'an."[1]

---

[1] Al-Dinawari, *Al-Akhbaar al-Tiwaal*, Pg. 191-192

Imam 'Ali (a) considered holy Qur'an as supreme authority in such conditions also. He told the son of Abu Sufyan:

"Remember that inequity and falsehood bring disgrace to a man in this world and in the Hereafter. The vicious character of a tyrant always betrays itself to those who carefully look into his actions. You must know that you can never get what has not been destined for you.

There are people who want to grab a thing without having any right or claim over it. To get the object they crave for, they try to interpret the commands of Allah to suit their purpose. But Allah has always given a lie to such people. Therefore, you should also fear the Day of Judgment, the day when only those who have done deeds deserving reward will be happy, and those, who have surrendered themselves to Satan and don't want to come out of its influence, will cut a sorry figure.

You invited me to let the Holy Book act as an arbitrator but you never believed that Book to be the Word of Allah. I, therefore, did not accept your invitation though I always accept the commands of that Book."

At another occasion, Imam 'Ali (a) told Muawiyah: "Allah has tested me through you and tested you through me. Each of us is a proof on other. You misinterpreted holy Qur'an for the sake of this world. You have asked me for a thing, in which neither my tongue nor my hands interfere.

You disobeyed me and asked the Syrians to do so. Your scholars deviated you and the rivals instigated people sitting in their houses against me."[1]

The above mentioned facts prove that Imam 'Ali (a) wanted the supreme authority of holy Qur'an. However, the circumstances in which Muawiyah invited him for Arbitration did not allow Imam

---

[1] Ibn Abil Hadid, *Sharh Nahjul Balagha*, Vol. 4, Pg. 113-160

'Ali (a) to accept the invitation. Also Imam 'Ali (a) had objected to appointment of Abu Moosa Ashari as the representative.

Amr ibn al-Aas was the most appropriate person to represent Muawiyah, whereas Abu Moosa Ashari was the most inappropriate one from 'Ali's side. However, because of insistence of the people of Iraq, Imam 'Ali (a) had to accept him. Imam 'Ali (a) hoped that perhaps Abu Moosa would make up for his past mistakes during the meeting of delegates.

Imam 'Ali (a) thought that the delegates would discuss the following points:

1. Was Uthman murdered unlawfully?

2. And Muawiyah had the right to avenge the death of Uthman?

3. If Uthman was innocent, how should the Caliph proceed with the case of his murder legally?

However, the delegates did not discuss the real topic and Amr ibn al-Aas brainwashed Abu Moosa saying that it is better for the Ummah that both Imam 'Ali (a) and Muawiyah should be dismissed. Abu Moosa Ashari was caught in the trap laid by Amr ibn al-Aas because of his foolishness and enmity to Imam 'Ali (a). He did not sense the wickedness of Amr ibn al-Aas till the end. Amr ibn al-Aas took full advantage of a simple and ignorant Bedouin and turned the lost battle in his own favor.

DIFFICULTIES OF 'ALI (A)

Khawarij came into being as a result of Arbitration. This group included extremist elements who did not care about logical reasoning and evidences.

Dr. Taha Husayn narrates the difficulties of Imam 'Ali (a) in the following words:

Khawarij had become a headache for Imam 'Ali (a). All Khawarij were not killed in the Battle of Nahrawan. Only a group of them was killed and the remaining lived in Kufa together. They also lived in Basra and the regions around Kufa and Basra.

They could not forget the killing of their brothers in the Battle of Nahrawan and it could not change their minds. It only increased their strength and they also got a terrific power whose source is hatred, jealousy and feeling of revenge.

The circumstances led the Khawarij to create such a front and a policy, from which they did not deviate in their long history. This policy was to oppose the caliphs, instigate people against them and not to support them in any matter. If they did not have power they invited people to their group and fought a battle secretly or openly by unsheathing their swords as soon as they gained power.

These people conspired against Imam 'Ali (a) from all sides in Kufa. They began deviating the thoughts and beliefs of the people, waiting in ambush. They did not offer prayer with Imam 'Ali (a). They did not listen to his sermons and talks and used to interrupt him on many occasions. In spite of all these things, they were happy with his verdict and did not fear getting arrested by him. They knew it very well that unless they provoke, they would not be troubled by Imam 'Ali (a) and their defects would not be exposed and they would continue to receive grants. They decided to make preparations for war with whatever grants they received.

The justice and forgiveness of Imam 'Ali (a) had raised the hopes of Khawarij. He was completely aware of their intentions. Occasionally, he used to point at his beard and forehead and say: "This would be stained by this." When he used to become wary of the disobedience of Companions, he used to say: "Why is the unfortunate one delaying it?"[1]

---

[1] A reference to Abdur Rahman Ibn Muljim

Often Khawarij came to him and expressed their thoughts openly. One day Harith ibn Rashid came to him and said: "God is the witness to the fact that I have neither obeyed you nor prayed behind you."

Imam 'Ali (a) said: "May God curse you, you have disobeyed your Lord. You have broken your oath and you are deceiving yourself. Why are you doing this?"

In spite of such open hostility, Imam 'Ali (a) neither got angry with him nor arrested him, instead invited him for a debate with a hope that he returns to the right path.

Afterwards this man set out from Kufa at night with an intention of fighting. He and his companions met two persons on the way. They asked those two persons about their religion. One of them told that he was a Jew. He was spared considering that he was a protected citizen (*Zimmi*) of Islamic state. The other person was a non-Arab Muslim. He was asked about his opinion regarding Imam 'Ali (a). When the person praised Imam 'Ali (a), he was attacked by the group of Khawarij and killed on the spot.[1]

The allegiance breakers (*Nakitheen*), the unjust (*Qasiteen*) and the apostates (*Mariqeen*) were against Imam 'Ali (a). In addition, he had to bear the treachery of his own men. Ubaidullah ibn Abbas was the governor of Imam 'Ali (a) in Basra. He was also a cousin of Imam 'Ali (a) and had a vast knowledge of religious and worldly matters. He had a special honor in Quraish in general and in Bani Hashim in particular. He also did not remain faithful to Imam 'Ali (a).

Abul Aswad Duali was the treasurer of Muslim treasury in Basra. He wrote to Imam 'Ali (a) regarding the financial irregularities of Ubaidullah Ibn Abbas. Imam 'Ali (a) wrote to Ibn Abbas saying:

"I have come to know certain things about you. If they are true you have angered you Lord. You have been untrustworthy. You have

---

[1] Dr. Taha Husayn, *Al-Fitnah al-Kubra 'Ali wa Banuh*, Pg. 133

disobeyed your Imam. Hence it is your duty to come to me with your accounts. Remember that the account of Allah is even stricter."

Imam 'Ali (a) never forgave financial discrepancies and did not bear being facile to the wealth of Muslims.

However, Ubaidullah Ibn Abbas left the governorship of Basra and went to Mecca instead of submitting the accounts. It is even more remorseful to know that he did not go from Basra empty-handed. Instead he took away the whole Muslim treasury with him. Bani Tameem decided to confront him. Fearing the circumstances, Ubaidullah took refuge with his uncles i.e. the tribe of Bani Azd. As a result, a war was about to start between Bani Azd and Bani Tameem. At last, Ubaidullah succeeded in taking the wealth away in spite of knowing that it did not belong to him.[1]

The Difficulties of Imam 'Ali (a) increased by the day. The governor showed his distrust and enemies showed their opposition. In spite of these hopeless conditions, Imam 'Ali (a) did not turn away from the right path. He did not deviate even a little bit from commandments of Qur'an. Calamities befell him one after the other but the lion of God had not learnt to fear in such times.

Imam 'Ali (a) did not let the banner of truth bow down till his last breath. He accepted the oceans of calamities for the sake of right till Ibn Muljim, the accursed one martyred him. We should review the justice of Imam 'Ali (a). He did not like being unjust to even his killer. He willed to his son: Provide good food to your prisoner. If I survive, only I would have the right to punish him or forgive him. If I die, do not strike him more than once because he struck me only once. Do not disfigure his body after killing him. Allah likes those who remain within the limits.

---

[1] Al-Fitnah al-Kubra *'Ali wa Banuh*, Pg. 129

GLIMPSES OF THE IMAM'S LIFE

I have pointed out many incidents in the previous sections which show the love of Imam (a) to the Book of Allah and Prophetic Practice (*Sunnah*). He always engaged himself in following the two.

His peace treaties and battles were in accordance with commandments of holy Qur'an. He behaved with his friends and enemies as ordered by holy Qur'an and Prophetic Practice.

Let me quote the following excerpts of the Imam's character, which are narrated by great Muslim historians.

CONSTITUTION OF HIS GOVERNMENT

The following letter was written to Malik Ashtar Nakhai. I would request the readers to read this letter of Imam 'Ali (a) carefully because Imam (a) has explained the constitution of Islam in this letter.

In the Name of Allah, the Beneficent, the Merciful.

These are the orders issued by the creature of Allah, 'Ali, the son Abu Talib (a) to Malik, the son of Ashtar when he appointed Malik as the Governor of Egypt to collect Zakat there, to combat the enemies of Islam and Egypt, to work for the welfare of its people and to look after its prosperity.

Be it known to you, O Malik, that I am sending you as Governor to a country, which in the past has experienced both just and unjust rule. Men will scrutinize your actions with a searching eye, even as you need to scrutinize the actions of those before you, and speak of you even as you did speak of them. The fact is that the public speaks well of only those who do good. It is they who furnish the proof of your actions. Hence the richest treasure that you may covet should be the treasure of good deeds. Keep your desires under control and deny yourself that which you have been prohibited, for by such abstinence alone you will be able to distinguish between what is good and what is not.

Develop in your heart the feeling of love for your people and let it be the source of kindliness and blessing to them. Do not behave with them like a barbarian, and do not appropriate to yourself that which belongs to them. Remember that the citizens of the state are of two categories.

They are subject to infirmities and liable to commit mistakes. Some indeed do commit mistakes. But forgive them even as you would like God to forgive you. Bear in mind that you are placed over them, even as I am placed over you. And then there is God even above him who has given you the position of governor in order that you may look after those under you and to be sufficient unto them. And remember you will be judged by what you do for them.

Do not set yourself against God, for neither do you possess the strength to shield yourself against His displeasure, nor can you place yourself outside the pale of His mercy and forgiveness. Do not feel sorry over any act of forgiveness, nor rejoice over any punishment that you may mete out to anyone. Do not rouse yourself to anger, for no good will come out of it.

Do not say: "I am your overlord and dictator, and that you should, therefore, bow to my commands," as that will corrupt your heart, weaken your faith in religion and create disorder in the state. Should you be elated by power, or feel in your mind the slightest symptoms of pride and arrogance, then look at the power and majesty of the divine governance of the Universe over which you have absolutely no control. It will restore the sense of calmness and affability. Beware! Never put yourself against the majesty and grandeur of God and never imitate His omnipotence; for God has brought low every rebel of God and every tyrant of man.

Let your mind respect through your actions the rights of God and the rights of man, and likewise, persuade your companions and relations to do the same. For, otherwise, you will be doing injustice to yourself and to humanity. Thus both man and God will become your enemies. There is no hearing anywhere for one at war with God until he repents and seeks forgiveness. Nothing deprives man of divine blessings or excites divine wrath against him more easily than oppression. Hence it is, that God listens to the voice of the oppressed and waylays the oppressor.

Maintain justice in administration and impose it on your own self and seek the consent of the people, for the discontent of the masses sterilizes the contentment of the privileged few and the discontent of the few loses itself in the contentment of the many. Remember, the privileged few will not rally round you in moments of difficulty: they will try to side-track justice, they will ask for more than what they deserve and will show no gratitude for favors done to them. They will feel restive in the face of trials and will offer no regret for their shortcomings. It is the common man who is the strength of the state and of religion. It is he who fights the enemy. So live in close contact with the masses and be mindful of their welfare.

Keep at a distance he who exposes the weakness of others. After all, the masses are not free from weaknesses. It is the duty of the ruler to shield them. Do not bring to light that which is hidden, but try to remove those weaknesses, which have been brought to light. God is watchful of everything that is hidden from you, and He alone will deal with it. Cover up the faults of the public to the best of your ability and God will not disclose your faults to the public gaze. Loosen the tangle of mutual hatred between the public and the administration and remove all those causes, which may give rise to strained relations between them. Protect yourself from every such act as may not be quite correct for you. Do not make haste in seeking confirmation of tale telling, for the taleteller is a deceitful person appearing in the garb of a friend.

Never take counsel of a miser, for, he will vitiate your magnanimity and frighten you of poverty. Do not take counsel of a coward also for he will weaken your resolutions. Do not take counsel of the greedy too, for he will instill greed in you and turn you into a tyrant. Miserliness, cowardliness and greed deprive man of his trust in God.

The worst counselor is he who has served as a counselor to unjust rulers and shared their crimes. So, never let men who have been companions of tyrants or shared their crimes be your counselors. You can get better men then these, men gifted with intelligence and foresight, but unpolluted by sin, men who have never aided a tyrant in his tyranny or a criminal in his crime. Such men will never be a burden to you.

On the other hand, they will be a source of help and strength to you at all times. They will be friends to you and strangers to your enemies. Choose such men alone for companionship both in private and in public. Even among these, show preference for those who have a habitual regard for truth however trying to you at times their truth may prove to be, and who offer you no encouragement in the display of tendencies, which God does not like His friends to develop.

Keep close to you the upright and the God-fearing and make clear to them that they are never to flatter you and never to give you credit for any good that you may not have done: for, the tolerance of flattery and unhealthy praise stimulates pride in man and makes him arrogant.

Do not treat the good and bad alike. That will deter the good from doing, and encourage the bad in their bad pursuits. Recompense everyone according to what they deserve. Remember that mutual trust and good will between the ruler and the ruled are bred only through benevolence, justice and service. So, cultivate goodwill amongst the people; for, their goodwill alone will save you from troubles. Your benevolence to them will be repaid by their trust in you, and your ill-treatment by their ill will.

Do not disregard the noble traditions set by our forbearers, which have promoted harmony and progress among the people; and do not initiate anything which might minimize their usefulness. The men who had established those noble traditions have had their reward; but responsibility will be yours if they are discarded. Try always to learn something from the experience of the learned and the wise, and frequently consult them in state matters so that you might maintain the peace and goodwill, which your predecessors had established in the land.

Remember that the people are composed of different classes. The progress of one is dependent on the progress of every other; and none can afford to be independent of the other. We have the army formed of the soldiers of God, we have our civil officers and their establishments, our judiciary, our revenue collectors and our public officers. The general public itself consist of Muslims and Zimmis and among them are merchants and craftsmen, the unemployed and the indigent. God has prescribed for them their several rights, duties and obligations. They are defined and preserved in the Book of God and in the traditions of His Prophet.

The Army, by the grace of God, is like a fortress to the people and lends dignity to the state. It upholds the prestige of Faith and maintains the peace of the country. Without it the state cannot stand. In its turn, it cannot stand without the support of the state. Our soldiers have proved strong before the enemy because of the privilege God has given them to fight for Him; but they have their material needs to fulfill and have therefore to depend on the income provided for them from the state revenue.

The military and civil population who pay revenue, both need the co-operation of others-the judiciary, civil officers and their establishment. The Qazi administers civil and criminal law; the civil officers collect revenue and attend to civil administration with the assistance of their establishment. And then there is the class of the poor and needy, whose maintenance is an obligation on the other classes.

God has given appropriate opportunity of service to one and all; and then there are the rights of all these classes over the administration which the administrator has to meet with an eye to the good of the entire population, a duty which he cannot fulfill properly unless he takes personal interest in its execution and seeks help from God. Indeed, it is obligatory on him to impose this duty on himself, and to bear with patience the inconveniences and difficulties incidental to his task.

Be Particularly mindful of the welfare of those in the army who in your opinion, are staunchly faithful to their God and Prophet and loyal to their chief, and who in the hour of passion can restrain themselves and listen coolly to sensible remonstrance, and who can succor the weak and smite the strong, whom violent provocation will not throw into violent temper and who will not falter at any stage.

Keep yourself in close contact with families of established reputation and integrity and with a glorious past, and draw to yourself men brave and upright in character, generous and benevolent in disposition; for such are the select of the society.

Care for them with the tenderness with which you care for your children, and do not talk before them of any good that you might have done to them, nor disregard any expression of affection, which they show in return; for, such conduct inspires loyalty, devotion and goodwill. Attend to every little want of theirs not resting content with what general help that you might have given to them, for sometimes, timely attention to a little want of theirs brings them immense relief. Surely these people will not forget you in your own hour of need.

It behooves you to select for your commander-in-chief one who imposes on himself, as a duty, the task of rendering help to his men, and who can excel in kindness every other officer who has to attend to the needs of men under him, and look after their families when they are away from their homes; so much so, that the entire army should feel united in their joys and in their sorrows.

This unity of people will give them added strength against the enemy. Continue to maintain a kindly attitude towards them so that they might feel ever attached to you. The fact is that the real happiness of administrators and their most pleasant comfort lies in establishing justice in the state and maintaining affectionate relations with the people. Their sincerity of feeling is expressed in the love and regard they show to you, on which alone depends the safety of the administrators.

Your advice to the army will be of no avail, unless and until you show affection to both men and officers, in order that they might not regard the government as an opposite burden or contribute to its downfall.

Continue to satisfy their needs and praise them over and over again for the services they have rendered. Such an attitude, God willing will require the brave to braver actions and induce the timid to deeds of bravery.

Try to enter into the feelings of others and do not foist the mistake of one another and do not grudge dispensing appropriate rewards. See to it that you do not show favors to one who has achieved nothing but merely counts on his family position; and do not with-hold proper reward from one who has done great deeds simply because he holds a low position in life.

Turn to God and to His Prophet for guidance whenever you feel uncertain regarding your actions. There is the commandment of God delivered to those whom He wishes to guide aright: "O people of faith! Obey God and obey His Prophet and obey those who hold authority over you. And refer to God and His Prophet whenever there is difference of opinion among you." To turn to God is in fact to consult the Book of God; and to turn to the Prophet is to follow his universally accepted traditions.

Select for your chief judge one from the people who is by far the best among them-one who is not obsessed with domestic worries, one who cannot be intimidated, one who does not err too often, one who does not turn back from a right path once he finds it, one who is not self-centered or avaricious, one who will not decide before knowing the full facts, one who will weigh with care every attendant doubt and pronounce a clear verdict after taking everything into full consideration, one who will not grow restive over the arguments of advocates and who will examine with patience every new disclosure of fact and who will be strictly impartial in his decision, one whom flattery cannot mislead or one who does not exult over his position. But it is not easy to find such men.

Once you have selected the right man for the office, pay him handsomely enough, to let him live in comfort and in keeping with his position, enough to keep him above temptation. Give him a position in your court so high that none can even dream of coveting it and so high that neither back biting nor intrigue can touch him.

Beware! The utmost care should be exercised in his selection: for it is a high office, which adventurous self-seekers aspire to secure and exploit in their selfish interests. For the selection of your chief judge, give careful consideration to the selection of other officers. Confirm them in their appointments after approved apprenticeship and probation. Never select men for responsible posts either out of any regard for personal connections or under any influence, for that might lead to injustice and corruption.

Of these, select for higher posts men of experience, men firm in faith and belonging to good families. Such men will not fall an easy prey to temptations and will discharge their duties with an eye on the abiding good of others. Increase their salaries to give them a contented life. A contented living is a help to self-purification. They will not feel the urge to tax the earnings of their subordinates for their own upkeep. They will then have no excuse either to go against your instructions or misappropriate state funds.

Keep a watch over them without their knowledge. Perchance they may develop true honesty and true concern for public welfare. But whenever any of them is accused of dishonesty, and the guilt is confirmed by the report of your secret service, then regard this as sufficient to convict him. Let the punishment be corporeal and let that be dealt with in public at an appointed place of degradation.

Great care is to be exercised in revenue administration to ensure the prosperity of those who pay the revenue to the state; for it is on their prosperity depends the prosperity of others, particularly the prosperity of the masses. Indeed, the state exists on its revenue. You should regard the proper upkeep of the land in cultivation as of greater importance than the collection of revenue, for revenue cannot be derived except by making the land productive.

He who demands revenue without helping the cultivator to improve his land, inflicts unmerited hardship on the cultivator and ruins the State. The rule of such a person does not last long. If the cultivators ask for reduction of their land tax for having suffered from epidemic or drought or excess of rains or the barrenness of the soil or floods damaging their crops, then, reduce the tax accordingly, so that their condition might improve.

Do not mind the loss of revenue on that account for that will return to you one day manifold in the hour of greater prosperity of the land and enable you to improve the condition of your towns and raise the prestige of your state. You will be the object of universal praise. The people will believe in your sense of justice. The confidence, which they will place in you in consequence will prove your strength, as they will be found ready to share your burdens.

You may settle in land any number of people but discontent will overtake them if the land is not improved. The cause of the cultivator's ruin is the rulers who are bent feverishly on accumulating wealth at all costs, out of fear that their rule might not last long. Such are the people who do not learn from examples or precedents.

Keep an eye on your establishment and your scribes; and select the best among them for your confidential correspondence, such among these as possess high character and deserve your full confidence, men who may not exploit their privileged position to go against you, and who may not grow neglectful of their duties, and who in the drafting of treaties may not succumb to external temptation and harm your interests, or fail to render you proper assistance and to save you from trouble, and who in carrying out their duties can realize their serious responsibilities, for he who does not realize his own responsibility can hardly appraise the responsibilities of others.

Do not select men for such work merely on the strength of your first impressions of your affection or good faith; or as a matter of fact, the pretensions of a good many who are really devoid of honesty and good breeding may cheat even the intelligence of rulers. Selection should be made after probation which should be the test of righteousness.

In making direct appointments from people, see to it that those selected possess influence with the people and who enjoy the reputation of being honest; for such selection is agreeable both to God and the Ruler. For every department of administration, let there be a head, whom no trying task might cause worry and no pressure of work annoy.

And remember that every weakness of anyone among your establishment and scribe, which you may overlook, will be written down against you in your scroll of deeds.

Adopt useful schemes placed before those engaged in trade and industry, and help them with wise counsels. Some of them live in towns, and some move from place to place with their ware and tools and earn their living by manual labor. Trade and industry are sources of profit to the state. While the general public are not inclined to bear the strain, those engaged in their professions take the trouble to collect commodities from far and near, from land and from across the sea, and from mountains and forests and naturally derive benefits.

It is this class of peace-loving people from whom no disturbance need be feared. They love peace and order; indeed they are incapable of creating disorder. Visit every part of the country and establish personal contact with this class, and enquire into their condition. But bear in mind that a good many of them are intensely greedy and are inured to bad dealings.

They hoard grain and try to sell it at a high price; and this is most harmful to the public. It is a blot on the name of the ruler not to fight this evil. Prevent them from hoarding; for the Prophet of God (pbuh) had prohibited it. And see to it that trade is carried on with utmost ease, that the scales are evenly held and that prices are so fixed that neither the seller nor the buyer is put to a loss. And if, inspite of your warning, should any one go against your commands and commit the crime of hoarding, then inflict upon him a severe punishment.

Beware! Fear God when dealing with the problem of the poor who have none to patronize them, who are forlorn, indigent and helpless and are greatly torn in mind victims to the vicissitudes of Time. Among them there are some who do not question their lot in life and who not withstand their misery, do not go about seeking alms.

For God's sake, safeguard their rights; for on you rests responsibility of protecting their interests. Assign for their upliftment, a portion of the state exchequer (*Baitul-maal*), wherever they may be, whether close at hand or far away from you. The rights of the two should be equal in your eye. Do not let any preoccupation slip them from your mind; for no excuse whatsoever for the disregard of their rights will be acceptable to God. Do not treat their interests as of less importance than your own, and never keep them outside the purview of your important considerations, and mark the persons who look down upon them and of whose condition they keep you in ignorance.

Select from among your officers such men as are upright and God-fearing and who can keep you properly informed of the condition of the poor. Make such provisions for these poor people as shall not oblige you to offer an excuse before God on the Day of Judgment;

for, it is this section of people more than any other which deserves benevolent treatment.

Seek your reward from God by giving to each of them what is due to him and enjoin on yourself as a sacred duty the task of meeting the needs of such aged among them as have no independent means of livelihood and are averse to seeking alms. And it is the discharge of this duty that usually proves very trying to rulers, but is very welcome to societies, which are gifted with foresight. It is only such societies or nations who truly carry out with equanimity their covenant with God to discharge their duty to the poor.

Meet the oppressed and the lowly periodically in an open conference and, conscious of the Divine Presence there, have a heart-to-heart talk with them, and let none from your armed guard or civil officers or members of the police or the Intelligence Department be by your side, so that the representative of the poor might state their grievances fearlessly and without reserve.

For I have heard the Prophet of God say that no nation or society in which the strong do not discharge their duty to the weak will occupy a high position. Bear with composure any strong language which they may use, and do not get annoyed if they cannot state their case lucidly, even so, God will open for you His door of blessings and rewards. Whatever you cannot afford to give, make that clear to them with utmost sincerity.

There are certain things, which call for prompt action. Accept the recommendations made by your officers for the redress of the grievances of the clerical staff. See to it that petitions or applications submitted for your consideration are brought to your notice the very day they are submitted, however much your officers might try to intercept them. Dispose the day's work that very day, for the coming day will bring with it its own task.

And then do not forget to set apart the best of your time for communion with God, although every moment of yours is for Him only, provided it is spent sincerely in the service of your people. The special time that you give to prayer in the strict religious sense is to be devoted to the performance of prescribed daily prayers.

Keep yourself occupied with prayers during the day and in the night and to gain perfect communion, do not as far as possible, let your prayers grow tiresome. And when you lead in congregation prayer, do not let your prayer be so lengthy as to cause discomfort to the congregation or raise in them the feeling of dislike for it or liquidate its effect: for in the congregation there may be invalids and also those who have to attend to pressing affairs of their own.

When I had asked of the Prophet of God on receiving an order to proceed to Yemen, how I should lead the people over there in prayer, he said, "Perform your prayers even as the weakest among you would do; and set an example of consideration to the faithful."

Alongside of the observance of all that I said bear one thing in mind. Never for any length of time keep yourself aloof from the people, for to do so is to keep oneself ignorant of their affairs. It develops in the ruler a wrong perspective and renders him unable to distinguish between what is important and what is not, between right and wrong, and between truth and falsehood.

The ruler is after all human; and he cannot form a correct view of anything, which is out of sight. There is no distinctive sign attached to truth, which may enable one to distinguish between the different varieties of truth and falsehood. The fact is that you must be one of the two things. Either you are just or unjust. If you are just, then you will not keep yourself away from the people, but will listen to them and meet their requirements.

On the other hand, if you are unjust, the people themselves will keep away from you. What virtue is there in keeping aloof? At all events aloofness is not desirable especially when it is your duty to attend to the needs of the people. Complaints of oppression by your officers or petitions for justice should not prove irksome to you.

Make this clear to yourself that those immediately about and around you will like to exploit their position to covet what belongs to others and commit acts of injustice. Suppress such a tendency in them. Make a rule of your conduct never to give even a small piece of land to any of your relations. That will prevent them from causing harm to the interests of others and save you from courting the misappropriation of both God and man.

Deal justice squarely regardless of the fact whether one is a relation or not. If any of your relations or companions violates the law, mete out the punishment prescribed by law however painful it might be to you personally; for it will be all to the good of the State. If at any time people suspect, that you have been unjust to them in any respect, disclose your mind to them and remove their suspicions. In this way, your mind will become attuned to the sense of justice and people will begin to love you. It will also fulfill your wish that you should enjoy their confidence.

Bear in mind that you do not throw away the offer of peace, which your enemy may himself make. Accept it, for that will please God. Peace is a source of comfort to the army; it reduces your worries and promotes order in the state. But beware! Be on your guard when peace is signed; for, certain types of enemies propose terms of peace just to lull you into a sense of security only to attack you again when you are off your guard.

So you should exercise the utmost vigilance on your part, and place no undue faith in their protestations. But, if under the peace treaty you have accepted any obligations, discharge those obligations scrupulously. It is a trust and must be faithfully upheld and whenever you have promised anything, keep it with all the strength that you command, for whatever difference of opinion might exist on other matter, there is nothing so noble as the fulfillment of a promise.

This is recognized even among the non Muslims, for they know the dire consequences which follow from the breaking of covenants. So never make excuses in discharging your responsibility and never break a promise, nor cheat your enemy. For, breach of promise is an act against God, and none except the positively wicked acts against God.

Indeed divine promises are a blessing spread over all mankind. The promise of God is a refuge sought after, even by the most powerful on earth; for there is no risk of being cheated. So, do not make any promise from which you may afterwards offer excuses to retract; nor do you go back upon what you have confirmed to abide by; nor do you break it, however galling it may at first prove to be. For it is far better to wait in patience for wholesome results to follow than to break it out of any apprehension.

Beware! Abstain from shedding blood without a valid cause. There is nothing more harmful than this, which brings about one's ruin. The blood that is willfully shed shortens the life of a state. On the Day of Judgment it is this crime for which one will have to answer first. So, beware! Do not wish to build the strength of your state on blood; for, it is this blood, which ultimately weakens the state and passes it on to other hands. Before me and my God no excuse for willful killing can be entertained.

Murder is a crime, which is punishable by death. If on any account the corporeal punishment dealt by the state for any lesser crime results in the death of the guilty, let not the prestige of the state stand in any way of the deceased's relations claiming blood money.

Do not make haste to do a thing before its time, nor put it off when the right moment arrives. Do not insist on doing a wrong thing, nor show slackness in rectifying a wrong thing. Perform everything in its proper time, and let everything occupy its proper place. When the people as a whole agree upon a thing, do not impose your own view on them and do not neglect to discharge the responsibility that rests on you in consequence.

For, the eyes of the people will be on you and you are answerable for whatever you do to them. The slightest dereliction of duty will bring its own retribution. Keep your anger under control and keep your hands and tongue in check. Whenever you become angry try to restrain yourself or else you will simply increase your worries.

It is imperative that you study carefully the principles, which have inspired just and good rulers who have gone before you. Give close thought to the example of our Prophet Muhammad (peace be on him), his traditions, and the commandments of the Book of God and whatever you might have assimilated from my own way of dealing with things.

Endeavor to the best of your ability to carry out the instructions which I have given you here and which you have solemnly undertaken to follow. By means of this order, I enjoin on you not to succumb to the prompting of your own heart or to turn away from the discharge of duties entrusted to you.

I seek the refuge in the Almighty and His unlimited sphere of blessings, and invite you to pray with me that He may give us together the grace to surrender willingly our will to His will, and to enable us to acquit ourselves well before him and His creation; so that mankind might cherish our memory and our work survives. I seek of God the culmination of His blessings and pray that He may grant you and me His grace and the honor of martyrdom in His cause. Verily, we have to return to Him. I invoke His blessings on the Prophet of God and his pure Progeny.

ALI AND THE PUBLIC TREASURY

Imam 'Ali (a) was very careful regarding Muslim wealth. He always considered Muslim treasury as the property of Muslims only and he never used it for his personal purpose.

We have seen in the incident of Aqeel how he did not give even a single dirham more to his own brother.

Have a look at the following incidents in addition those mentioned above:

Haroon ibn Antara narrates from his father that he saw Imam 'Ali (a) at a place called Khoornaq in winter. He was wearing old clothes and was shivering in cold. He asked the Imam:

"O Master of faithful! Allah has allotted to you and your family a share from the Muslim treasury. In spite of this, why didn't you get a warm blanket to protect yourself from cold?"

Imam 'Ali (a) replied: "I am not ashamed of saying that I brought this simple blanket from Medina."[1]

Imam 'Ali (a) never resided in the Ruler's Palace at Kufa. He lived in a small house with unplastered walls and gave shelter to the poor in Darul Imarah (royal quarters). He sold his sword many times to buy clothes and feed the poor. Uqbah ibn al-Qama narrates that he saw Imam 'Ali (a) eating a dry piece of bread. He asked: "O Master of faithful! Do you eat dry bread?"

Imam replied: "O Abul Junoob! The Prophet used to eat bread even drier than this. His clothes used to be coarser than mine. If I leave the way of the Prophet, it is possible that I will get separated from him."[2]

Ibn Athir narrates that some wealth was brought to Imam 'Ali (a) from Isfahan. Imam 'Ali (a) divided it into seven parts and took a draw to decide who would be the first to get the share.[3]

Yahya ibn Musailaima narrates that Imam 'Ali (a) made Amr ibn Musailaima the governor of Isfahan. He came back to Imam 'Ali (a) after some time with a lot of wealth. This wealth included some water skins filled with honey and butter.

Umme Kulthum, Amirul Momineen's daughter sent a message to Amr to send the butter and honey, which he had brought along to her.

---

[1] Aqqad, *Abqariyat al-Imam 'Ali*, Pg. 13 and Al-Kamil Ibn Athir
[2] Abbas Mahmood al-Aqqad, *Abqariyat al-Imam 'Ali*, Pg. 20
[3] *Al-Kamil fit Tarikh*, Vol. 3, Pg. 200-202

Amr sent two bags to her. Imam 'Ali (a) began counting the wealth on the next day. He found that two bags were missing. He asked Amr about them and Amr kept quiet. Imam 'Ali (a) told him to reply for the sake of Allah. He said: "I had sent two bags to your daughter." Imam 'Ali (a) ordered the bags to be brought back from home. When they were brought to him, the content worth three dirhams was less in them. He bought honey and butter worth three dirham and added to the bags. Then he distributed them among eligible persons.

Sufyan says that Imam 'Ali (a) neither built palaces nor usurp the right of any one.

It is narrated that Imam 'Ali (a) had sold his sword and said: "If I had four dirhams, I would not have sold my sword."

Imam 'Ali (a) did not buy provisions from a shopkeeper who knew him well. He used to put a seal on the bag of containing barley flour. He used to say that he liked to eat only that food, which was completely pure according to his knowledge. He did not like eating food whose purity was doubtful.[1]

HUMILITY AND JUSTICE OF ALI (A)

Ibn Athir Shobi narrates: Imam 'Ali's (a) armor got lost somewhere and he found it with a Christian. He brought that Christian to the court of Qazi Shurai and began debating with him in the Qazi's presence. Imam 'Ali (a) said that the armor belonged to him, which was neither sold nor gifted by him.

Shurai asked the Christian: "What have you got to say regarding the claim of Amirul Momineen (a)?

The Christian said: "This armor is mine and Amirul Momineen (a) is lying.'

Shurai turned to Imam 'Ali (a) and asked: "Do you have any proof?"

---

[1] *Al-Kamil fit Tarikh*, Vol. 3, Pg. 203

Imam 'Ali (a) smiled and said that he did not have any proof. Shurai handed the armor to the Christian. He went away with the armor and returned after walking a few steps and said: "I bear witness that it is the decision of the prophets. Amirul Momineen (a) brought me to the court in spite of having power. His judge gave a verdict against him and he accepted the decision silently. This armor belongs to Amirul Momineen (a)." Then he recited the formula of faith and became a Muslim.

Dr. Taha Husayn writes: Imam 'Ali (a) did not buy provisions from a shopkeeper of his acquaintance so that the shopkeeper does not favor him because of his being a ruler. He used to carry loaves of bread on his back at night and distribute it among the poor secretly. They never knew who supplies food to them at night. When he was martyred, the poor came to know who their nocturnal helper was.

Imam 'Ali (a) did not become satisfied until he fulfilled his duty of helping people in religious matters. He used to lead congregational prayers. He used to teach them through his words and deeds. He used to feed poor and needy. He used to search for the needy and fulfill their needs. He used to separate from the people and involve himself in worship alone. He offered the midnight prayer and rested only after a major part of the night had passed.

Again he used to go to the mosque before the darkness disappeared. He used to call out to the people who were sleeping, for prayer. In this way he kept himself occupied in Allah's worship all night. He used to remember Allah while he was alone and when he addressed the public. He used to encourage people to question him about religious matters.

He used to remain careful in his words and deeds regarding equity in distribution of wealth. He also was careful regarding equity in distribution whenever someone asked for something. One day two women came to him and expressed their helplessness. Imam 'Ali (a) ordered them to be given clothes and food for they were needy. He also gave them some money. One of them asked for more as she was an Arab and the other woman was not.

Imam 'Ali (a) handed over a little dust to her and said: "I don't know whether Allah has given more excellence to someone because of anything except obedience and piety."[1]

ANALYSIS OF 'ALI'S GENERAL POLICIES

The People who are unaware of the truth and excellence of Imam 'Ali (a) are of the opinion that Umar ibn Khattab was far better than Imam 'Ali (a) in politics even though Imam 'Ali (a) had more knowledge than him.

Abu 'Ali Sina and followers of his school have this opinion and their argument is that Imam 'Ali (a) did not get success in the field of politics because he confined himself to the boundaries of Islamic law. He considered general requirements in wars, peace treaties and common policies.

On the other hand, Umar considered general requirements and resorted to personal exertions. He used to go for Express Text (*Nass*) if the situation demanded and used to deceive his enemies. He used to use his whip excessively and forgive criminals in certain situations. The practice of Imam 'Ali (a) was completely different from this. He never made changes to the texts of Shariah. He did not believe in personal exertions (*Ijtihaad*). He performed all worldly actions according to religious commandments. He used to control everyone with a single rod. He used to follow the book of Allah and Prophetic Practice (*Sunnah*) in all matters. He did not consider it lawful to oppose Shariah for the sake of worldly gains.

The example of his worldly politics is that a person wanted to kill him and he had expressed this desire in public. However, when this person was brought in the court of Imam 'Ali (a), he ordered that he could not punish anyone before he committed a crime.

---

[1] Al-Fitnah al-Kubra *'Ali wa Banuh*, Pg. 109

Here is an example of his religious policies. A person convicted of theft was brought in the court of Imam 'Ali (a). Imam 'Ali (a) said: "I would not charge him because of doubt; without a proof or confession."

Imam 'Ali (a) did not appoint any hypocrite as a governor. He considered Muawiyah ibn Abi Sufyan a hypocrite and did not stand him even for a moment.

He was advised by Mughaira ibn Shoba and other such politically-minded persons that he should not have any conflict with Muawiyah at that moment and dismiss him once the government has stabilized.

But Imam 'Ali (a) said: "I cannot bear a hypocrite like Muawiyah ruling an Islamic province. Then too I would not consider any deceit lawful in this matter." Talha and Zubair paid allegiance to Imam 'Ali (a) and then broke their oaths. They came to Imam 'Ali (a) and took his permission to perform Umrah. Imam 'Ali (a) asked them to promise that they would not divide the Muslims. When they promised, Imam 'Ali (a) permitted them to go.

Imam 'Ali (a) did not force them to stay in Medina only because of doubt.

Imam 'Ali (a) always worked for the benefit of principles of justice. The period of his rule was short but the world got to see the picture of a divine government with their own eyes. People could see the picture of a functioning government based on divine politics in accordance with Qur'an in the mosque of Kufa.

SOME OF HIS GOLDEN SAYINGS

1. When this world favors somebody, it lends him the merits of others, and when it turns its face away from him it snatches away even his own excellences and fame.

2. A time will come after me when there would be nothing more concealed than truth and nothing more explicit than falsehood. Many

people will swear falsely by Allah. Good deeds will be considered bad and vice versa.

3. Maintain such relations with people that they cry after you are dead and remain eager to meet you when you are alive.

4. Beware of an honest person who is hungry and a dishonest person whose stomach is full.

5. Two kinds of people will be damned on my account; those who form an exaggerated opinion about me and those who under-estimate me because they hate me.

6. Keep away from hypocrites because they are misguided and they misguide others.

7. Fulfilling wishes cannot be done without three things viz. it should be considered a small act so that it is proved great, it should be hidden so that it comes out on its own and it should be done soon so that it gives happiness.

8. Keep away from all those acts which are liked by the doer for himself and not for other Muslims. Keep away from all those deeds, which are done in solitude and cannot be done openly. Keep away from all those acts about which when a person is asked, he denies or seeks pardon.

9. A person who does good is better than that deed and a person who does evil is worse than that deed.

10. Patience is of two kinds: patience over what pains you, and patience against what you covet.

11. A leader should educate himself before teaching others and should learn etiquettes before preaching them to others.

12. The world and the hereafter are opposed to each other. They are two separate things. Either a person loves this world or he loves the

hereafter. The world and the hereafter are like east and west. If a person gets nearer to one, he moves far away from the other.

13. A companion of a king is like a person riding a lion. People envy him but he knows very well what he is riding.

14. If a person respects his self, he does not value his desires.

15. Justice has one form and injustice has many forms. Hence it is easy to adopt injustice instead of adopting justice. Justice is like a target of a sharp shooter and injustice is like a missed aim. Hitting the target requires a lot of effort and it is quite easy to miss the aim.

16. The world makes people forget about other things. When a person acquires one thing, he becomes greedy about other things.

17. You are living in the age where goodness is turning back and falsehood is moving forward.

Glance at different classes of people. You will find beggars complaining about their poverty and you will find rich who deny the bounties of Allah. You will find such misers are miserly in giving rights of Allah. You will find disobedient ones who are deaf when it comes to listening at advices. May Allah's curse be on those who preach good but do not act upon it and those who preach abstinence from evil but do not act upon it.

18. The tongue of a believer is behind his heart and the heart of a hypocrite is behind his tongue. A believer thinks well before speaking. He speaks only if the words are worth speaking. He keeps quiet if the point is not good. A hypocrite speaks whatever comes to his mind. He does not care about whether a statement is beneficial for him.

19. By Allah! Muawiyah is not cleverer than me but he is a betrayer and deceives others.

HIS WILL TO IMAM HASAN (A)

Upon his return from Siffeen, he made the following will and testament to his son, Imam Hasan (a), whose main points are as follows:

After praise to Allah and the Holy Prophet (s.a.w.s) let it be known to you that decay of health, passing away of time and nearness to death have made me realize that I should give more thought to my future (next world) and to my people, advise them more and spend more time in equipping them mentally to face this world. I felt that my own sons and my near ones have as much right to utilize my experiences and knowledge, all the ups and downs of life, all the realities of life and the hereafter.

I decided, therefore, to spend more time and to prepare you for your future. This was neither selfishness nor self-esteem, nor any mental luxury of giving away advices, but it was the sincere desire of making you see the world as I found it, looking at the realities of time as I looked at them, and doing the right thing at the right time and the right place as it should be done, which made me write down these advices to you. You will not find anything but truths and realities in them.

My dear son, you are a part my body and soul. Whenever I look at you I feel as I am looking at myself. If any calamity happens to you, I feel as if it has happened to me. Your death will make me feel as if it was my own death. Your affairs are like my own affairs. Therefore I commit these advices to you. I want you to pay attention to them and to guard them so that they may remain in your life (to personally guide you).

My first and foremost advice to you, my son, is to fear Allah. Be His obedient servant. Keep His thought always fresh in your mind. Be attached to and carefully guard the rope, which connects you to Him (Islam). Can any other connection be stronger, more durable and more lasting than this to command greater respect and consideration or to replace it?

Accept good advices and refresh your mind with them. Adopt piety and kill inordinate desires with its help. Build your character with the help of sincere faith in religion and Allah. Subjugate your self-willed, obstinate and refractory nature with the vision of death, make it see the mortality of life and of all that it holds dear, to realize the actuality of misfortunes and adversities, the changes of circumstance and times, and compel it to study the histories of past people.

Persuade it to see the ruined cities, the dilapidated palaces and decaying signs and relics of fallen empires and past nations. Then meditate over the activities of those people over what all they have done, when they started their careers; where, when and how they were actually brought to an end; where are they now? What have they actually gained out of life, and what was their contribution to human welfare. If you carefully ponder over these problems, you will find that each one of these people parted with all that they cherished and loved and are now in a solitary abode alone and unattended, and you will also be like them.

Be sure to provide well for your future abode. Do not lose eternal blessings for the sake of worldly pleasures.

Do not talk about things you do not know. Do not speculate and pass judgment over subjects, which you are not in a position to form an opinion about. Give up when there is a possibility of your going astray. It is better to give up the quest than to advance forward facing uncertain dangers and unforeseen risks.

Fight, whenever required, to defend the cause of Allah. Do not be afraid that people will laugh at you, censure your action or slander you. Fearlessly and broadly help truth and justice. Bear patiently the sufferings and face bravely the obstacles, which come your way when you try to uphold them. Adhere to the cause of truth and justice whenever you find them. Try to be well-versed in Islamic jurisprudence and theology, and acquire a thorough knowledge of the laws of this religion.

Develop patience against sufferings, calamities and adversities. This virtue of patience is one of the highest values of morality and nobility of character, and is the best habit one can develop. Trust in Allah and let your mind seek His protection in every calamity and suffering. You will thus entrust yourself and your affairs to the Best Trustee and to the Mightiest Guardian. Do not seek help and protection from anybody but Allah. Reserve your prayers, your requests, your solicitations and your entreaties to Him and Him alone because to grant as well as to withhold lies in His and only in His power. Ask as much of His favors and seek as much of His Guidance as often as you can.

Try to understand my advices, ponder over them deeply; do not take them lightly and do not turn away from them. The best knowledge is that which benefits the listener. Knowledge, which does not benefit anyone, is useless to learn or remember.

My dear son, when I realized that I was getting old and when I felt that weakness and feebleness were gradually creeping over me, I hastened to advise you on the best ways of leading a noble, virtuous and useful life. I hated the idea that either death overtakes me before I tell you all I want to tell or my mental capacities, like my body strength, fall prey to deterioration. I convey all this knowledge to you, otherwise inordinate desires, temptations and inducements may influence you, or adverse changes of times and circumstances may drag you into their mire, and I would leave you like an unbroken and untrained colt.

A young and fresh mind is like virgin soil, which allows things sown in it to grow verdantly and to bear luxuriantly. Therefore, I have made use of early opportunity to educate and train you, before your mind loses its freshness, before it gets hardened and warped, before you start facing life unprepared for the encounter, and before you are forced to use your decisions and discretions without gaining advantages of cumulated traditions, collected knowledge and experiences of others.

These advices and counsels that I give will save you from the worry of acquiring knowledge, gathering experiences and soliciting others for advice. Now you can easily make use of all the knowledge men acquired with great care, trouble and patience; things which were hidden and which only experiences and sufferings could bring to light are made easily available to you through these advices.

My dear son! Though the span of my life is not as large as that of others who have passed away before me, I took great care to study their lives. Assiduously I went through their activities, I contemplated over their deliberations and deeds, I studied their remains, relics and ruins; and I pondered over their lives so deeply that I felt as if I had lived and worked with them from early ages of history down to our times.

I know what did good and what brought harm to them. Sifting the good from the bad, I am concentrating within these pages the knowledge that I gathered. Through these advices I have tried to show you the value of honest living and high thinking, and the dangers of a vicious and sinful life. I have covered and guarded every aspect of your life since it is my duty as a kind, considerate and loving father.

From the very beginning I wanted to help you develop a noble character and prepare you for the life, which you will have to lead. I wanted to train you to grow up to be a young man with a noble character, an open and honest mind, and a clear and precise knowledge of things around you. Originally my desire was only to teach you the Holy Book thoroughly, to make you understand its intricacies, to impart you with the complete knowledge of His Orders and interdictions and not to leave you at the mercy of the knowledge of other people.

But after having succeeded in this task, I felt nervous that I may leave you untrained and uneducated in those subjects which themselves are subject to so much confusion and so many contradictions; whose confusions have been worse confounded by selfish desires, warped minds, wicked ways of life, and sinful modes of thinking. Therefore, I have noted down, in these lines, the basic principles of nobility, piety, truth and justice.

You may feel they are overbearing and harsh, but my desire is to arm you with this knowledge instead of leaving you unarmed to face the world where there is every danger of loss and damnation. As you are a noble, virtuous and pious young man, I am sure you will receive Divine Guidance and Succor. I am sure He will help you to achieve your aim in life. I want you to promise yourself to follow my advices carefully.

Remember my son, the best advices are those which tell you to fear Allah, to confine yourself to the performance of those duties which have been incumbent upon you by Him, and to follow the footsteps of your ancestors (The Holy Prophet and Imam 'Ali), and your pious relatives. Verily they carefully scanned their thoughts and deeds, as you must try to do. This kind of deliberation made them take from life what was really the best and forsake that which was not incumbent upon them.

If your mind refuses to accept my advices and you persist to try own experiments, then you are at liberty to arrive at your conclusions, but only after carefully studying the subject and acquiring the knowledge necessary for such decisions. You must not allow uncertainties and doubts to poison your mind and skepticism or irrational likes and dislikes to affect your views. Remember that before you start thinking about a problem, seek guidance from the Lord and beseech Him to give you a lead in the right direction; avoid confusion in your ideas and do not let disbelief (about the truth of the teachings of religion) take hold of your mind, because one will lead you towards agnosticism, and other towards error and sin.

When you are thus prepared to solve any problem and you are sure that you posses a clear mind, a sincere and firm desire to reach the truth, to say the correct thing and to do the correct deed, then carefully go through the advices that I am leaving you. If your mind is not as clear and free from doubts as you wish it to be, then you will be wandering in the wilderness of uncertainties and errors like a camel suffering from night blindness. Under these circumstances it is best that you give up the quest, because with such limitations, none can ever reach the truth.

My dear son, carefully and very carefully remember these sayings of mine, that the Lord, Who is the Master of death, is also the Master of life. The Creator is the Annihilator. And the One who annihilates has the power to bring everything back to existence again. The One who sends you calamities is the One who will bring you safe out of them.

Remember that this world is working under laws ordained by Him and it consists of the sum total of actions and reactions, causes and effects, calamities and reverses, pains and pleasures; and reward and punishment; but this is not all which the picture depicts; there are things in it which are beyond our understanding, things which we do not and cannot know and things which cannot be foreseen and foretold.

For instance, the rewards and punishments of the Day of Judgment: Remember that your lack of understanding is due to the insufficiency of your knowledge. Remember that when you came into this world your first appearance was that of an ignorant, uneducated and unlearned being, then you gradually acquired knowledge. There are several things (in this world), which were beyond your knowledge, which perplexed and surprised you and about which you did not understand "why" and "how"; gradually you acquired knowledge about some of those subjects and in future, your knowledge and vision may further expand. Therefore, the best thing for you to do is to seek guidance of One Who has created and Who maintains and nourishes you. You must fear His Wrath as well as His punishments.

Your requests and solicitations should be to Him alone; you should be afraid of Him and nobody else.

Be it known to you, my son, that nobody has given mankind such detailed information about Allah (His mercy, His kindness, His glory, His might and His power) as our Holy Prophet (s). I advise you to have faith in his teachings, to make him your leader and to accept his guidance for your salvation. Thus advising you, I have done the best that I can do as a sincere and loving adviser, and I assure you, however you may try to find a better way for your good, you will not find any superior to the one advised by me.

Remember my son that had there been any other God, beside the One, he would have also sent his messengers and prophets and they would have pointed out to mankind the domain and glory of this second god and you would have also seen them. But no such incident ever took place. He is one God whom we all should recognize and worship. He has explained Himself. Nobody is a partner to Him in His domain, might and glory. He is eternal, has always been and shall remain when every other thing will disappear into nothingness and there shall be no end to His existence.

His glory and His Existence is so supreme, pre-eminent, transcendent, incomparable and excellent that it is beyond the grasp of minds and intellects. None can understand or visualize Him. When you have accepted these truths and realities, your behavior so far as His orders and interdictions are concerned, should be that of a person who realizes that this status, power and position is nothing when compared to that of his Lord, who wants to gain His favor through Prayers and obedience who fears His Wrath as well as His punishments, and Who is absolutely in need of His help and protection. Remember my son, that God has not ordered you to do anything but that which is good and which propagates and distributes goodness, and He has not interdicted you from anything but that which is bad and will bring about bad effects.

My Dear son, through this message of mine, I have explained everything about this world, how fickle and quick changing is its attitude, how short-lived and evanescent is everything that it holds or offers, and how fast it changes its moods and its favors. I have also explained about the life to come; the pleasures and blessings provided there are the everlasting peace, comfort and happiness arranged for in the heaven. I have given enough examples of both aspects of life, before and after death, so that you may know the reality and lead life on the basis of that knowledge.

The Truth is that people who have carefully studied the conditions of life and the world pass their days as if they know that they are travelers who have to leave a place which is barren (practically a desert with the extreme scarcity of food and water), unhealthy and uncongenial and they have to go towards lands which are fertile, healthy, congenial and where there is abundant provision of all comforts and pleasures. They have eagerly taken up the journey, happy in the hope of future blessings and peace.

They have willingly accepted the sufferings, troubles and hazards of the way, parting of friends, scarcity of food and comfort during the pilgrimage so that they may reach the journey's end and a happy place. They do not refuse to bear any discomfort and do not grudge any expenditure on the way (giving out alms and charities), and helping the poor and needy. Every step which they put forward towards their goal, however tiring and exhausting it may be, is a happy event of their lives.

On the contrary the condition of those people, who are staying in fertile and happy regions and who have to undertake a journey, knowing full well that the journey is going to end in an inhospitable, arid and unfertile land: can anything be more loathsome to them than this journey? How they would hate to leave the place where they are and to arrive at the place, which they so much hate, and which is so dismaying, dreadful and frightening.

My dear son, so far as your behavior with other human beings is concerned, let your 'self' act as scales to help you judge its goodness or wickedness. Do unto others as you wish others to do unto you. Whatever you like for others, and whatever you dislike to happen to you, spare others from such happenings. Do not oppress and tyrannize anyone because you surely do not like to be oppressed and tyrannized. Be kind and sympathetic to others, as you certainly desire others to treat you kindly and sympathetically.

Whatever habits you find objectionable, and loathsome in others, abstain from developing those traits of character. If you are satisfied or feel happy in receiving a certain kind of behavior from others, you may behave with others exactly in the same way. Do not speak about them in the way that you do not like others to speak about you. Do not speak on the subject about which you know little or nothing, and if you at all want to speak on anything or about anyone of whom you are fully aware then avoid scandal, libel and aspersion, as you do not like yourself to be scandalized and libeled in the same manner.

Remember, son, that vanity and conceit are forms of folly, these traits will bring to you serious harm and will be a constant source of danger to you. Therefore, lead a well-balanced life (neither be conceited nor suffer from inferiority complex), and exert yourself to earn an honest living. But do not act like a treasurer for somebody.

And, whenever you receive guidance of the Lord to achieve the things you desire, do not get proud of your achievement but be humble and submissive to Him and realize that your success was due to His mercy and favor.

Remember, my son, that before you is a long and arduous journey (life). The journey is not only very long, exhausting, laborious and onerous, but the route is mostly through dismal, dreary and deserted regions, where you will be sadly in need of refreshing, renovating and enlivening aids and you cannot dispense with such provisions as to keep you going and to maintain you till the end of your journey, the Day of Judgment.

But remember that you do not overload yourself (do not entrust yourself with so many obligations and duties that you cannot honorably fulfill them or with such luxurious life as to be wicked and vicious) because if this load is more than what you can conveniently bear, your journey will be very painful and toilsome. If you find yourself around poor, needy and destitute people who are willing to carry your load for you as far as the Day of Judgment, consider this to be a boon, engage them and pass burden on to them, (distribute your wealth amongst the poor, destitute and needy - help others to the best of your ability and be kind and sympathetic to human beings).

Thus, relieve yourself of the heavy responsibility and liability of submitting an account on the Day of Reckoning of how you have made use of His favors (of health, wealth, power and position). Thus you may arrive at the end of your journey, light and fresh, and may have enough provision for you there (reward for having done your duty to man and God in this world). Have as many weight carriers as you can (help as many people as you can) so that you may not miss them when you very badly need them (when your sins of commission and omission will be balanced against your good deeds.

You must have enough good deeds to turn the scales in your favor). Remember that all you give out in charities and good deeds are like powerful loans, make use of your wealth and power in such a way that you get all that back on the day when you will be poor and helpless (The Day of Judgment). Be it known to you, my son, that your passage lies through an appalling dreadful valley (death or grave) and the journey is extremely tiring and arduous.

Here a man with light weight is far better than an overburdened person and one who can travel fast will pass through it quicker that none whom encumbrance forces to go slow. You shall have to pass through this valley. The only way out of it is either in the Heaven or in the Hell; (there is no other way out of it and no possibility of retracing one's step). Therefore, it is wise to send your things there before you, pre-arrange for the place of your stay before you reach there; because after death there is no repentance and no possibility of coming back to this world to undo the wrong done by you.

Realize this truth, my son, that the Lord Who owns and holds the treasures of the heaven and the earth has given you permission to ask and beg for them, and has promised to grant your prayers. He has told you to pray for His favors that they may be granted and to ask for His blessings that they may be bestowed. He has not appointed guards to prevent your prayers from reaching Him.

Nor there is any need for anybody to intercede before Him on your behalf. If you go back upon your promises, if you break your vows or start doing things that you have repented from, He will not immediately punish you, neither He refuses you His favors and grants in haste; and if you repent once again He neither taunts you nor betrays you, though you may fully deserve both, but He accepts your repentance and forgives you.

He never grudges His forgiveness nor refuses His mercy; on the contrary He has decreed repentance as a virtue and pious deed. The Merciful Lord has ordered that every evil deed of yours will be counted as one and a good deed and pious action will be rewarded tenfold. He has left the door of repentance open. He hears you whenever you call Him. He accepts your prayers whenever you pray to Him.

You beg of Him to grant you your heart's desires; you lay before Him the secrets of your heart; you tell Him about the calamities that have befallen you and misfortunes, which face you and beseech His help to overcome them. You invoke His help and support in difficulties and distress. You implore Him to grant you a long life and sound health; you pray to Him for prosperity you request of Him such favors and grants that none but He can bestow and award.

Think that by simply granting you the privilege of praying for His favors and mercies, He has handed over the keys of His treasures to you. Whenever you are in need, you pray and He confers His favors and blessings.

But some times when you find that your requests are not immediately granted, you need not be disappointed. Because grant of prayers often rests with the true purpose and intention of the implorer. Sometimes the prayers are delayed because the Merciful Lord wants you to receive further rewards patiently bearing calamities and sufferings and still believe sincerely in His help. Thus, you may be awarded better favors than you requested. Sometimes your prayers are turned down, and this is also in your interest; because you often, unknowingly, ask for things that are really harmful to you.

If your requests are granted, they will do more harm than good, and many of your requests may be such that if granted they will result in your eternal damnation. Thus, the refusal to accede to your solicitations is a blessing in disguise for you. But very often your requests, if they are not really harmful in this world or in the hereafter, may be delayed but they are granted in quantities much more than you had asked for, bringing more blessings than you could ever imagine.

So you should be very careful in asking Allah for His favors; only pray for such things which are really beneficial to you, and these benefits are lasting and in the long run they do not end in harm. Remember, my dear son, that wealth and power (If you pray for them) are such things that they will not always be with you and may bring harm to you in the Hereafter.

Be it known to you, my son, that you are created for the next world and not for this. You are born to die and not to live forever. Your stay in this world is temporary. You live in a place, which is subject to decay and destruction. It is a place where you will have to be busy getting ready for the next world. It is a road (to the next world) on which you are standing. Death is following you. You cannot run away from it. However hard you may try to avoid it, it is going to catch you sooner or later. Therefore, take care that it may not catch you unaware and unprepared and no chance is left to you to repent the vices and sins committed and undo the harm done by you. If death catches you unaware, you are eternally dammed.

Therefore, my son, always keep three things in mind; death, your deeds and actions and the Hereafter. In this way you will always be ready to face death and it will not catch you unaware.

My dear son, do not be carried away and do not be lured by the infatuations of worldly people in this vivacious life and its pleasures.

Do not be impressed by the sight of their acute struggle to possess and own this world. God has very mercifully explained to you everything about this world, not only the Merciful Lord but this world has told you everything; it has disclosed to you its mortality; it has openly declared its weakness, its shortcomings and its vices.

Remember that these worldly people are barking dogs, and hungry and ferocious beasts. Some of them are constantly barking at others. Their mighty lords massacre the poor and weak. Their inordinate desires and their greed have such a complete hold over them that you will find some of them like animals tamed and tied with the rope round their feet and neck. (They have lost freedom of thought and cannot come out of the enslavement of desire and habit). There are others whom wealth and power have turned mad.

They behave like unruly beasts, trampling, crushing and killing their fellow beings and destroying things around them. The history of this world is merely a record of such incidents, some big and some small; the difference is of might, but the intensity is the same. These people have lost the balance of their minds. They do not know what they are doing and where they are going; scan their activities and study their ways of thinking as you find them confused and irrational.

They appear like cattle wandering in the dreary desert, where there is no water to drink and no food to eat, no shepherd to care for them and no guardian to look after them. What has actually happened to them is that the vicious world has taken possession of them; it is dragging them wherever it likes and is treating them as if they are blind because it has really blindfolded them against divine lights of true religion.

They are wandering without true aims and sober purposes in the wonderful show that the world has staged for them; they are fully drunk with the wine and pleasures amassed around them. They take this world to be their god and nourisher. The world is playing with them and they are playing with it, and have forgotten and forsaken everything else.

But the nights of enjoyment and pleasures won't last forever for anybody; the dawn of realities will break sooner or later. The caravan of life will surely reach its destination one day. One, who has nights and days acting as piebald horses for carrying him onward to his journey's end, must remember that though he may feel as if he is enroute to his destination, every day is carrying him a step further in his journey towards death.

Be it known to you, my son, that you cannot have every wish of yours granted, you cannot expect to escape death; and you are passing through your days of life as others before you have done. Therefore, control your expectations, desires and cravings; be moderate in your demands; earn your livelihood through scrupulously honest means; be concentrated with what you get honestly and honorably; go slow and do not let your desires drive you madly, because there are many desires which will lead you to disappointments and loss.

Remember that everyone who prays for a thing will not always get what he prays for, and everyone who controls his desires, has self respect and does not pray for things, will not always remain unlucky or disappointed. So, do not bring down your self-respect; do not be mean and submissive. Do not subjugate yourself through these vile and base traits, though they may appear to make it possible for you to achieve your heart's desires because nothing in this world can compensate for the loss of self-respect, nobleness of mind and honor.

Take care, my son, and be careful not to make yourself a slave for anybody. God has created you a free man. Do not sell away your freedom in return for anything. There is no actual gain and real value in benefits that you derive by selling your honor and self-respect or by subjugating yourself to disgrace, insults and indignities. There is no real good wealth and power that is acquired by foul means. Beware my son, that avarice and greed may not drive you to destruction and damnation. If you can succeed in having nobody as your benefactor but God, then try your best to achieve this nobleness of character because He will grant you your share whether or not you try to gather around you donors, patrons and benefactors.

Remember that the little given to you by God is going to be more useful, serviceable, honorable and respectable than what is granted by man in copious and abundant quantities. What can a man give but part of that which God has granted him?

The losses that you suffer because of your silence can be easily compensated, but the losses, which arise out of excessive and loose talk are difficult to requite. Do you not see that the best way of guarding a bay is by closing its mouth?

To guard what you already possess is better than to ask for what others possess.

The bitterness of disappointment, deprivation and poverty is actually sweeter than the disgrace and humiliation of begging.

Returns of hard but respectable work, though small in quantity, are better than the wealth acquired through sin and wickedness.

Nobody can guard your secrets better than you.

Often a man tries his best to acquire a thing, which is the most harmful to him. Often one does himself the worst harm.

One who talks too much makes most mistakes.

One who often thinks and reflects develops foresight and vision.

By socializing with good people you will develop goodness in your character, and by avoiding the company of wicked persons you will abstain from wickedness.

Livelihood acquired by foul means is the worst form of livelihood.

To oppress a weak and helpless person is the worst form of tyranny and wickedness.

If your kindness or indulgence is going to bring forth cruel results then severity or strictness is real kindness.

Often, medicating results in disease; sometimes diseases prove to be health preservers.

Often you obtain warnings and advices from the people who are fit to warn and advise you, and often you will come across advisers who are not sincere.

Do not rely on vain hopes because vain hopes are assets of idiots and fools.

Wisdom is the name of the trait of remembering experiences and making use of them. The best experience is one, which gives the best warning and advice.

Take advantage of opportunities before they turn their backs upon you (make hay while the sun shines).

All who try cannot succeed.

Those who die will not come back.

The worst form of folly is to waste the opportunities of life as well as to lose salvation.

For every action there is a reaction.

Shortly you will get what has been destined.

There is an element of risk and speculation in every trade as well as danger of loss.

Often small returns prove as beneficial as big profits.

An accessory or accomplice who insults you and a friend who has not formed a good opinion of you will not be of any help or use to you.

Treat those with consideration and kindness over whom you have power and authority.

Do not run the risk of endangering yourself through irrational, unreasonable and extravagant hopes.

Take care and do not be fooled by flattery.

Do good to your brother when he is doing harm to you. When he declines to recognize the kinship, befriend him, help him and try to maintain relations. If he is miserable and refuses to give you monetary help, be generous and support him financially. If he is harsh and cruel, be kind and considerate to him. If he harms you, accept his excuses. Behave as if he is a master and you are a slave and he is a benefactor and you are a beneficiary. But be careful that you do not thus behave with undeserving and mean persons.

Do not develop friendship with the enemy of your friend, otherwise your friend will turn into an enemy.

Advise your friends sincerely and to the best of your ability though he may not like it.

Keep a complete control over your temper and anger, because such control produces good results at the end.

Be mild, pleasant and lenient with he who is harsh, gross and strict with you. Gradually he will turn to your way of behavior.

Grant favor and be considerate with your enemy, because you will thus gain either one or the other of the two kinds of victories: (one rising above your enemy, the other of reducing intensity of his enmity).

If you want to cease relations with your friend, do not break off totally, let your heart retain some consideration (if not love) for him, so that you will still have (at least) some regard for him if he comes back.

Do not disappoint a person who holds a good opinion of you, and do not make him change his opinion.

Under the impression that you, as a friend, can behave as you like, do not violate the rights of your friend, because when deprived he will no longer remain your friend.

Do not ill-treat members of your household (wife, children and dependants), and do not behave with them as if you are the worst tempered and the most cruel man alive.

Do not run after one who tries to avoid you.

The greatest achievement of your character is that the enmity of your brother against you dare not overcome the consideration and friendship you feel towards him, and his ill-treatment cannot over balance your kind treatment to him.

Do not get too worried and depressed over oppressions and cruelties, because whoever oppresses or tyrannizes you is in reality doing harm to himself.

Never ill-treat a person who has done good unto you.

Know it well, son, that there are two kinds of livelihood: one which you are searching for and the other which wants you (which has been destined for you); it will reach you even if you do not try to obtain it.

To be submissive, humble and begging when one is powerless and poor, and to be arrogant, oppressive and cruel when in power and opulence are two ugly traits of human character.

Nothing in this world is really useful and beneficial unless it has some utility and benefit in the next world. If you want to lament over things, which you have lost in this world, then worry about the loss of things, which had immortal value for you.

The past and almost all, which was in your possession during the past is not with you now. You may thus rationally come to the conclusion that the present and all which is in your possession now will also leave you.

Do not be like a person on whom advices have no effect; they require punishment to correct them. Sensible and reasonable men acquire education and culture through advice; brutes always accept correction through punishment and chastisements.

Overcome your sorrows, worries and misfortunes through hard work and patience and faith in the Merciful Lord. One who gives up a straight path, honest and rational ways of thinking and working will harm himself.

A friend is like a relative and a true friend is one who speaks well of you even behind your back.

Inordinate desires have close relations with misfortunes and calamities.

Often close relatives behave more distantly than strangers and often those strangers help you more than your nearest relatives.

Poor is he who has no friends. Whoever forsakes truths finds that his path of life has become narrow and troublesome.

He who wants to retain his prestige and position, through contentment and honesty, will find them lasting assets.

The strongest relation is one between man and God.

One who does not care for you is your enemy.

If there is a danger of death or damnation in achievement of an object then your safety lies in your failure to achieve it.

Weaknesses and shortcomings are not things to talk about.

Opportunities do not repeat themselves.

Sometimes very wise and learned persons fail to achieve the object they aim for, and foolish and uneducated people attain their purposes.

To sever your relations with ignorant and uneducated people is itself like keeping company with wise and learned persons.

Whoever trusts this world is betrayed by it, and whoever gives it importance and exalts its position is disgraced and humiliated by it.

Every arrow of yours will not hit the bull's eye (every scheme will not succeed).

With a change of status and position your condition will also change.

Before ascertaining the conditions of a route, find out what kind of persons will accompany you.

Instead of inquiring about the condition of a home, in which you are going to live, try to find out what kind of people your neighbors are.

Do not introduce ridiculous topics in your talk even if you have to repeat sayings to others.

Divide and distribute work amongst your servants, so that you can hold each one responsible for the work entrusted to him. This is a better and smoother way of carrying on work, than giving them an opportunity to throw work on somebody else.

Treat your family with love and respect, because they act as wings with which you fly, and as hands, which support you and fight for you. They are the people whom you turn to in trouble and in need.

My dear son, after having given you these advices, I entrust you to the Lord. He will help, guide and protect you in this world and Hereafter. I pray and beseech Him to take you under His protection in both the worlds.

ALI (A) IN THE VERSES OF HOLY QUR'AN

There are a number of verses in holy Qur'an praising Imam 'Ali (a). According to Ibn Abbas, Almighty Allah revealed three hundred and sixty verses regarding him. The following verses perfectly fit the life of Imam 'Ali (a).

1.

(وَمَن يُطِعِ اللَّهَ وَالرَّسُولَ فَأُوْلَٰئِكَ مَعَ الَّذِينَ أَنْعَمَ اللَّهُ عَلَيْهِم مِّنَ النَّبِيِّينَ وَالصِّدِّيقِينَ وَالشُّهَدَاء وَالصَّالِحِينَ وَحَسُنَ أُولَٰئِكَ رَفِيقاً.)

And whoever obeys Allah and the Apostle, these are with those upon whom Allah has bestowed favors from among the prophets and the truthful and the martyrs and the good, and a goodly company are they![1]

2.

(إِنَّ الَّذِينَ قَالُوا رَبُّنَا اللَّهُ ثُمَّ اسْتَقَامُوا تَتَنَزَّلُ عَلَيْهِمُ الْمَلَائِكَةُ أَلَّا تَخَافُوا وَلَا تَحْزَنُوا وَأَبْشِرُوا بِالْجَنَّةِ الَّتِي كُنتُمْ تُوعَدُونَ. نَحْنُ أَوْلِيَاؤُكُمْ فِي الْحَيَاةِ الدُّنْيَا وَفِي الْآخِرَةِ وَلَكُمْ فِيهَا مَا تَشْتَهِي أَنفُسُكُمْ وَلَكُمْ فِيهَا مَا تَدَّعُونَ.)

(As for) those who say: Our Lord is Allah, then continue in the right way, the angels descend upon them, saying: Fear not, nor be grieved, and receive good news of the garden which you

---

[1] Surah Nisa 4:69

were promised. *We are your guardians in this world's life and in the hereafter, and you shall have therein what your souls desire and you shall have therein what you ask for.*[1]

3.

(وَأَمَّا مَنْ خَافَ مَقَامَ رَبِّهِ وَنَهَى النَّفْسَ عَنِ الْهَوَىٰ فَإِنَّ الْجَنَّةَ هِيَ الْمَأْوَىٰ.)

And as for him who fears to stand in the presence of his Lord and forbids the soul from low desires, then surely the garden-that is the abode.[2]

---

[1] Surah Fussilat 41:30-31
[2] Surah Naziyat 79:40-41

GLIMPSES OF MUAWIYAH'S CHARACTER

After describing the life of Imam 'Ali (a), there is no necessity to talk about his opponents because things can be judged by their opposites. Yet, I would like to have a glance at the character of the severest enemy of Imam 'Ali (a), Muawiyah because the bright light of a day cannot be valued without the presence of a dark night. If a person has not experienced burning hot sun it would be difficult for him to understand the value of cool shade.

Similarly, if a person is not aware of the filth of Abu Jahl he cannot value the actual compassion of Muhammad. Therefore, unless Muawiyah's character is put forward, it will be difficult to value of justice of Imam 'Ali (a).

Comparing Muawiyah with Imam 'Ali (a) is like comparing two opposite things. The difference between the character of Imam 'Ali (a) and Muawiyah is like the difference between heaven and earth. In short, Muawiyah's life was full of injustice as much as the life of Imam 'Ali (a) was full of justice. Imam 'Ali (a) was the true successor of the Prophet. Similarly, Muawiyah was the perfect inheritor of his father's character.

Imam 'Ali (a) possessed the excellences of Lady Fatima bint Asad and Lady Khadija. Muawiyah was the inheritor of the horrible activities of his mother, who chewed human liver.

Muawiyah fulfilled his ambitions through deceit and Islamic Ummah is still suffering from its evil effects.

Muawiyah revived the enmity between tribes. He enflamed evil thinking whose heat is still experienced by Islamic Ummah. I have presented a small picture of Muawiyah's character so that justice-loving minds can distinguish between the politics of Imam 'Ali (a) and Muawiyah.

PLIGHT OF HUJR IBN ADI

Historian Ibn Athir writes in *Tarikh Kamil:* Hujr ibn Adi and his companions were martyred in 51 A.H. because Muawiyah had made Mughaira ibn Shoba the governor of Kufa in 41 A.H. and had advised him: "I want to give you many advices but I would not give you so many advices because of your good understanding. However keep one thing in mind. Do not keep away from troubling 'Ali and do not avoid praying for Uthman's salvation. You should oppress the friends of 'Ali and befriend the friends of Uthman and grant them lots of gifts."

Mughaira obeyed Muawiyah's order. He always troubled Imam 'Ali (a). Hujr ibn Adi used to criticize him saying: "You and your Amir are accursed ones. The one you are troubling is full of excellences." Mughaira stopped grants to Hujr ibn Adi and his friends. Hujr used to say: "O servant of God! You have stopped our grants without any cause. You do not have any right to do so. You should start paying us our grants."

When Mughaira died, Ziyad ibn Uqbah became the governor of Kufa. Ziyad followed the footsteps of Muawiyah and Mughaira. He used to trouble Amirul Momineen (a). Hujr ibn Adi always defended the right. Ziyad imprisoned Hujr ibn Adi and twelve of his companions. He convicted them of certain crime and brought in four witnesses to sign the testimony. Those who testified against Hujr ibn Adi included Talha ibn Ubaidullah's two sons – Ishaq and Moosa, Zubair's son Manzar and Imad ibn Uqbah ibn Abi Muit. Ziyad handed the prisoners to Wail ibn Hujr al-Hadhrami and Kathir ibn Shahab and sent them to Syria.

Both the trusted agents of Ziyad took the prisoners and set out for Syria. They reached a place called Gharrain. Ziyad had given a letter to Wail addressed to Muawiyah. The caravan reached a place called Marj Uzra in the outskirts of Syria and halted there. Wail and Kathir went to Muawiyah and handed Ziyad's letter to him. Ziyad had written that Hujr ibn Adi and his companions were the severest enemies of Muawiyah and they loved Abu Turab very much. They did not obey any orders of the government. They were making the land of Kufa bitter for Muawiyah. Hence it was upto him to punish them so that others could learn a lesson from them.

After that, Wail gave the letter of Shurai ibn Hani to Muawiyah. It was written therein: I have come to know that Ziyad has also mentioned my testimony in his statement of case. My opinion regarding Hujr is that he is a person who offers prayers, pays charity, performs Hajj and Umrah. He enjoins good and stops others from evil. It is prohibited for you to take his life or wealth.

The followers of Imam 'Ali (a) arrested by Ziyad were:

- Hujr ibn Adi Kindi
- Arqam ibn Abdullah Kindi
- Shareek ibn Shadad Hadhrami
- Saifi ibn Faseel Shaibani
- Qabisa ibn Sanee Abasi
- Karim ibn Afif Khathami
- Aasim ibn Auf Bajali
- Waraqa ibn Sami Bajali
- Kadam ibn Hassan Unzi
- Abdur Rahman ibn Hassan ibn Hassan Unzi
- Muhrir ibn Shahab Tamimi
- Abdullah ibn Hauya Saadi

The above mentioned twelve persons were arrested first and then two more persons viz. Utbah ibn Akhmis ibn Saad ibn Bakr and Saad ibn Namran Hamadani were also arrested and sent to Syria. In this way the number of oppressed prisoners was fourteen.

The incident of Hujr ibn Adi is described by Tabari as follows:

Qais ibn Ibad Shaibani came to Ziyad and said: "A person from Bani Hashim named Saifi ibn Faseel is the leader of the group of Hujr. He is your severest enemy." Ziyad summoned him and said: "O enemy of God! Are you related to Abu Turab?"

He said that he did not know any person by that name.

Ziyad said: "Don't you know 'Ali ibn Abi Talib also?"

Saifi said: "Yes, I know him."

Ziyad: "He is father of dust (Abu Turab)."

Saifi: "It is not possible because he is the father of Hasan and Husain."

A police officer told him: "The Chief calls him Abu Turab, how dare you call him father of Hasan and Husain?"

Saifi: "I should also lie if the chief does so?"

Ziyad: "You are committing one crime after another, bring my stick."

When the stick was brought to him, Ziyad asked: "What is your belief about Abu Turab?

Saifi: "I would say that he is the most virtuous servant of Allah."

Hearing this, Ziyad hit him madly and oppressed him very much. When he was tired of inflicting atrocities, he asked Saifi: "What is your opinion about Imam 'Ali (a) now?"

He said: "Even if my body is broken into pieces, I would say the same about him."

Ziyad: "Don't do it or I will kill you."

Saifi: "If you do so, I will attain martyrdom and this misfortune will be included in your scroll of deeds forever."

Ziyad ordered him to be arrested and he was shackled in chains and took to the prison. After that, Ziyad prepared a charge-sheet against Hujr ibn Adi and friends. The bitterest enemies of Imam 'Ali (a) signed the testimony against these innocent persons.

Abu Moosa's son Abu Burda writes in this testimony: "I testify by the Lord of the worlds that Hujr ibn Adi and friends isolated themselves from the community. They disobeyed the Chief and invited people to break their allegiance to Amir Muawiyah. They invited people to the love of Abu Turab."

Ziyad said: "I want others also to write similar testimonies as I am trying to end the life of this dishonest and foolish person."

Inaq ibn Sharjil ibn Abi Daham al-Tamimi came forward to give his testimony but Ziyad said: "No, I would start taking testimonies from the tribe of Quraish only and will take the testimonies of only those honorable persons who are known to Muawiyah." Hearing this, Ishaq ibn Talha ibn Ubaidullah, Moosa ibn Talha, Ismail ibn Talha, Manzar ibn Zubair and Imarah ibn Uqbah ibn Abi Muit, Abdur Rahman ibn Hunad, Amr ibn Saad ibn Abi Waqqas, Amir ibn Saud ibn Umayyah, Muriz ibn Rabia ibn Abdul Aza Ibn Abdush Shams, Ubaidullah ibn Muslim Hadhrami, Unaq ibn Sharjil, Wail ibn Hujr Hadhrami, Kathir ibn Shahab Harthi, Qatan ibn Abdullah and Sari ibn Waqqas Harthi signed the testimony.

In addition to this, Ziyad included the testimony of Shurai Qazi and Shurai ibn Hani Harthi. Qazi Shurai says that Ziyad asked him about Hujr. He told Ziyad that Hujr stood up for prayer at night and fasted during day.

When Shurai ibn Hani Harthi came to know that his testimony is also present in the charge-sheet, he came to Ziyad and disapproved his action. He said: "Why did you mention my testimony without my permission and knowledge? I have nothing to do with it in this world and the hereafter." Then he came to the prisoners and handed a letter to Wail ibn Hujr and said: "This is my letter and it should reach

Muawiyah without fail." He had written: "I have come to know that Ziyad has written down my testimony against Hujr ibn Adi. You should know that I testify that Hujr ibn Adi offers prayers, gives alms, performs Hajj and Umrah, he enjoins good and forbids evil. His life and property is worth respect."

The Prisoners were halted at a place called Marj Uzra near Damascus; six of them were killed on the order of Muawiyah viz.

1. Hujr ibn Adi (r.a.)

2. Sharik ibn Shaddad Hadhrami

3. Saifi ibn Faseel Shaibani

4. Qabisa ibn Zaibia Abasi

5. Muhraz ibn Shahab al-Saadi

6. Kudam ibn Hayyan al-Ghazi

Abdullah ibn Hassan Unzi was sent back to Ziyad and Muawiyah ordered Ziyad that he should be killed in the worst manner. Ziyad buried him alive.[1]

God's mercy be upon these pure lovers.

Hind bint Zaid recited following elegy at the death of Hujr and companions:

"O bright moon! Look Adi is going. Hujr is going to Muawiyah ibn Harb. Amir Ziyad says that Muawiyah will kill him. O Hujr ibn Adi! May you remain safe and happy. Muawiyah considers it his birthright to kill innocent people. His vizier is the worst person in this Ummah."

Dr. Taha Husayn writes: A Muslim ruler considered it legal to kill those whose protection was desired by Allah. The ruler ordered them

---

[1] *Tarikh Tabari*, Vol. 6, Pg. 155

to be killed without meeting them or giving them a chance to defend themselves or say something.

This grievous story has moved Muslims far and wide. When Ayesha came to know that this group was being sent to Syria, she sent Abdur Rahman ibn Harith Ibn Hisham to Muawiyah to talk to him about them. However, when Abdur Rahman reached Syria, the group was already martyred.

When Abdur Rahman ibn Umar came to know about this remorseful incident, he took off his turban and asked the people to turn away from him; then he began to weep audibly.

Hujr's martyrdom is a tragic incident. None of the seniors of that time doubt the fact that it was a big crack in the wall of Islam. Even Muawiyah could not forget Hujr till the time of his death. He used to remember Hujr the most on his death-bed. Historians are of the opinion that Muawiyah used to murmur on his death bed: "O Hujr! You have spoilt my hereafter. My account with Ibn Adi is very long."[1]

OTHER EXAMPLES OF MUAWIYAH'S DECEIT

Muawiyah did not feel anything wrong in crushing human beings in order to achieve his ambition.

He came to know that Imam 'Ali (a) has made Malik Ashtar the governor of Egypt in the place of Muhammad ibn Abi Bakr, so he conspired with a landlord and promised him that if he killed Malik before he reaches Egypt, he would be exempt from paying taxes on his land.

When Malik passed by that region, the landlord invited him for lunch and gave him poison mixed in honey, because of which Malik got martyred.

---

[1] Al-Fitnah al-Kubra *'Ali wa Banuh*, Pg. 243

After this incident, Muawiyah and Amr ibn al-Aas used to boast: "Honey is also an army of Allah." Muawiyah openly flouted the terms of the treaty signed with Imam Hasan (a). He conspired with the Imam's wife, Judah bint Ashath to poison the Imam and said that if she poisoned him he would grant her a huge amount of wealth and marry her to his son Yazid.

Imam Hasan's wife poisoned him on Muawiyah's instigation and the Imam was martyred.

Masoodi writes that Ibn Abbas went to Syria for some work and he was sitting in the mosque when he heard a loud 'Allaahu Akbar' (God is the greatest) from Muawiyah's Green Palace. Muawiyah's wife, Fakhta bint Qarza asked Muawiyah the reason of his happiness. Muawiyah said: "I have just got the news of Hasan's death."[1]

TAKING ZIYAD IBN ABIH AS HIS BROTHER

Ziyad was a very cunning person. He was only a servant during the Imam's Caliphate, but Muawiyah wanted to involve him in his mischievous activities. He wrote to Ziyad: "Leave 'Ali and come to me because you were born of my father, Abu Sufyan."

Ziyad's father was unknown. Therefore people used to call him Ziyad ibn Abih i.e. the son of his father. When Imam 'Ali (a) got the news of this wickedness of Muawiyah, he wrote to Ziyad:

"I am given to understand that Muawiyah has been corresponding with you. Beware, he wants to make a fool of you, to blunt your intelligence and to harm your self-respect. Remember that it is Satan which will attack an imprudent and incautious Muslim from behind and from right and left so that finding him unwary it may overpower him and enslave his reasoning."[2]

The fact is that during the Caliphate of Umar, Abu Sufyan unwisely gave utterances to something which was unjustifiable and

---

[1] *Murujuz Zahab*, Vol. 2, Pg. 307
[2] *Nahjul Balagha*, Letter no. 44

unreasonable. It was one of those evil suggestions of Satan which are not only an insult to a self-respecting man but which cannot help in proving the descent (according to the laws of Islam) or in legalizing heritage. The condition of a man claiming such a lineage is that of a gate crasher in a party from which he may be thrown out with humiliation.

Masoodi narrates: "Muawiyah made Ziyad his brother in 40 A.H. Ziyad ibn Asma, Malik ibn Rabia and Munzir ibn Awwam testified that they had heard Abu Sufyan saying that Ziyad was born out through him. After that, Abu Maryam Sulooli testified that: Ziyad's mother was the slave-girl of Harth ibn Kaldah. She was married to a person named Ubaid. She led a disgraceful life in the Haratul Baghaya area of Taif. People with ill character used to visit that area. Once Abu Sufyan visited that area and stayed there. I used to be a bartender in a wine house. Abu Sufyan asked me to arrange a woman for him.

I searched a lot but did not find anyone except the slave-girl of Harith i.e. Sumayya. I informed Abu Sufyan that there is no woman except a dark complexioned slave-girl. Abu Sufyan asked me to bring that woman.

Then I took Sumayya to Abu Sufyan that night and Ziyad was born of the union. Therefore I bear witness that he is Muawiyah's brother." Hearing this, the brother of Sumayya's mistress Safiya, Yunus ibn Ubaid stood up and said:

"Muawiyah! It is the decision of Allah and His Messenger that a child belongs to a person at whose house he is born and a fornicator must be stoned to death. You are associating a child with a fornicator, which is clearly against the Book of Allah." Abdur Rahman ibn Ummul Hakam quoted following lines regarding this incident:

Give the message of a Yemeni to Muawiyah ibn Harb. Are you angry with the fact that your father should be called chaste? Do you like the fact that he is called a fornicator? I bear witness that your relation with Ziyad is same as the relation of an elephant with a donkey.

Ibn Abil Hadid has narrated the words of his teacher, Abu Uthman in the following incident:

Ziyad was Muawiyah's governor in Basra and he had just become the son of Abu Sufyan. He passed by a gathering where a blind person called Abul Uryan al-Adadi was sitting. Abul Uryan asked about the passers by.

People told him that he was Ziyad ibn Abi Sufyan passing along with his companions. The blind person said: "By Allah, Abu Sufyan had given birth to Yazid, Muawiyah, Utbah, Ambasa, Hanzala and Muhammad. Where did this Ziyad come from?"

When Ziyad came to know about his words, he became angry. One of the companions asked him to silent him by giving him wealth instead of punishing him.

Ziyad sent two hundred dinars to him. Next day, Ziyad passed by and saluted the gathering.

The blind, Abu al-Uryan started crying on hearing the voice of salutation. People asked the reason of his weeping. He said: "Ziyad's voice is very similar to Abu Sufyan's."[1]

Hasan Basri used to say that Muawiyah did four such things; each of which is enough for destruction:

1. He acquired power by tying up with people who loved this world in spite of the fact that Companions with knowledge and virtues were present.

2. He made his drunkard son, Yazid his heir apparent who used to wear silk and play a tambourine.

---

[1] *Sharh Nahjul Balagha*, Vol. 4, Pg. 68

3. He made Ziyad his brother. While Allah has said that the child belongs to a person on whose bed he is born and a fornicator should be stoned to death.

4. He unlawfully eliminated Hujr ibn Adi and companions.[1]

SAYINGS OF MUAWIYAH

Muawiyah called Yazid at his death-bed and willed: "O my dear son! I have fastened the load of pain and have warded off rebellion from you, and have straightened up matters. I have tamed the enemies, have brought the reins of the Arabs in your hands, and have accumulated for you that which no father can do for his son. I don't fear anyone opposing or fighting you on the question of Caliphate except four persons.

These being Husain ibn 'Ali, Abdullah ibn Umar, Abdullah ibn Zubair and Abdul Rahman ibn Abu Bakr. As regards Abdullah ibn Umar, (excessive) worship has broken him, if no one remains to assist him, he shall succumb to you. As regards Husain ibn 'Ali, he is a light-minded person, and the people of Iraq will betray him until they force him to rebel and you will have to fight with him.

As regards the son of Abu Bakr, he follows what his companions like, and his aspires only for women and fun. While the one who like a lion lies in ambush, and the fox who is playing a game with you and is in track of an opportunity to pounce upon you, is the son of Zubair. And if he revolts and you gain victory over him, separate every joint of his.[2]

2. Tabari has narrated the words of Abu Masadah Farazi as follows:

Muawiyah told me: "O Ibn Masadah! May Allah's mercy be on Abu Bakr. He did not seek this world nor did the world seek him. Ibn Hantama was sought by the world but he did not seek the world.

---

[1] Al-Fitnah al-Kubra *'Ali wa Banuh,* Pg. 248
[2] *Al-Kamil fit Tarikh,* Vol. 3, Pg. 259-260

Uthman sought this world and the world sought him. As far as I am concerned, I have already enjoyed this world."

3. When Malik Ashtar was martyred through Muawiyah's conspiracy, he said: 'Ali had two arms Ammar ibn Yasir, which was cut in the Battle of Siffeen and his other one is cut today.

4. Muawiyah was cursed by the Prophet that Allah will not fill his stomach. This curse came into effect later on when Muawiyah used to eat seven times a day and say: "By God, I get tired of eating, but my stomach does not fill up!"

ALI'S DISCOURSE REGARDING BANI HASHIM AND BANI UMAYYAH

I would like to conclude this book with the discussion about mutual differences between Bani Hashim and Bani Umayyah. Thus, I have selected a letter of Imam 'Ali (a) to Muawiyah from *Nahjul Balagha* for this purpose, regarding which the compiler of *Nahjul Balagha*, Sayyid Razi says, "This lesson is one of the best lessons of Amirul Momineen (a):

After glorifying Allah and praising the Prophet (s) let it be known to you that I am in receipt of your letter wherein you write to me that Almighty Allah selected Muhammad (s), the Prophet as the Messenger of His revelations and He helped those Companions of the Prophet (s) who sincerely exerted themselves to assist him. Is it not an irony of fate that circumstances have favored you to such a position that you dare remind us of the favors which Allah bestowed upon us and the Blessings conferred by Him upon His chosen Prophet (s) who was one of us. You have nothing to do with them and you have no share in these Blessings and Favors.

Your condition is like that of a man who carries dates to "Hujr"[1] or that of a man who tries to teach archery to the master from whom he has learnt the art. You believe that the best of the people amongst the

---
[1] 'Hujr' is a place, which has abundant dates

Muslims are so and so and you have started discussing a subject (superiority of Emigrants over Helpers) which if it is proved correct will not be of any use to you, will not enhance your status and if it is repudiated, this repudiation will not harm you because you are neither an Emigrant nor a Helpers.

What have you to do with their respective status and prestige? What is that for you if one is considered superior to the other? How are you considered in their affairs? You are a freed and liberated slave, and slaves and their sons, though freed and liberated, cannot aspire to the status of Emigrants and Helpers and they have no right to introduce unholy classification amongst the Emigrants and Helpers. Do you realize your limitations? You do not belong to either group, you are a liberated slave and son of liberated parents and you want to introduce an unhealthy division between these two groups.

The false status you have tried to grasp is not going to enhance your prestige (before Allah or the people). Can you not think of remaining at the place where your old hostility towards Islam and the Prophet (s) has kept you? How is the lower status or defeat of one class or a person of that class, to whom you do not belong going to harm you and how is the success or higher status of the other going to do you good? You have gone astray from the straight path and from the real teachings of Islam. Listen! I want to give you a short description of the Blessings of Allah upon us.

A party of Emigrants met martyrdom. They were killed in the cause of Islam and Allah. Every one of them was blessed by Allah with a status and rank. Out of them those who belonged to my family and tribe, Bani Hashim, were granted an excellent status by Allah. Hamza (the uncle of the Prophet and 'Ali) received the title of Chief of Martyrs (*Sayyidush Shuhada*).[1]

The Prophet (s) himself called him by this name after his martyrdom and at his funeral ceremony. The Prophet (s) recited 'Allaahu Akbar'

---

[1] Holy Prophet had given the title of 'Chief of martyrs' to Hamza (r.a.)

(God is the greatest) seventy times as a mark of distinction for him, which is not for any other Muslim. Some Emigrants lost their hands in the battlefield but when one of us (Ja'far, cousin of the Prophet (s) and brother of Imam 'Ali (a)) lost both of his hands and died in the battlefield, Allah granted him angelic wings and the Prophet (s) informed us that this martyr has received the title of Tayyar (one who glides in Paradise).[1]

If Allah had not disapproved man's habit of eulogizing and praising himself, I would have given several such instances which speak of the enhancement of my prestige and status before Allah, instances which are accepted and can be testified by faithful Muslims about which the hearers will have no reason to doubt. Do not be like a man whom the Devil has laid astray. Accept the obvious truth when it faces you.

Listen O' Muawiyah! We (Ahlul Bayt, the progeny of the Prophet) are unique examples of the creation of Allah. For such a status, we are not under obligation to any person or tribe but the Almighty Allah Who granted us these blessings. Human beings have received and will receive perfection through us. The perpetual supremacy and inherent superiority do not prevent us from making contact with human beings or with your clan, we have married amongst you and have established family connections with your (as well as with others) clan, though you do not belong to our class. How can you be our equal when the Prophet (s) belongs to us and Abu Jahl, the worst enemy of Islam was from amongst you.[2]

---

[1] "Ali's elder brother, Ja'far lost his both arms in the battle of Muta. Holy Prophet said: I have seen Ja'far flying along with angels in Paradise. Allah has granted him two emerald wings to fly by.
[2] Abu Sufyan, the father of Muawiyah was on the forefront among those who denied.

Asadullah (lit. "The Lion of Allah" - a title of 'Ali) is from amongst us, while Asadul Ahlaaf (lion of the opposing groups, who had sworn to fight against Islam and the Prophet) was from you.[1]

The two foremost leaders of the youth of Paradise (Hasan and Imam Husain) are from us and the children of Hell are from you.[2] The best woman in the world (title bestowed by Allah upon Fatima, the beloved daughter of the Prophet (s) is from us, and the slanderer and the wood-carrying woman who tried to spend every hour of her life in causing harm to the Prophet of Islam (s), was your aunt.[3]

There are so many other things similar to the few mentioned, which praise us and speak ill of your clan and which show how far and superior we are to you.

We were faithful followers of the commandments of Allah and you and your clan always opposed Islam and accepted it out of sheer expediency simply to save yourselves from humiliation and disgrace.

Our sincerity in Islam and our services to its cause are the facts of history and history cannot deny your enmity against Islam and the Prophet (s).

The credit which you want to take away from us and the honor which you want to deprive us of is the one which the Holy Qur'an is carefully guarding for us. It says:

---

[1] The Holy Prophet had given the title of 'Lion of Allah' to Hamza. Utbah bin Rabia, Muawiyah's grandfather was proud of being called 'lion of those who take oath'.
[2] A famous tradition of the Holy Prophet (s) about Hasan and Husain is: Hasan and Husain are the chiefs of the youth of Paradise. He had pointed out the sons of Utbah bin Abi Muit calling them with youth of hell. Holy Prophet told Utbah: You and your sons will go to hell.
[3] A famous saying of the Holy Prophet (s) regarding Lady Fatima is: Fatima is the chief of the women of the worlds. 'Hammalat al-hatab' (carrier of firewood) implies Umme Jameel bint Harb, the paternal aunt of Muawiyah and wife of Abu Lahab. She used to collect thorns and spread them on the way of Holy Prophet. Holy Quran has cursed her along with Abu Lahab in the following verse: He shall soon burn in those flames. And his wife, the bearer of firewood.

"Some relatives are superior and have excellence over others, according to the Book of Allah" [Qur'an, 33:6]

And in another place in the very same Book, Allah informs mankind that:

"The nearest people to Abraham, are those who follow him and those who follow the Prophet (s) and the true believers. Allah is the guardian of the true believers" [Qur'an, 2:68].

Therefore we hold two excellences: That of close relationship to the Prophet (s) and that of loyally accepting his teachings. Do you know on the day of Saqifah, Emigrants told Helpers that they were superior to them because they in one way or the other, were related to the Prophet (s) and therefore they deserved the Caliphate and with the aid of this argument, the Emigrants carried the day.

If success can be achieved with the help of this argument and if it has got a grain of truth in it then according to it, we and not you, deserve the Caliphate. If not, then the Helpers still hold their claim over the Caliphate.

You want to impress the world with the idea that I envied all the previous caliphs and that I was jealous of them. Even if I grant this, I want to know what right and authority have you to ask for an explanation from me? You have no place in religion to talk of such things. You also want to taunt me by saying that when I refused to accept the Caliphate of the First Caliph I was dragged like a camel with a rope round my neck and every kind of cruelty and humiliation was leveled against me. I swear by my life that by talking like that you want to bring disgrace to me but you are actually doing the greatest service to me and are disgracing yourself as well as the cause that you pretend to support.

There is no disgrace for a Muslim, if he is subjected to tyranny and suppression so long as he is firm in his faith and belief in Allah and religion. This is exactly what I say that every cruelty and tyranny was leveled against me to deprive me of the right which Allah and the Prophet (s) have given me and this is exactly what you do not want to acknowledge and accept. Your taunts against me go a long way to prove that in reality there was no election, it was a coup d'etat followed by brutal force which decided the fate of Caliphate by making it neither hereditary nor elective but possessive. I have no desire to go into these details but you brought in the subject and I was forced to explain a few points about it.

Then you have referred to Uthman's murder, and declaring yourself to be his relative, you claim vengeance and blood (and want me to arrange for it as if I was responsible for the murder). I want to say something about the insinuation and false propaganda carried on by you in this respect.

My reply to you is that first of all, you should try and find out who was the arch-enemy of Uthman. Can the arch-enemy be he who offered his help and services to Uthman and Uthman refused to have anything to do with him and told him plainly to go and sit at home as his help was not required and his services were not needed or the worst enemy of Uthman is he whom Uthman asked to come to his succor and who purposely and intentionally delayed the help and allowed the events to take their course till what was to happen, happened? No, these two persons cannot be considered in the same category. I swear by the Omniscient Allah that He very well knows everything as He says in the Holy Book:

"Allah certainly knows the people who put obstacles in the path of those who wanted to go to war and also to those who did not stay to face a battle." [Qur'an, 33:18].

I do not want to offer any excuse for having objected to his introducing innovations in religion. If my objections to the introduction of innovation and my advice to him to give it up was considered by him a sin committed by me, then I do not attach any importance to his opinion, because well-wishers are often blamed, and their good advice is misconstrued but they do their duty to man and religion. Allah in the Holy Book repeats the saying of a prophet which appropriately represents my position. He says,

"I only intend to reform you as much as I can. My success lies with Allah. I have faith in Him and trust in His help." [Qur'an, 11:88].

Then you have tried to frighten me by saying that there is nothing with you for me and my Companions but your sword. Well, Muawiyah! You made the people laugh at your words, they were feeling very sad and depressed at the standard of mental depravity exhibited by you.

When did you find the sons of Abdul Muttalib (grandfather of the Prophet and 'Ali) timid in facing their enemies or getting afraid of brandishing swords?

Just wait a little; you will, in the near future have to face the attack of a brave soldier. He will shortly invite you for the encounter you desire for. The thing which you apparently wish for is not as far away as you imagine it to be. I am coming to you with an army of Emigrants, Helpers and those Companions who have sincere faith in me. Theirs is a powerful congregation. Their movements will raise huge clouds of dust (indicating the strength of the army). They are prepared to die or to kill. They believe that the best that could happen to them is to receive the Blessings of the Lord by their good deeds. Sons of those warriors who routed your clan in the Battle of Badr are with them.

The swords of Bani Hashim are with them. And you have already realized the sharpness of these swords when your brother, your maternal uncle, your grandfather and kinsmen were killed (those people were killed by Imam 'Ali (a) in the battles of Badr and Uhud). These swords are now nearing the despots who have tyrannized the Muslim world."[1]

---

[1] *Nahjul Balagha*, Letter 28

BIBLIOGRAPHY

TRADITION BOOKS

Sahih Muslim: Imam Abul Hasan Muslim ibn Hajjaj Qushiri Nishapuri, d. 241

Sahih Bukhari: Imam Abu Abdullah Muhammad ibn Ismail Bukhari, d. 256.

BIOGRAPHY BOOKS

Siratun Nabi: Abdul Malik ibn Hisham Himyari, d. 218.

Ansabul Ashraf: Ahmad ibn Yahya ibn Jabir Balazari, d. 279.

Usd al-Ghaba fee Marifatus Sahaba: Abul Hasan Izziddin 'Ali ibn Abil Karam Jazari (Ibn Athir), d. 630.

Al-Isabah fee Tamizus Sahaba: Qadi Shahabuddin Ahmad ibn 'Ali Kanani (Ibn Hajar Asqalani), d. 852.

Insanul Uyoon Siratul Amin wal Mamoom (Sirate Halabiya): Allamah 'Ali ibn Burhan Halabi, d. 1044.

Hayat Muhammad: Muhammad Husain Haikal.

Al-Fitnatul Kubra: Taha Husayn, d. 1393.

HISTORY BOOKS

At-Tabaqatul Kubra: Muhammad ibn Saad Katib Waqidi, d. 230.

Al-Imamah was Siyasah: Abdullah ibn Muslim Dinawari (Ibn Qutaibah), d. 276.

Tarikh Yaqoobi: Ahmad ibn Abi Yaqoob (Ibn Qazwh Yaqoobi), d. 292.

Tarikhul Umam wal Mulook: Imam Abu Ja'far Muhammad ibn Jurair Tabari, d. 310.

Al-Iqdul Farid: Abu Amr Ahmad ibn Muhammad ibn Abde Rabbeh Andulusi, d. 327.

Murujuz Zahab wa Madinul Jauhar: 'Ali ibn Husain Masudi, d. 346.

Tarikh Baghdad: Hafiz Abu Bakr Ahmad ibn 'Ali Khatib Baghdadi, d. 463.

Al-Kamil Fit-Tarikh: Abul Hasan Izzuddin 'Ali ibn Abil Karam Jazari (Ibn Athir), d. 630.

Sharh Nahjul Balagha: Izuddin Abu Haamid ibn Haibatullah Madaini (Ibn Abil Hadid), d. 655.

Al-Mukhtasar fee Akhbaril Bashar: Allamah Abul Fida Ismail ibn 'Ali (Abul Fida), d. 732.

Al-Bidaya wan Nihaya: Hafiz Imaduddin Abul Fida Ismail ibn Umar Damishqi (Ibn Kathir), d. 774.

MISCELLANEOUS

Dalailun Imamah: Imam Abu Ja'far Muhammad ibn Jurair Tabari, d. 310.

Manaqib 'Ali Ibn Abi Talib (a): Shaykh 'Ali ibn Muhammad ibn Maghazali Shafei, d. 483.

Al-Milal wan Nahal: Abul Fath Muhammad ibn Abdul Karim ibn Abi Bakr Ahmad Shahristani, d. 548.

Sharh Nahjul Balagha: Shaykh Muhammad Abduh Misri, d. 1323.

www.ingramcontent.com/pod-product-compliance
Lightning Source LLC
LaVergne TN
LVHW091720070526
838199LV00050B/2483